The Jarrow Crusade: The Issue
Protest and Legend

Matt Perry

**University of
Sunderland Press**

© Matt Perry

ISBN 1 873757 60 3

First published 2005

Cover Image by Permission People's History Museum

Cover Design by Tim Murphy Creative Solutions
Copy edited by Felicity Hepburn

Published in Great Britain by
The University of Sunderland Press
in association with Business Education Publishers Limited
The Teleport
Doxford International
Sunderland
SR3 3XD

Tel: 0191 5252410
Fax: 0191 5201815

British Cataloguing-in-Publications Data
A catalogue record for this book is available from the British Library

Printed in Great Britain by the Alden Group, Oxford.

Acknowledgements

This book could not have been achieved without the help of many friends and acquaintances. I would like to thank those who have kindly agreed to sit for interviews: John Badger, Harry Clarke, Con Shiels and the late Con Whalen. Thanks also to those who had the unenviable task of reading my manuscript in draft form: John Charlton, Richard Croucher, Stuart Howard, David Martin, Archie Potts and Graham Potts. The staff at Colindale Newspaper Archive, Gateshead Local Studies, the Geffrye Museum, the National Museum of Labour History, Newcastle Local Studies, the Public Record Office, Sheffield Archives, South Shields Library, South Shields Museum, Tyne and Wear Archive Service, the Working-Class Movement Library have all been patient and helpful. I'm very grateful to all those that have assisted me in the collection of information: Gillian Fake, Alex Ferguson, Peter Flannery, Tony Hepburn, Jarrow and Hebburn Local History Society, Tom Kelly, Terry Kelly, Don MacRaild, Alan Plater, Rose Reeve, George Smith and Malcolm Smith. And special thanks to Christine.

Contents

Preface

Is it possible to say anything new about the Jarrow Crusade? I hope to surprise those who approach this book with a certain amount of scepticism on this count. Going beyond the standard sources – the *Shields Gazette*, the *Evening Chronicle*, *The Town that Was Murdered* and the odd interview with march leaders – provides a fuller and richer account of the Jarrow Crusade than the one that is currently on offer. Based on five years' research, this work will bring together a wide range of sources that have not as yet seriously informed the debate on the Jarrow Crusade. I have secured the release of Home Office papers about the hunger marches of 1936. Archival sources such as the Bishop of Durham's papers, Sir John Jarvis's papers, Special Branch and Board of Trade papers at the Public Record Office, the British Newspaper Library, Colindale, the town clerk's files and council minutes at the Tyne and Wear Archive, Labour Party material at the Sheffield Archives, as well as Ellen Wilkinson's press cuttings at the National Museum of Labour History have been consulted. A host of non-archival sources – the works of Ellen Wilkinson, film, folk song, opera, and photographs have been used. The oral testimony of the Crusade was also carefully sifted, including an interview with the last survivor of the Crusade.

Telling the story in all its detailed richness questions the legend of the Crusade and the uses to which it has been put. Very little critical discussion has taken place. No serious work has been done on the cultural impact of the Crusade, or its 'sites of memory' or the political controversies of the Crusade. No major account has sought to challenge the legend which has been founded on a series of myths: the myth of success, the myth of universal support, the myth of 'no politics' and the myth of uniqueness. This analysis will be incorporated into the narrative of events.

First and foremost in the book there is an account of the Crusade. Its sub-plots possess a delicious quality: the confused identity of the mascot dog, the so-called kidnap attempt, the squabbling steel barons, the cat-fighting Bishops, the 'gate-crashing' communists, the contested relics, the support of patricians and plebs, the gifts of cherry cake in Ferryhill and underwear in Nottingham. The reflections of the marchers, the weather and impressions of the places on the route give a taste of the experience of the Crusade. It is also about the unaccountable decisions that in Ellen Wilkinson's words 'murdered' the town.

The approach adopted here is also to weave the contemporary events, the major features of the Crusade's background and elements of the myth-making process into a day-by-day account of the march. This involves a consideration, prompted by the narrative of the journey itself, of the social circumstances of Jarrow in the 1930s: crime, health, social struggles, housing and class. Examination of the Crusade's context also encompasses a consideration of English society in the 1930s. The marchers trekked the length of England encountering very different parts of the country. They witnessed spa towns, palaces, town halls, cathedrals, industrial cities, coalfields, workplaces, workhouses and slums. Contemporary social commentators – J.B. Priestley, D.H. Lawrence, George Orwell, A.D.K. Owen, the Pilgrim Trust, David Goodfellow, G.C.M. M'Gonigle – are deployed to give a flavour of the places through which they passed. Their journey was rich in contrasts both in the imagination and social reality.

At times the narrative will break to scrutinise the main protagonists in the story of Jarrow: Ellen Wilkinson, Jarrow's MP; the march leaders (Jock Hanlon, David Riley, Paddy Scullion, Joe Symonds) who rebelled against their own Labour Party, on their return to Jarrow; Sir John Jarvis MP, Jarrow's charitable benefactor; the Bishop of Durham, who condemned the men from his own diocese as a revolutionary mob and Sir Walter Runciman, who disappointed the town's delegation in July over the proposed steelworks for Jarrow, an event which directly provoked the march to London. Far from giving their support, the Labour Party leadership, in the words of Labour Councillor and March Marshal David Riley, 'stabbed' the Crusade 'in the back' and it did so on more than one occasion. The condemnation of the Bishop of Durham is well known but his motivations and the fact that he worked behind the scenes to undermine the Crusade are not. The local non-partisanship is a celebrated aspect of the Crusade but less well known is Sir John Jarvis's and the local Conservative's 'humanitarian-political' double-game or that the march leaders acrimoniously left the Labour Party within a month of the Crusade's return. Ellen Wilkinson, because of the complexity of her politics and the importance of her career, deserves some careful consideration. Her political campaigning and journalism connect the Crusade with other issues of the day: women's rights, Spain, Germany and the Empire. If she is only remembered for her leadership of the Jarrow Crusade or as Minister of Education, that memory compares poorly to her life. Also, where possible, the voices of the Crusaders are introduced through the numerous interviews that have taken place and through the folklore from Jarrow itself.

Connections between the tramp to London and the making of the legend are also sought. Sometimes comparisons with other myths, such as the original Crusades, Saint George, Robin Hood, allow insight into the manufacturing of a modern legend. Particular attention is paid to the question of the memory, relics and cultural representations of the Crusade.

Timing, locality and personality bind the Crusade together with other contemporary events, allowing the narrative to pass naturally between them. The Jarrow Crusade was one of four roughly simultaneous marches to London – the National Hunger March, the National League of the Blind march and the Scottish veterans' march. They passed through the same towns and occasionally crossed paths. These marches faced the same intransigence from the Baldwin Government and the same surveillance from the police. Throughout the month of October, the Spanish Republic's fate was in the balance as Franco's armies advanced towards Madrid, Hitler's Condor Legion landed at Cadiz and the pro-republican International Brigades were formed. The Crusade started as the Labour Party held its conference in Edinburgh. Days earlier, there had been major clashes between Mosley's blackshirts and anti-fascists in the East End of London. Perhaps most intriguingly, a constitutional crisis over the abdication of Edward VIII imperceptibly developed. There were many intersections between the Crusade and these events as two minor examples illustrate. Ellen Wilkinson was on the reception committee of the National Hunger March and sought the advice of Wal Hannington the leader of the NUWM on how to organise the Jarrow Crusade. Jock Hanlon, one of Crusade leaders, met up with his brother who was on the National League of the Blind March in Northampton.

The Jarrow Crusade:
Protest and Legend

Introduction

The Jarrow Crusade's fame and its legendary status are undisputed. Time has turned the Crusade into something it was not. The march leaders of 1936 never intended to create a legend. They might have used considerable presentational care and had a sense of theatre to dramatise their protest but publicity was not their criterion of success. Fame was a means to an end, not an end in itself. However, the passage of time has transformed the Jarrow Crusade from a historical event into a potent talisman, with which many apparently seek association. My aim is to establish how the legend was formed and to restore it as a historical act enmeshed in the flow of events and personalities. The Jarrow Crusade mutated into more than a myth. Myth suggests a simple story or a single (sometimes false) assumption. The Crusade is more a collection of elusive myths prone to subtle variations following over the years a vast array of different pathways. Having said that, the legend possesses a core consistency. Wherever one finds the Crusade one discovers the following myths: its non-political character, its superior organisation, its success, its universal support, its essentially English and religious (or Crusade-like) character. These myths are bound up with its symbolism: 'wee Ellen', the banners, its bowler-hatted marshal, the mouth organ band and the black dog.

From children's story to opera, cultural representations have transmitted the Jarrow Crusade into our collective memory, to an extent we are not necessarily even aware of. The image of the Crusade has as a result become highly suggestive and deeply embedded in our cultural subconscious. While this book was in preparation three exhibitions featured the event. There are – to my knowledge – five plays, two musicals, an opera, three pop songs, two folk songs, several paintings and poems, a short story, performance art, a mural, two sculptures, glassware, four television documentaries (three British, one German), four radio programmes, a children's story, a cuddly toy, a real ale, a public house, an election poster, street names, innumerable pieces of journalism and historical references, and of course hundreds of often-reproduced photographs.[1] I would be surprised if this was an exhaustive list. Perversely, given the attention lavished on it, there are only two book-length accounts exclusively about the Crusade; neither by an academic historian, both at the time of writing out of print. It seems odd that academic historians should have neglected an event of such cultural significance. Artists and dramatists are less concerned with the cold empirical detail of the past than historians and their media are necessarily freer, looser and more elastic. For this reason, the Crusade legend has been largely taken as it was found.

There is a regional basis to some of the cultural celebration of the Crusade. Charlie Hardy, the South Shields-born folk singer and songwriter who wrote 'The Song of the Jarrow Marchers' in 1964 connected the Crusade to his own regional identity as a reaction to the experience of living in the South of England. He explained, 'I try to keep the Geordie flag flying in this outpost of civilisation.'[2] In 1974, local lad Alan Price, of sixties pop band The Animals fame, released the 'Jarrow Song' as a single, a song that extolled local pride (the chorus begins 'Oh, come on the Geordie boys') and the lingering threat of militancy ('and if they don't give them a second glance, Geordie with my blessing burn them down.').[3] In October 1986 the Bede Gallery, Jarrow hosted the 'Impressions of a Town' exhibition with such artists as Thomas C. Dugdale, Paolo DiPaolo, George Patterson and Dave Pearson depicting the Crusade.[4] These representations of Jarrow Crusade and the assumptions on which they are based help to forge a regional identity. Having said that, its impact stretches well beyond the North East to a national and even a global level.

If scrutinised, do our assumptions about the Crusade hold? What was known about this event came from the mouths of the march leaders, from the pages of Ellen Wilkinson's book, *The Town that Was Murdered*, and from newspaper accounts of the *Shields Gazette* and the *Evening Chronicle*. The multitude of cultural references to the Crusade echoed, recycled and authenticated this particular view providing a highly uniform account. These form the ubiquitous assumptions of the Crusade. This is what we take to be the truth about the Crusade providing the standard content of the legend.

The commonplace preconceptions we accept as true, however, falter when assessed against the fullest range of historical sources. This study has examined the official documents of the town council, Special Branch, MI5, the cabinet and Home Office, local newspapers of the towns along the route, national newspapers, and newspapers of the North East, interviews with marchers, local folklore, Labour Party and trade union records, and cultural representations of the Crusade. The participants themselves allow a richer understanding. Profiles of key participants can be reconstructed through their interviews, diaries, archival deposits and writings. In particular the enigmatic Ellen Wilkinson, the undisputed heroine of 1936, left a prodigious literary legacy – letters, journalism, political works and novels. Taken together these sources reveal clues to the first line of the riddle of the Crusade: how such a seemingly minor event should assume such notoriety and significance. At the time, the Jarrow Crusade was a relatively unimportant issue but over time its meaning has gathered greater weight. To take one illustration of this lately acquired significance, British Embassies' websites recently provided a chronology of history of the British people. For the 1930s there are only two entries, the Jarrow Crusade and the beginning of the Second World War. Was the Crusade really the most important event of the decade apart from the outbreak of war? This book will address the tendency to amputate the Crusade from its proper historical context, to promote it and elevate it in very stylised form. Returning the Crusade to its context allows a more vivid history, a more engaging narrative, one full of intrigue, irony, folklore and simmering emotion. The richness of the sources allows a magical realism much more preferable than the hollow romanticisation that is all too easy. Rather than this being a trivial event, we discover that the Crusade was part of great historical moment when social and political crises came together – the Depression, appeasement, anti-fascism, the abdication, and the threat of war.

It is one of History's ironies that we know more of the men of high civic office who were persuaded, sometimes with reluctance, to greet the Crusade, or the industrialists who dispensed an Olympian benevolence, or the MPs from whom the Crusade received a moment's sympathy, than the men who tramped their way to London, let alone the women they left behind. This account, of all accounts, should be about them, but injustice and class difference remains in death as it did in life. Wherever possible I have sought out information about the actual marchers, sometimes relying on folk knowledge. Nonetheless, understanding the 'who was who' of powerful admirers and detractors of the Crusade is in itself revealing.

For sociologist Max Weber, a modern legend is a contradiction in terms. He defined modernity as a rational-bureaucratic age. Legends – Saint George, Robin Hood and the Crusades – belong to a bygone world before scientific investigation disenchanted the world and robbed it of its mythologies. How could a legend of this type grow in the twentieth century? All and sundry have raised the banners of the Crusade aloft: Labour and Conservative, supermarket magnates and the workless, fuel protesters and Tony Blair. It has evicted almost every other event of the 1930s from collective memory, including other larger and more successful marches of the unemployed.

To Remember or to Forget?

Opinion divides over whether to remember or forget the Jarrow Crusade. As early as 1967, a bitter argument took place about this on Jarrow council.[5] The remembering of the Crusade has already been amply catalogued; the effort to suppress the memory is less familiar. Former director at Hebburn Palmer's, the ship-repair yard, Leslie Champness believed, 'It's passed from generation to generation, which is a mistake. You should forget the past and look to the future.'[6] Rhodes Boyson, the Conservative MP, complained of Labour's Jarrow nostalgia which had the purpose of obscuring their failures during a decade of conservatism and affluence.[7] Sir John Hall, developer of the MetroCentre shopping complex, contributed to the case for forgetting in a television documentary, *Beyond Jarrow*, screened in March 1988. Piers Merchant, Conservative Newcastle Central MP, said that the Jarrow 86 march was 'a disservice to the region' and, 'If this region wants help it is no use projecting images of the past'.[8] In South Tyneside, this debate continues in new form: whether there should be a permanent exhibition of the Crusade.[9]

For several decades, the Crusade seemed to be a suppressed memory and it simply failed to register in the national imagination. During the decades of silence that by no accident coincided with post-war prosperity, the Crusade was not forgotten but lived a subterranean existence. Within families and amongst workmates, *some* Crusaders and their relatives told the tales of the march.[10] Jarrow-born playwright Alan Plater remembered:

> I learned storytelling in the back yard of my grandparents' house in York Street, Jarrow, on those lovely days when the family gathered for a bit crack. The family tales involved a huge and diverse cast of characters, from Palmer the shipbuilder to Buchan the footballer, from Wee Ellen the agitator to Wee Geordie Wood the comedian.[11]

John Miles, the celebrated musician, whose grandfather, Cuddy Errington, was one of the Crusade's cooks, remembered his father telling of his grandfather's escapades.[12] Family traditions of story-telling, keepsakes and heirlooms have shaped the legend of the Crusade and kept it alive at a local level. Pubs, cafés and homes in Jarrow are adorned with photographs and other commemorations of the Crusade. Jarrow's cultural intelligentsia – Alan Plater, John Miles, Tom Kelly, Peter Flannery and Alex Ferguson – have transformed these oral family traditions into part of the local and national culture. The significance of the local memories of the Crusade, their transmission from generation to generation and their refashioning into popular culture means that official or institutional versions of the Crusade legend have not gone unchallenged.

Peter Flannery, interviewed in BBC television's *The Road from Jarrow* contended, 'Maybe this was the generation that began to think it had been cheated, but you look at the generation now, they not only know that they have been cheated, it is in their blood that they have been cheated, and they are angry.' In contrast, a BBC spokesperson for the programme revealed the underlying post-industrial message: 'Sixty years on, service industries have overtaken manufacturing and new technology has revolutionised the workplace. People are materially better off.'[13] In other words, the protests and class conflicts of the past were no longer relevant to the present. The Crusader Con Whalen commented, 'I'll be watching all the series but the first part just seemed to show how rich Sir John Hall is. But Jarrow writer Peter Flannery is in the series, which is good because when a researcher came to see me from the BBC about the series, I said they should get in touch with him.'[14] Here then, authentic voices of the Crusade provided a counter-current to the tide of convention.

In a sense, to ask us to forget the Crusade is like Canute forbidding the advance of the tide, but the very fact that there are those who advocate that it should be forgotten illustrates the contested character of memory of the Crusade.

Historians and the Jarrow Crusade

Several historians have noticed that the Jarrow Crusade has achieved the status of legend. Michael Polley described the 'touchstone memory' of the Jarrow Crusade as a part of the confused 'internal mythology' of the 1930s.[15] Bill Purdue has explained Jarrow's fame as one aspect of the Labour Party's propaganda version of the 1930s which emphasised hardship and militancy, which they imposed during the 1940s, their most successful decade.[16] However, whilst it is true that the 1930s saw both prosperity and penury, Purdue was wrong to propose that the Jarrow myth exaggerated the militancy of the times. Quite the reverse. The Jarrow Crusade has come to signify moderation and deference. John Saville was much nearer the mark when he pointed out that the Jarrow myth has served to partially eclipse other, more significant, unemployed protests. In similar fashion, Richard Croucher described the historians who downplayed the achievements of the hunger marches as the Jarrow Crusade School.[17] Historians have disputed the character of the Crusade because they contest this decade as a whole. The Crusade's part in this debate has been largely allegorical or exemplary rather than the subject of historical analysis.

Historians have fuelled the myth of the Jarrow Crusade in two distinct senses. First, by its use to symbolise unemployment, hardship, and protest. Secondly, some presented it as a successful protest in contrast to the other misguided efforts of the unemployed. In the first category, Noreen Branson and Margot Heinemann's *Britain in the Nineteen Thirties* has a photograph of the Crusade on the front cover of the 1973 paperback edition; curiously, in his *Labour and the Left in the 1930s*, Ben Pimlott's opening paragraph talked of the 1930s as 'the decade of the Jarrow Crusade...' though the events are not worthy of a mention in the rest of the book; and Ronald Blyth's chapter on the Depression in his *The Age of Illusion* is entitled 'Jarrow'.[18] Dozens of such examples could be cited. For other historians, Jarrow is more than simply a metaphor. Stevenson and Cook, in their *Britain in the Depression*, described the Jarrow Crusade as 'the publicity triumph' whilst National Unemployed Workers' Movement demonstrations 'faded into obscurity'.[19] Harmer counterpoised communist disappointment with 'the simultaneous success of Jarrow'.[20] Andrew Thorpe stated that none of the hunger marchers 'achieved the publicity accorded to the 1936 Jarrow March.'[21] The Crusade's myth of success is the corollary of the contention that the hunger marches were futile, a view which in my opinion is seriously flawed.[22]

Myths present historians with a dilemma. One the one hand, historians have exposed the invented character of myths, their artificiality and their manipulated character. However the danger with such an approach is that it devalues and underestimates the power, social function and the depth of penetration of myths.[23] On the other, there is the temptation in taking myths more seriously to abandon the notion that the people's capacity to reason, challenge and transform myths for their own purposes and in their own interests. This perspective views popular consciousness in an irrational unchanging way too exclusively in terms of folk devils, myths and moral panics. Bringing together both these approaches and appreciating their limitations is necessary for understanding the significance of the Jarrow Crusade.

My intention is to reach a popular audience, including both North-Easterners interested in their ancestors and those more widely interested in the history of labour and to write in a scholarly manner. This may at times frustrate these two constituencies but I beg a little patience from both. There is nothing novel in this and I acknowledge a tradition of writing people's history. It is an approach to history that asks uncomfortable questions of those who ruled and sympathises with those who were ruled.

The narrative approach adopted here has many advantages. Writing of the Crusade on a day-by-day basis makes it an accessible story with a comprehensible structure and plot. The concurrence of events allows the historian to show the context of the Crusade. Jarrow's march coincided with three other marches, the third and fourth month of the Spanish Civil War, the 'Battle of Cable Street' and the abdication crisis. However, as the account reveals, these were more than mere coincidence. There were countless real connections between these events and they could only be separated artificially. This is an important point because a central myth of the Jarrow Crusade is its exceptional character: that it was superior to other marches, that it was more successful than them, that it was not a hunger march. The events were tied together through personalities, through common strategic dilemmas, by common enemies, and shaped profoundly by the moment.

Historical opinion about the 1930s is sharply divided and the Jarrow Crusade takes on an exaggerated significance in these debates without detailed investigation. Greater insight into the Crusade will change the role that it plays in that debate because the claims made for it, in my opinion, are not sustainable. Given that the

Crusade is often used as an illustration supporting a wider position, an updated interpretation of the march does not necessarily threaten the overall position of the revisionists. However as the approach adopted here is to examine the weave of contemporary events, this study can throw further light on these more general arguments.

One of the drawbacks with the narrative approach and the examination of protest is that it can obscure the more profound, slower-paced changes that were taking place at the time. Connecting events is much easier but these structural connections are no less significant in explaining the Crusade. When we encounter individuals they are part of wider intellectual traditions, they line up in different sides in the arguments of the day, they represent great global trends of capitalism at that time. They undeniably have choice but their options are limited by circumstance, by who they are and what they can achieve. The danger then is to meet individuals, like for instance Sir John Jarvis, and to see in him nothing other than a philanthropist trying to improve things in Jarrow. He was that, but he was much more. His patronage stood in the traditions of charitable works for the deserving poor and employer paternalism rather than in the spirit of the right to work and the modern welfare state. He was a politician with a conscious strategy to prevent dangerous territorial losses for his party. He was also a businessman with an eye on the great economic trends of the day – rearmament and the drift to war, rationalisation, the closer relationship between the state and big business, the growing interpenetration of the banks and industry – and how he could most effectively seize upon them.

Making sense of the trends of the capitalist system in 1936 is crucial to the story of the Crusade and its context. This was the year in which Charlie Chaplin used his comic genius to question the dehumanising effects of rationalised mass production in the film *Modern Times*. In this year, the fault-lines of great industrial powers and their empires were shifting in the Mediterranean, in Eastern Europe and in the Far East. But the contradictions of age were not just international; patterns of capitalist development profoundly affected British society. Historians have debated the 'condition of England' in the 1930s and the Crusaders witnessed the contrasts

9

and complexities of English society as they tramped through cathedral towns, manufacturing cities, the affluent Home Counties and the distressed coalfields.

Sir Ian Kershaw in his acclaimed biography of Hitler sought to write a 'structural biography' meaning one that paid great attention to the environment that shaped the Nazi leader. Similarly this is an attempt to write a narrative history of the Jarrow Crusade that picks out its structural connections: contexts of wider social relationships, contexts of the culture and legend of the Crusade, contexts of contemporary events and the contexts of the past's relationship to the present.

The Backdrop of Events

At the heart of Jarrow's woes of course were the fortunes of the shipbuilding industry. The worst of the slump in shipbuilding coincided with the global economic recession of the early 1930s. Other industries, for example coalmining, were also devastated in this economic environment. However, the problems of shipbuilding began before the onset of this recession. With declining profit margins, overcapacity and international competition, the shipbuilding industry witnessed the closure of 36 shipbuilders from 1920 to 1930. Whilst the North East built 81.7% of the world's ships in 1892, in 1934, a trough year, it had fallen to 6.8%.[24] The industry employed 104,631 in 1921; ten years later there were only 29,525 jobs. Sir James Lithgow, chairman of the Shipbuilding Employers' Federation implemented a 'scrap and build' plan to restore the profits of shipbuilding magnates. Funded by a levy on members and Bankers' Industrial Development Company (BIDC) money, in March 1929 the Shipbuilders Employers' Federation created the National Shipbuilders' Security Ltd (NSS), a holding company to eliminate overcapacity. It scrapped 38 yards, over a quarter of all berths.[25] The intention was to avoid the damaging uncertainty of cut-throat price competition. That was cold comfort to unemployed shipbuilding workers in towns where the yards had been closed and 'sterilised'.

Sir Charles Mark Palmer (1822-1907) had created modern Jarrow with his shipyard and the influx of labour that it required. Jarrow was in effect a company town, nicknamed Palmersville. Between 1852 when it opened and 1932, Palmer's Yard had built over 1,000 ships.[26] Referring to Palmer's manager McGowan of the 1920s, the people of Jarrow summed up their history thus: 'St. Bede founded it, Sir Charles Palmer built it, and McGowan buggered it'.[27] Despite being reputedly one of the most efficient in the country, financial difficulties had crippled the yard. The management had over-optimistically misread the market in the immediate post-war years when they had bought a yard at Amble, Northumberland and the South Pelaw colliery. They also updated the steelworks, thereby piling up large debts. In effect, at the roulette wheel of competitive capitalism, the management were gambling with their workers' and the town's futures. From 1921 the firm suffered large losses with only three years in the black before closure.[28] The last ship, the destroyer HMS Duchess, was launched on 19 July 1932. In 1933 because of its overdraft at the bank and lack of orders, the receiver was called in. In the following year, the receiver sold the yard to Lithgow's National Shipbuilders' Security.[29] Palmer's in Jarrow was closed and was not to be re-opened for 40 years under the NSS terms to any buyer of the site. The moment that symbolised the greatest despair was when Palmer's distinctive forward-leaning square cranes with elliptical heads were pulled down. Their toppling was to be remembered as a terrible day of heartbreak for Jarrow.

For governments between the wars, the economic and social conditions were a recurrent concern. At the time of the Jarrow Crusade, two aspects of the Government's policy towards unemployment attracted public controversy: the so-called 'special' or distressed areas like the North East, South Wales and Scotland and the Unemployment Assistance Board, which provided relief for the unemployed through the hated means test. The National Unemployed Workers' Movement (NUWM, 1920-46) was the main organisation of the unemployed to organise protests against government policy. The movement was subject to ups and downs with peaks of activity reached in 1920-23 and 1931-6. Through the NUWM, the unemployed themselves built a movement, which organised marches, demonstrations, factory protests against overtime and casework for claimants. This organisation, whose key figures were communists such as Wal Hannington and Harry MacShane, found itself persistently shunned by the official Labour movement and was affected by the shifting line of the Communist International. Its leaders were willing on occasion to ignore or dilute communist instructions which they thought were against the interests of the movement. The NUWM organised six national hunger marches, the last of which coincided with the Jarrow Crusade. The National Hunger March of 1936 targeted the Unemployment Assistance Board scales and the means test. By 1936, largely as a result of the endeavours of the NUWM, the idea of marching on London had caught on so that along with the Jarrow Crusade and the National Hunger March, there were also simultaneously marches organised by the National League of the Blind and by Scottish veterans.

If the means test and the Special Areas were to the fore in domestic politics, the Baldwin Government faced a series of challenges in terms of foreign affairs: the territorial claims of Hitler, the Spanish Civil War, a general strike in Palestine, a coup in Iraq and nationalism in India. The British Empire was an ailing giant. The Government's answer to German and Italian expansionism was to appease and hopefully contain. The Spanish Civil War acted as a beacon to anti-fascists who enlisted in the International Brigades to fight Franco. Several of those who marched to London in October and November enlisted in the International Brigades. The British Government, on the other hand, pursued a policy of non-intervention throughout. This stance aimed to prevent international involvement in the war in order to avoid an escalation of the conflict to the European level. Non-intervention failed miserably to stop arm sales to Franco's rebels and the maintenance of this policy increasingly became a hypocritical fiction.

Behind the curtain of press silence, while all this was happening, a serious constitutional crisis was beginning to unfold. The King at the time was Edward VIII whose brief reign ended in abdication over his relationship and eventual marriage to American divorcee Wallis Simpson. The First World War had seriously shaken the royal family. Their European cousins (not only in metaphor) had lost power in Russia, Austria-Hungary and Germany. The Palace feared that the days of the monarchy were numbered. In order to preserve the monarchy, the strategy of Sir Arthur (later Lord) Stamfordham, George V's Private Secretary, was to win for the heir to the throne a special place in the affection of the working class. As Prince of Wales, Edward had gained the reputation as the 'People's Prince' and was by far the most popular of George V's children. He had earned his nickname because of tours of mining communities and depressed working-class areas, and because of his sponsorship of veterans' organisations like the Toc H and charitable bodies such as the National Council of Social Services. The unemployed were a particular target of Edward's charm offensive. By the time of the death of George V in January 1936, the Palace had succeeded in creating a genuinely popular heir for the old King. The problem was that behind the public face, Edward was a playboy with a penchant for married women and suspect political views (Hitler's Ambassador to Britain called him 'a kind of English National Socialist').[30] His relationship with Wallis Simpson set Edward on a collision course with Palace officials and the Prime Minister. On 15 October Alec Hardinge, the King's Private Secretary (unbeknown to His Majesty) held a meeting with Stanley Baldwin asking the latter to prevent the divorce of Wallis Simpson. If that divorce took place it would be completed in time for Edward's coronation so that she might be crowned alongside him. The abdication crisis added to the worries of the Government. Moreover, as Edward's popularity swelled because of his sympathy for those in the distressed areas, it meant the abdication and the plight of Special Areas might be brought together in a way that would present an intractable crisis for Stanley Baldwin's Government.

The Backdrop of Personalities

Ellen Wilkinson (1891-1947) was Jarrow's MP at the time of the Crusade and one of its leaders. German refugee and left-wing academic Edward Conze described her as an undersized fiery red-headed agitator, a British Rosa Luxemburg from the slums of Manchester, who, for a while, had been an elementary school teacher. Her physical courage made me gasp when I saw it in Spain.[31]

Because of her association with the respectable and non-political Crusade, representations of Ellen Wilkinson often tend to water down her radicalism. Several schools have adopted her name and a metro on the Tyne and Wear network is named after her. As an example of the dilution of her politics, her membership of the Communist Party (1920-23) is dismissed as 'brief'.[32] The newspapers too made light of or sidestepped the MP's politics: 'Red Ellen' became 'Wee Ellen'. Special Branch were not so dismissive of her politics; their report on the march underlined her former membership of Communist Party and the fact that she had maintained a long-standing association with the party's campaigns. They were also well aware that she was on the reception committee of the National Hunger March.

Born in Salford into a working-class home, Ellen Wilkinson possessed a long and impressive *curriculum vitae* as a political activist. She joined the Independent Labour Party at the age of 16. After university, with her great vitality as the best possible recommendation, she became in 1913 Manchester organiser of Millicent Fawcett's National Union of Women Suffrage Societies and then in 1915 a national organiser of Amalgamated Union of Co-operative Employees (which later became National Union of Distributive and Allied Workers, NUDAW, and then Union of Shop, Distributive and Allied Workers, USDAW). Sympathetic to the Russian revolution, especially its achievements on the road to women's liberation, she visited the Soviet Union in 1921 and a portrait of Lenin looked down over her bed.[33] When she was first elected to the Commons in October 1924, Ellen was one of only four women MPs.

When she lost her Middlesbrough East seat in 1931, Ellen Wilkinson worked for the NUDAW until her electoral victory in Jarrow in 1935. Her career blossomed after the Crusade. She was to join the Labour Party National Executive Committee in 1937. In 1940, as the Labour Party joined with Churchill's coalition government she became Parliamentary Secretary to the Minister of Pensions and then Parliamentary Secretary to the Ministry of Home Security from 1940 to 1945.

The pinnacle of her career was reached during the Labour Government of 1945 when she became Minister of Education. As such she was responsible for the implementation of the 1944 Education Act. Her friend Edward Conze believed that Ellen Wilkinson was out of her depth at the Ministry of Education and that Attlee had put her there to neutralise her politically. In truth Ellen Wilkinson was out of her element, a natural poacher rather than gamekeeper. These were the contradictions of Labour in office that she had eloquently exposed previously.[34] Her record at the Ministry of Education has had a mixed reception amongst labour historians.[35] Whilst she increased the school-leaving age to 15, introduced free school milk and established university scholarships, she opposed the introduction of comprehensive schools, arguing against teaching unions and those within her own party along lines suggested to her by the top civil servants at the Ministry of Education. In her novel *Division Bell Mystery*, she described the Whitehall mandarins 'who let the puppets [i.e. the Ministers] play' and observed, 'There is no wine so intoxicating as the feeling of being on the inside when big events are moving'.[36] Could Ellen Wilkinson in office be immune to the pressures that she herself had earlier recognised? David Rubinstein reflected:

> The qualities required of left-wing rebels and of reforming ministers are seldom identical, and Ellen Wilkinson was not the first nor the last socialist to raise the spirits of the political enemy after assuming the mantle of office.[37]

Ellen Wilkinson was an enigmatic figure, like an unstable volatile compound. Her ideas were an eclectic and evolving blend of Fabianism, Methodism and Marxism. Likewise, her political career freely mixed passionate and energetic opposition to capitalism and an ambition for high office in party and government.

As the President of the Board of Trade in the mid-1930s, Sir Walter Runciman (1870-1949) held Jarrow's fortunes in his ministerial hands. When petitioned to help Jarrow in July 1936, Sir Walter had infamously declared to the delegation from the striken town 'Jarrow must work out its own salvation'. Sir Walter's comment was according to David Riley 'seven curt and heartless words [that] started this Crusade'.[38] Ellen Wilkinson's frosty appraisal of Runciman had not thawed by the time of writing *The Town That Was Murdered*. 'Icily correct, icily polite, apparently completely indifferent to the woes of others, Runciman as a minister in each office he held was one of England's minor disasters' was her verdict.[39] Indeed, Sir Walter junior had had a long political career as an MP that had began in the last year of the old century. He served as the President of the Board of Trade twice (1914-16 and 1931-7). Sir Walter the elder, the President of the Board of Trade's father, had been Hartlepool MP during the war years and received a baronetcy in the honours list of 1933. His lodgings did not bear comparison to those of the overcrowded whitewashed former miner's cottages and red-brick coal-blackened back-to-back terraces of Jarrow. He would stay where business or whim took him: the impressive Fernwood House, in leafy Jesmond, Newcastle; or his London apartment, 53 Leadenhall Street, in fashionable EC3; or the grand 300-year-old country mansion, Shoreston Hall, Northumberland.[40] His son, who became Viscount Runciman of Doxford, was born in South Shields, but this local connection with Jarrow counted for little and failed to narrow the greater distance of class. In the story of the Crusade, he deservedly became the villain of the piece and this infamy was compounded when he featured as one of the 'guilty men' who appeased Hitler over the dismemberment of democratic Czechoslovakia in 1938.[41] Of his role as Head of the Mission to Czechoslovakia in August-September 1938, Ellen caustically observed, 'Runciman's words sealed Palmer's of Jarrow's fate as later he was to seal Prague's.'[42] Sudeten Nazis saluted the Runciman mission to Czechoslovakia with the chant 'we need no Christmas-man, we have our Runciman'.[43]

Sir Andrew Duncan (1884-1952) was the Chairman of the British Iron and Steel Federation from 1935 to 1940. Here was a ruling-class insider who was very well connected and wielded a considerable if half-concealed influence over Jarrow's fate. When the Bank of England turned down the finance for the Jarrow steel works in 1936 because of the objections of the BISF, Sir Andrew was the intermediary between these bodies being both a Director of the Bank of England (1929-40) and the Chairman of the BISF. Formerly head of the Central Electricity Board, chosen because of that industry's modern and rational reputation, he had also been the Vice-President of the Shipbuilding Employers' Federation during the 1920s when the industry was devising the policy of rationalisation that ultimately set Jarrow's fate. Imagine the local consternation then, when this same individual became the President of the Board of Trade and the Minister of Supply in 1940, once again having Jarrow's future in his hands.[44] T.P. Scarborough, the chair of Barnet Urban District Council who interviewed Sir Andrew on Jarrow's behalf the month before the Crusade, came away with the impression that 'He is a charming man, genuinely concerned for the unemployed, but too much obsessed with the question of profits!' She was in reality being fobbed off and when he was pressed about trying to find the finance for the Jarrow project he objected that if this was done for Jarrow, then what about Dunbarton? He told her that whilst he sympathised with Jarrow's plight, he thought that the march would do a 'great deal of harm'.[45] It certainly did a great deal of harm to the reputation of the BISF which car manufacturer Lord Nuffield described as 'a perfect ramp, an absolute ramp, big cigars and nothing to do'.[46] Not everyone was so generous to Sir Andrew as Miss Scarborough. H.P. Everett, the Tyne Improvement Commissioner, held a meeting with the President of the Board of Trade at which he 'detected lurking somewhere in the vaults of the Bank of England another sinister figure Sir Andrew Duncan'.[47]

Hensley Henson, the Bishop of Durham (1863-1947) is a key figure in the story of the Jarrow Crusade. As one of the leading Bishops of the land, Hensley Henson was a member of the British establishment with a seat in the House of Lords and was at the right hand of King George VI at the Coronation in 1937. One instance of his lofty social status and upper-class connections was his position in the Masonic movement. Although he believed himself to be a poor Mason because he found the 'feeding and functions intolerable', Lord Harewood, the sitting Provincial Grand Master, proposed the Bishop to HRH the Duke of Connaught as his successor; the Bishop declined because of his advanced years.[48]

His condemnation of the Crusade is infamous. Less well known are his private actions to undermine the Crusade and the hidden conflicts amongst Anglican clergy of which the Jarrow Crusade became one more subject. The Bishop of Durham was a controversial priest who sought office in order to combat both Anglo-Catholicism and Christian Socialism within the Church of England. Henson's relations with several other Bishops were strained and the public support for the Crusade of other clergy has these differences as a subtext. In his memoirs and letters, he was derogatory about several of his fellows. The previous Bishop of Ripon who had 'hurl[ed] cocoanuts at me' was 'polemical, garrulous, and humourless', and made 'foolish utterances'.[49] Thus factional intrigue hid behind the mixed Anglican clerical reactions to the Crusade.[50] The Church, however, had greater concerns at the time. The abdication crisis was a particular threat to the Church of England as an institution because the coronation of Edward might have required the Church to ignore its own doctrines during the coronation ceremony over which it had to officiate.[51] The acuteness of this problem for the Church was sharpened when a reference in the Bishop of Bradford's address precipitated the end of the press silence on the matter. The newspapers put senior churchmen under intense scrutiny during the whole affair and there was a danger that clerical moralising against a popular king would make a further blow to the standing of the Church.

Sir John Jarvis (1876-1950) tried to rescue Jarrow by a combination of philanthropy, new industries and government subsidies. Sir John initiated the Surrey Fund for the relief of Jarrow in 1934. That this Surrey MP, with no known connection with the North East, should take such an interest in Jarrow is not quite as strange as it first seems. Sir John, a well-connected and influential businessman, was considered to be an expert in labour issues. He had advised the government on industrial relations during the First World War and subsequently on financial matters. For his services he received a baronetcy in 1922.[52] With interests in publishing, construction and manufacturing, Sir John was the chairman of J & A Churchill Ltd. (Publishers) and Armstrong Whitworth (Ironfounders) Ltd. Like many of London's political and business élite, he was a member of the exclusive Carlton Club and had even represented England at curling. With an enhanced profile as High Sheriff of Surrey (1934-35), Sir John's election to the Commons in 1935 (where he served as MP for Guildford until his death in 1950) marked his breakthrough as a national political figure. This man has come to occupy a privileged place in lowly Jarrow's history. He did much to promote his self-image as selfless benefactor, he ploughed over £40,000 into the town's recovery, and his fame is second only to Ellen Wilkinson in the fight against distress in Jarrow. His obituary in *The Times* stated that 'He earned the gratitude of a town by his unselfish work for and help to the people of Jarrow during the worst days of economic depression.'[53] *Who Was Who?* noted that he started '5 new industries on Tyneside employing over 5,000 men'. He is remembered, albeit less reverentially, in oral testimony. Robert Maughan, a Jarrow Crusader, recalled: 'He helped the town a lot that man, I must be honest, well he tried to help. He got me a fortnight's work anyway. (Laughter).'[54] He is also remembered for stealing the limelight with his announcement of the establishment of a tube metal works in Jarrow at the Crusade's London public meeting.

Sir Percy Malcolm Stewart OBE (1872-1951) is a less significant character but integral to the drama of the Jarrow Crusade. Malcolm Stewart divided his energies between philanthropy and business. He was the President of the National Council of Social Services, the government-sponsored charitable network that organised various efforts to relieve the Depression. He was a major cement manufacturer, President of the Cement Makers' Federation. In contrast to coal or shipbuilding, this industry profited from the construction boom of the mid- and late 1930s.[55] During the Jarrow Crusade he resigned from his post as the Commissioner for the Special Areas in England and Wales. This role had been set up under the Special Areas Act of 1934 to deal with those regions that the economic slump had devastated and that the economic recovery of the mid- and late 1930s was slow to reach. The Jarrow Crusade and the National Hunger March along with King's visit to South Wales in November 1936 increased the pressure on the Government to do something about the special areas. As pressure mounted on the Government, Stewart publicly associated himself with Jarrow's cause and had lobbied Government to intervene to save the steelworks project.

Far away from the tramping boots of the marchers, these individuals provide the cast list of the Crusade and its unfolding drama. Upon their actions depended the livelihoods of the inhabitants of Jarrow. Their largely unaccountable decisions constitute the real history of the Crusade beyond its familiar legend.

Week One: Jarrow to Ripon

Monday 5 October: Marching to the Promised Land
Jarrow to Chester-le-Street (pop. 18,390), 12 miles

After two months of preparation, the Jarrow Crusade was ready. The organisers had carefully choreographed the day of departure. Mayor of Jarrow Billy Thompson, sporting his two-cornered hat, robes and gold chain, beside the Town Clerk, C.S. Perkins, in wig and gown, led other town dignitaries in procession to Christ Church. Sitting in the congregation, tightly packed into the pews, were many of the wives of the men who were about to leave them for a month's quest for justice. Reverend H.T. Hood, the congregational minister, read the lesson, Proverbs: 4. More than just an arbitrary choice, this matched Mayor Thompson's vision of the Crusade. He had insisted on the religious aspect of the march and its non-political character. He had hoped to persuade a local clergyman to lead the march with a crucifix but was unable to find one willing to do so.[1]

To read this lesson, is to understand the Crusade, at least in part. Proverbs Four was an 'instruction of a father', just as the marchers were under the fatherly guidance of the town's leaders. On their journey, they were advised to tread the path of righteousness. Unlike other hunger marches, they were not to 'drink the wine of violence'. The lesson counselled listeners not to speak out of turn with 'forward mouth, and perverse lip', just as the town officials kept tightly controlled what was said to the press.[2] Here, in the lesson, key features of the Crusade could be discerned in cameo.

Opening a prayer, the Church of England Rector of Jarrow, the Reverend S. Harvie Clark urged, 'Guide those in posts of responsibility and leadership in our town and country that they may wisely take counsel to heal our distress'.[3] The choice of hymns – 'Through the night of doubt and sorrow' and 'O God, our help in ages past' – was also apt. The former took up the crusading imagery so central to presentation of the march to the press and public. The first and final verses expounded the virtues of a religious crusade, and reverberated with poignancy in the dark wooden rafters:

Onward goes the pilgrim band,
Singing songs of expectation,
Marching to the promised land.
Clear before us through the darkness
Gleams and burns the guiding light:
Brother clasps the hand of brother,
Stepping fearless through the night.

…

Onward, therefore, pilgrim brothers,
Onward, with the cross our aid!
Bear its shame, and fight its battle,
Till we rest beneath its shade.
Soon shall come the great awaking,
Soon the rending of the tomb;
Then the scattering of all shadows,
And the end of toil and gloom.

The blessing of Dr James Geoffrey Gordon followed, an act that organisers correctly calculated would receive wide press coverage. He was a senior figure in the diocese having become the Bishop Suffragan of Jarrow, Archdeacon and Canon Residentiary of Durham Cathedral in 1932 and although he was the Bishop of Jarrow, he lived at the College, in Durham. The clergy of all Jarrow's denominations – Church of England, Roman Catholic, Baptist and Presbyterian – were witnesses to this consecration of Jarrow's pilgrimage. Organisers stressed that the Crusade was unsectarian but as the established church, the Church of England held a privileged position in its rituals throughout.

After the church service, Mayor Thompson inspected the men. Seven of those selected had dropped out as the march was about to begin; one of them had found a job. Given that 1,200 had volunteered and only 200 were chosen, the seven replacements were easily found, amongst them neighbours: Billy Beattie, who did not have a chance to ask his wife and left a note on the mantelpiece, and Bob Burns of Morpeth Avenue.[4] The mayor solemnly cautioned them, 'Remember, you are going to London for Jarrow and we depend on you to maintain the credit of the town'.[5]

March leaders repeatedly insisted that theirs was not a hunger march but a crusade. Over eight centuries earlier, after papal deliberations at the Council of Clermont in the centre of France, an immense crowd gathered at the opening of the First Crusade on 27 November 1095. With its official solemnity, religious ritual and teeming streets, if not the mystical illusions, Jarrow emulated that fateful day. In the presence of the clerical and noble dignitaries, as well as those from the lower orders, Pope Urban II appealed to all those present to take the sign of the cross, make an oath of allegiance and venture forth to the Holy Land. For their endeavours, a papal decree of penitent remission would cleanse their sins. Seething with religious euphoria and spontaneous enthusiasm, many pledged themselves to the enterprise and sewed makeshift crosses onto their garments.

From Christ Church, at around 10.30 am, Ellen Wilkinson, Jarrow's MP, Mayor Thompson, Charles Perkins, the Town Clerk, Councillor A.E. 'Gompy' Gompertz, secretary of South Shields Labour Party, and Jarrow town councillors led the Crusade through the town accompanied by Palmer's band.[6] Thousands squeezed either side of the first few hundred yards through Jarrow and Hebburn along Grange Road, Hill Street, Albert Road, Victoria Road, moving into Pelaw on the Shields Road.[7] The whole town bid them on their way. The crowds were cordoned onto the pavements while the men, marching four abreast their 'Jarrow Crusade' banner aloft, threaded through the centre of Jarrow. The whole town was abuzz with excitement.

For the first time in years, not a soul watched from the public gallery of the Jarrow Police Court, where the unemployed could bank on drama and local intrigue.[8] Apart from road traffic offences, much of the court's time was consumed with grim routine of the crimes of poverty. Regular complainants were coal companies – Harton Coal Company and John Bowes & Partners – prosecuting those who were trespassing on their slagheaps taking coal to keep their hearths warm. Inspector Kay of the London and North Eastern Railway likewise regularly snatched men pilfering coal from the railway's depots. Such transgressors typically received fines of six or ten shillings. Another major part of the court's time was taken up with the non-payment of bills. Sunderland and South Shields Water Company and South Shields Gas Company placed its customers in front of the justices of the peace to secure warrant orders so that they could send in the bailiffs. Defendants also faced the courts for non-payment of rates. A proportion of these unfortunates returned to the courts for defaulting on their fines. The courts also witnessed petty, and exceptionally not so petty, theft. During the Crusade, a 16-year-old was tried for stealing £46 and sent to Netherton Training School. But the typical objects of larceny were potatoes, pigeons, scrap metal, milk bottles and, of course, the most common item, coal. Cases of dole abuse were rare, but there were fourteen on 14 December 1935. Given the tightness of the regulations, even petty infringements might result in prosecution. The Juvenile Court records suggest a degree of friction between the authorities and Jarrow's youth. Trespass, vandalism and riding bicycles without lights on were common infractions amongst youngsters.[9]

The departure of the Crusade, especially the Bishop's blessing, made a great impression on the press. All who were present remember it and stories pass from one generation to another. Sam Rowan, the council employee assigned to the Crusade on a full-time basis, remembered surveying the assembled marchers and townsfolk from the steps of the town hall and thinking, 'My God, what have I let myself in for?' Don (now Lord) Dixon, who became the town's MP in 1979, also recalled the day:

> I can vividly remember the start of the march. As a seven-year-old child I ran up our back lane to the Town Hall and saw crowds of people outside. Not knowing what it was all about I later asked my father why all the crowds were outside the Town Hall and why were the people marching. He told me they were going to London for work. I asked the innocent question: "Wouldn't it be better to fetch the work up here where the men are?"[10]

A newspaper photograph captured George Smith, a clerk at Jarrow office of the South Shields and Sunderland Water Company, peering through his office window at the sight. One of his bosses at Head Office must have scrutinised the image to check up on his drones or been told by a zealous colleague. Either way, this earned George a stern reprimand, 'Had you nothing better to do than watch this kind of thing?'[11] The departure provided another classic image of the Crusade. It pictured the Robb family at its centre – John Robb, former labourer at Palmer's, holding his son Bobby's hand, wife Emily and son Benny in her arms - alongside the banner. It has become probably the most commonly used photograph of the Crusade.[12] In its fiftieth anniversary coverage of the Crusade, *The Observer* again printed it and interviewed Eva Murray, Benny and Bobby's sister, next to the celebrated image.[13] The photograph has also acted as muse for artists. Both the sculpture in Jarrow metro station and in the car park of Morrisons in Jarrow are based on it. Its popularity and evocative power rest on its depiction of the Crusade as a family event showing that hardship affected entire households and that the Crusade touched different generations.

Harry Clarke, then aged 13 years, remembered skipping off school to be a camp-follower of the Crusade for the first five or so miles. He walked alongside George Cruikshank, a communist, and one of the banner-carriers on that day. Harry was a founding member of the Jarrow and Hebburn League of Labour Youth and then the Jarrow and Hebburn Young Communist League. At the time there were about eight members of the Communist Party in Jarrow and Hebburn, led by red-haired, red-faced Mick Boyle. When the Church Poverty Action Group (CPAG) organised a march through Jarrow in 1999, Harry addressed the marchers in a special church service. When local television covered the CPAG march they obligingly drew parallels with 1936. These re-enactments stirred a public controversy. The last surviving Crusader, Con Whalen, described the CPAG march as futile. He also challenged a central myth of the Crusade – that it (unlike other marches) was a success. On *North East Tonight*, Con explained that his march had made 'not a ha'porth of difference' as the closure of the shipyards testified.[14]

Walking in the brilliant autumn sunshine, the oldest man to accompany the marchers, Councillor Gordon, won his reputation as 'the singing councillor'. They reached Springwell Bank by 1 pm and the Crusade took its first pause for food: tea and corned beef sandwiches (consuming 50 loaves and 40 lbs of corned beef). In the afternoon the bright periods of sunshine continued but even this warmest part of the day did not get above 13ºC. Two miles from Chester-le-Street, borrowing a football from children, thirty or forty Crusaders enthusiastically played a match during their rest. They arrived at Chester-le-Street at 5 pm. Councillor G. Robson welcomed the Crusade and the women's section of Chester-le-Street Labour Party provided a meal of jam, bread and tea. The newspaper report did not however tally with what Sam Rowan would 'remember to his dying day' that 'he'd never seen men so disappointed in all me life' by the food after their long hike because they were fed corned beef sandwiches and tea exactly as they had had for their lunch. On the first evening, the medical students, D. Cargill and Joan Blake of the Inter-Hospital Socialist Society, were already busy with blistered feet and a workless hairdresser, known in the folklore of Crusade as the 'Jarra barber', was already plying his trade.[15] So not only were the Crusaders well fed, they were also well groomed. Sam Rowan remembered how they were desperately short of soap on the first day and Joe Symonds was frantically buying soap wherever he could. Although the *Shields Gazette* report at the time was upbeat about the response in Chester-le-Street, it was later described as 'cheerless' and 'ambivalent' and the men were a little disconcerted to be 'packed like sardines' into the Parish church hall.[16] The *Gazette* reporter was conscious that concerned family members back home would pore over this account and the positive gloss was probably to reassure Crusaders' kith and kin.

The Crusade certainly failed to make a great impression on Chester-le-Street's local newspaper. On 2 October the weekly *Chester-le-Street Chronicle and District Advertiser* had a brief report stating that Chester would be the first halt of the Crusade and printed a letter from Mayor Thompson appealing for sympathy. In the following issue a cursory report noted that the Crusade's passing received 'a good welcome' but this was buried in the 'We Know' column of miscellaneous local events below school scholarships, mothers' meetings and the Dean of Peterborough's visit. It even ranked below tales from leek shows about the 'pinched' prizes and leeks that circulated from one show to another.[17] Leeks and allotments played an important role in Jarrow. Arthur Barton remembered:

> The allotments ... were not only an economic asset to many a harassed father, but a refuge where he could get away from the accusing faces of his children, and his wife's incessant 'Will ye ever work again?' and find a measure of peace and contentment turning the loam on the side of the cemetery bank to grow vegetables for the eternal stews, and perhaps leeks for the annual shows at the little pubs along the High Street. Many a man kept his sanity this way and something of his manhood, and even a little pride when his leek outdid the others or his pigeon came back first from Rouen.[18]

Ellen Wilkinson accompanied the march to Chester-le-Street before leaving for the annual Labour Party conference in Edinburgh. The conference had opened that day. She missed the morning session that had debated 'Fascist disturbances in East London'. This referred to the previous Saturday, when a massive counter-mobilisation of anti-fascists had halted Oswald Mosley's Blackshirts, in the renowned 'Battle of Cable Street'. Despite Cable Street's status in working-class folk memory, Herbert Morrison, leader of the London Labour Party, arch-anti-communist and Ellen Wilkinson's lover, moving the motion calling for a government inquiry and a ban on political uniforms, condemned those who had organised the counter-demonstration.[19]

In the afternoon, the conference debated the situation in Spain and the National Council of Labour's support for the policy of non-intervention.[20] Since 28 September, the Labour and Socialist International (LSI) and the International Federation of Trade Unions (IFTU) backed Leon Blum's policy of non-intervention rather than the appeal of the Spanish centre-left Government.[21] Two days later, the NCL telegrammed Anthony Eden, at the Foreign Office, to inform him of their support for this position. Sir Charles Trevelyan's impassioned rebuttal countered Arthur Greenwood's opening speech. He demanded to know:

> ... when you talk of non-intervention, is it intervention to call for the operation of old-time sanctioned international law, that arms can be bought by a Government from nationals of another country? Is it intervention to say that law shall still operate? What we have been doing is to sanction the destruction of an international law which would probably have saved the Spanish people....

Rotherham MP, William Dobbie, who had recently returned from Spain, went further, declaring 'the democracy of Spain is being murdered and we are assisting in the assassination'. Despite Nye Bevan adding to this sentiment, speakers supporting the leadership's position – Clement Attlee, George Hicks, Ernest Bevin, Charles Dukes – held the line, with the aid of the block vote, 1,836,000 to 519,000.

***

These issues were close to Ellen Wilkinson's heart. She had already made a trip to Spain with Lord Listowel in 1934 in the aftermath of the Asturian miners' insurrection on behalf of the Relief

Committee for the Victims of Fascism (RCVF). The miners had risen in response to the formation of a centre-right coalition Government that included Gil Robles of the CEDA (*Confederación Española de Derechos Autónomos*) who menaced Spanish workers in a way that evoked an Iberian Hitler or Mussolini. Though desperately short of rifles, with their knowledge of explosives, their catapults and sticks of dynamite, the *dinamiteros* ('dynamiters') were a formidable and militant force. They fought under the slogan '*Uníos, Hermanos Proletarios!*' (Unite, Proletarian Brothers!) a reaction against the disunity that had allowed Hitler to gain power in Germany the year before. By the time Ellen Wilkinson arrived in Asturias, a counterrevolution was in full swing, costing the lives of around 2,000 workers. In this brutal campaign, General Franco gained his taste for spilling workers' blood to 'restore order'. Foreign eyewitnesses to the excesses of Franco's troops, even former members of the British House of Commons, were not welcome and Commandant Doval of Oviedo summarily deported Ellen Wilkinson to France. On her return from Spain, she used several speaking engagements to expose the repression in the Asturian province. She described villages bombed from the air, mass executions and the arrest of all left journalists.[22] The conclusion that she drew was that fascism had risen in countries because labour had failed to take power, that there was little left that capitalism could offer British workers and they should run industry on socialist lines. Much to its discredit, the National Executive Committee (NEC) of the Labour Party condemned Ellen Wilkinson for her courageous trip to Spain. Their perverse justification was that the right-wing Spanish Government was now scrutinising the documents of foreigners with a view to expelling them from the country.[23] Ellen Wilkinson was then an official of the National Union of Distributive and Allied Workers (NUDAW), and its EC called for a report on her activities in Spain.[24] Her association with the RCVF nearly cost Ellen her membership of the Labour Party. The Party put the RCVF on the list of proscribed organisations and then passed a motion at its 1934 conference stating that membership of that organisation was incompatible with Labour Party membership.[25] Ellen had protested against this to the press.[26] Having won the motion at the conference, the Labour Party NEC pursued the matter sending 28 ultimatum letters to individual members who were associated with the campaign, including Lord Marley, the Party's Chief Whip in the Lords, Aneurin Bevan and Ellen Wilkinson on 28 December 1934.[27] She immediately broke her association with the organisation. By the end of February all but four recipients of the letter had replied and bowed to the NEC.

Unashamed of his chilling intentions two years later, Franco declared just over a week into the Spanish Civil War to an American journalist in Tetuan:

> There can be no truce or treaty. I will continue preparing my advance on Madrid. I will advance. I will take the capital. I will save Spain from Marxism no matter what the price. Shortly, very shortly, my troops will have pacified the country and all of this will soon seem like a nightmare.

The journalist replied 'That means that you will have to shoot half of Spain?', at which Franco smiled, 'I repeat, at whatever cost'.[28] He had first used terror and repression as a commander of the Foreign Legion in Spanish Morocco where he tolerated decapitation and mutilation to instil dread in the Moroccan population.[29]

***

The Jarrow Crusade was not the only unemployed protest to start on 5 October. In some ways, more significantly, the 400-strong West Scotland Contingent of the National Hunger March left Glasgow for Kilmarnock that day. Led by Peter Kerrigan, the West Scotland group were to converge on London alongside other contingents totalling some 1,400 a full week after the Crusade. John Lochmore, a Scottish hunger marcher, observed several decades later:

> The Jarrow March which took place at the same time as ours equally was of significance, but over the years the media and the establishment have put it to the fore and have virtually ignored the NUWM march.[30]

Tuesday 6 October: Cherry Cake in Ferryhill
Chester-le-Street to Ferryhill (pop. 3,400), 12 miles

After what was for many a sleepless night on the floor of the Church Institute, the marchers had finished breakfast by 7.30 am. As they left the town, the main street lined with townspeople, Councillors C.H. Clayton and W.P. Watson wished the Crusaders well on their departure from Chester-le-Street. For Councillor Clayton, the Crusade did not signify simply one town's protest; he told the *Chronicle* reporter:

> This type of march has not in the past proved fruitful, but I sincerely hope that this will have a different result. It constitutes not only Jarrow's protest, but the combined protests against hardship of the whole of the North-East Community.[31]

So for those in the industrial north, Jarrow was not a special case but an extreme example of their own suffering. The pamphlet *A Derelict Area* described the blighted region in 1935.[32] The Durham coalfield was victim of high unemployment, though not as high as Jarrow. In the county as a whole, one in four insured workers was without work. In September 1936, a second powerful account of its conditions had been published, John Newsom's *Out of the Pit: a Challenge to the Comfortable*. He observed that the awful situation of the unemployed miners in County Durham should not obscure the fact that the working miners were also suffering terrible iniquity:

> The real tragedy of Durham lies not alone in the derelict pits and idle hands, but in villages which even when relatively prosperous were ugly, overcrowded and insanitary and in conditions of labour which force men to work for a weekly wage which is grossly inadequate by comparative, let alone any absolute standard.[33]

As the Crusade moved further south into more affluent and conservative territory, the welcoming messages of local dignitaries reversed. There Jarrow was an aberrant exception to the norm of prosperity caused by perverse and unique circumstance. Stressing that the Crusade was 'not like the other marches' and the exceptional suffering of the town was therefore necessary to secure the support of Conservative civic leaders whose government trumpeted the general and growing prosperity of the land.

On 6 October two 14-year-old lads from Hebburn or Chester-le-Street who had tagged along and hoped to participate in the march were sent home by bus. Like the previous day, bright sunny periods and broken cloud prevailed but the thermometer dropped further with the maximum temperature a chilly 10°C. Still, with a brisk pace and the sun on their backs, this was little hardship for the men. They travelled through Plawsworth, Pity Me, Framwellgate Moor, eating a hearty broth of carrot, leek, celery and turnip near Neville's Cross, the site of a battle 590 years earlier between Scots and English. Courtly chroniclers and local folklore embroidered legend into the historical fabric of this event too. Anticipating Ellen Wilkinson and the Jarrow Crusade banners, after a divine premonition, St. Cuthbert's chalice cloth was used as a talismanic banner for the English army who were led, according to some accounts, into battle by a great heroine, Queen Phillippa.[34]

The Jarrow banners too have become latter day talismans hoisted to bestow a sense of virtue, long-standing injustice and authenticity on many subsequent protests. Professional sign-writer John Badger designed the Crusade banners. John's brother Alfred marched and his son, also called John, led the Jarrow '86 march, literally following in his uncle's footsteps. In 1936, John senior acquired some wallpaper from a sympathetic shopkeeper and skilfully sketched the letters on it, cutting them out for a template. He then traced the letters on pieces of dark linen stretched across mat-making frames. Mrs Lydon, whose husband Valentine was a marcher, then hand-stitched the letters and bordering of the banners on the white canvas background. The banners became potent symbols of the Crusade, an ever-present part of the iconography. Not the typical red of working-class movement banners, Jarrow's black and white banners were both politically neutral as well as non-sectarian and proved to be highly photogenic; they have remained perfect for journalists and historians alike.[35] Nevertheless, given this care, several newspapers and the police misquoted the banners which, as we know, were neither inscribed with 'Jarrow Protest March' nor 'Jarrow Crusaders' but 'Jarrow Crusade'.[36]

These banners, four in total, became artifacts of disputed ownership and authenticity. In the exhibition of Jarrow Crusade at Bede's World, Jarrow Labour Party provided the banner that hung as an exhibit. The Labour Party believed this to be one of the four original banners. Vince Rea suggested that he possessed an authentic banner and that this exhibited banner was a replica that he had commissioned because there had been so many requests to borrow the banner in campaigns for jobs in the 1980s. The curators and archeologists at Bede's World reflected on the irony that when encountering the alien territory of twentieth-century history there was so much familiar to them: contested provenances, replica artifacts, mythology, and even religious relics. The banners had not always been such prized and disputed objects; for some years, as if camouflaged in its mundane domestic setting, the significance of one banner was lost and it was used as an ironing cloth in marcher Geordie Shearer's washroom.[37] John Badger senior also turned his sign-writing skills to the oak petition box upon which he inscribed 'Jarrow Petition' in gold leaf. Harry Stoddart, Ellen's agent, provided one penny from Jarrow Labour Party funds for a small tin of paint from Woolworths for the job.[38]

In stark contrast to the previous evening, the marchers received a wonderful response from the people of Ferryhill and hospitality from the Miners' Lodges. Someone had chalked on the square 'Welcome to the Jarrow Crusade. We are in solidarity with you'. The chairman of the Parish council, Councillor Bickerstaffe, officially greeted them. Con Shiels, the Crusade's cook, wrote home to his son saying, 'we got a better welcome as all the town was out'.[39] March leaders held an open air meeting in the market place with loudspeakers. After this, in what was to become part of the daily ritual of the Crusade, the petition box, treated as a precious object, was deposited in the safe in the Council Chambers. Meanwhile, the marchers ate a tea of ham sandwiches and scones in the Miners' Institute. Fellow Crusaders looked on bemused as a marcher took the ham from his sandwich, placed it in an envelope and posted it to his family explaining that they had not had meat for six weeks. The story is well known in Jarrow and has reappeared in various depictions of the Crusade.[40] For their night's sleep, the marchers divided into three groups: 60 stayed in Ferryhill Town Hall, 60 in the International Organisation of Good Templars Hall, and 80 in St. Luke's Parish Hall.

In Edinburgh, the Labour Party conference spent the morning and afternoon sessions discussing the worrying international situation. Also from Edinburgh, the East of Scotland contingent of the National Hunger March departed on its month-long journey arriving in Gorebridge that night. Harry McShane led this contingent. Forty years later he spoke at the age of 84 in the Albert Hall for the Right to Work Campaign which organised marches against unemployment.[41] There were mixed reactions amongst former Crusaders to more recent marches for jobs. As the European Marches against Unemployment, Insecurity and Exclusion passed through Jarrow in May 1997, Jimmy McCauley for one reflected:

> It seems like people will always have to march for jobs. A lot of people didn't support the first Jarrow march and then jumped on the bandwagon when it became famous. I've been a trade unionist all my life and I wanted to come along and support this march.[42]

Whilst there were always Crusaders who would support later ventures, others saw such marches as futile, or unable to match the 1936 march. Marchers drew mixed conclusions from the failure of their own actions, but they all agreed that the march did not achieve its objective. Herein lies the great riddle of the Jarrow Crusade: why did a failed march gain such celebrity?

Wednesday 7 October: The Workhouse is Waiting
Ferryhill to Darlington (pop. 70,000), 12 miles

The marchers breakfasted in the Ferryhill Miners' Institute consuming 70 pounds of bacon, 140 pounds of bread and three boxes of tomatoes. After the meal, the marchers cheered for Ferryhill in appreciation of the reception that they had received and the miners presented the Crusaders with 120 pounds of cherry cake. The Ferryhill police complimented the marchers on their conduct. Before setting out at 9.30, some of the younger marchers had time for a dance with the girls of Ferryhill in the market place.[43] Selwyn Waller, the reporter for the *Shields Gazette*, could already notice that the men were putting on weight; David Riley agreed. A newsreel company filmed the Crusade on its way to Darlington and this footage has been used in many subsequent documentaries. The Metropolitan Police Commissioner had tried to ban the filming of marches because they knew that it would generate more sympathy for the marchers. By 1936, their attitude had softened. When *Movietone News* requested police co-operation with their filming of the Crusade's rain-sodden entry into the capital, the authorities begrudgingly replied that 'it was not desired that facilities should be given for filming of the Jarrow marchers at Marble Arch, but that if any filming were done, it would be at the Company's risk and responsibility'.[44]

The statement from the Unemployment Assistance Board (UAB) that the dependants of the Crusaders would not receive UAB benefit had caused considerable anguish.[45] The wife of every Crusader received a letter from David Riley reassuring her that she would receive benefits and advising her to go to the Public Assistance Committee (PAC) the next day before noon.[46] The threat to benefits was one of the major ploys of the authorities to deter prospective marchers. The fear of going without was a serious worry for families already on the breadline.

The Crusaders reached Aycliffe at 12.30 pm where they took their midday meal of polony sandwiches and tea. The weather held throughout the uneventful five mile afternoon hike. They were counting themselves lucky on that score as there were nearly eight hours of sun that day, even more than the day before. The Crusade arrived in Darlington at around 6 pm. Despite this being a town with a Conservative council, and its MP Colonel Peat being a vocal opponent of the steelworks for Jarrow, the streets of the market town were lined with cheering folk.[47] Con Shiels reported to his son that after a 'fine' reception in Chester-le-Street, and a 'better welcome' in Ferryhill, Darlington was 'better again'.[48] Some marchers were beginning to experience difficulties with their feet. After the second night, three-quarters had blisters, one developing a septic heel, but he pleaded with Riley to stay on the march.[49] Reverend Y. Scott, the mayor's chaplain, said that the rivalry between the towns was forgotten because of their sympathy for the Crusade.[50] At a public meeting in the Co-operative Hall, Mayor Thompson told of the problems of having many townsfolk with ten or more years unemployment in addition to 300 to 400 youngsters leaving school each year with no prospect of work. David Riley spoke next, explaining that the Crusade was no stunt. Alderman Symonds and Councillors Scullion and Hanlon were also on the platform. Together they formed the march leadership and were on the left of the Labour Party. An MI5 agent reported 'only one of whom I know to have been closely identified with the Communist Party'.[51] In all likelihood this referred to Scullion or Symonds both of whom had been closely associated with the NUWM. All four were involved in campaigning for the unemployed. Con Shiels, the son of the Crusade's cook, remembered Jock Hanlon representing him at the Courts of Referees, helping him to overturn a decision and to get his benefit restored in 1937. But they were also involved in demonstrations and pickets to prevent evictions. Paddy Scullion was first elected to the council in 1935. His eldest daughter, Muriel Forrest, reflecting back on his life said:

> His whole life was socialism and trade unionism. The whole family was brought up on that. It was our bread and butter. I think he would love to be remembered as one of the men who led the Jarrow March.[52]

He, along with David Riley, Joe Symonds and Jock Hanlon were expelled from the Labour Party and formed a break-away rebel group on the council within weeks of returning to Jarrow.[53] But the group rejoined Labour and Paddy became mayor in 1947-9 and an alderman in 1949. Because of his diminutive stature, measuring only 5 feet 1 inch, he was nicknamed the 'bantam mayor'. In 1964, Paddy was made a Freeman of the Borough. Coincidentally, he was rebuffed by another Conservative PM – Ted Heath, in 1972 – just as he had been in 1936 when he was part of a delegation from the north-east region.[54] Joe Symonds had an even more successful political career than Paddy Scullion. Born on 17 January 1900, Symonds was first elected to the council in 1929 for Labour, though he had previously stood against Labour on an Unemployed Workers Committee ticket. He became an alderman in 1935 and mayor in 1945.[55] The following year he became a Durham County Councillor and was elected MP for Whitehaven, serving from 1959 until 1970. Besides unemployment, his abiding concern was housing. He was an executive member of the National Housing and Town Planning Council (1938-65) and its Chairman in 1948-50.[56] Despite its unofficial status at the time, the Crusade therefore later became a badge of credibility in Labour Party circles at both a local and national level. Moreover, the political ascent of the 'four laddies' and Ellen Wilkinson has helped establish the myth of institutional support of and within the Party.

The Crusaders bedded down in the workhouse, which despite its forbidding reputation, offered the men a hot bath, shave, roast beef, cabbage and potatoes for tea followed by boiled ham, jam, bread and tea for breakfast. Marcher Mick McDermott, however, recalled seeing the other guests of the workhouse: 'Lots of tramps were coming in broken-hearted. The man who was in charge was directing them into the bath with a stick.'[57] Under the workhouse regulations, these inmates had a diet of bread, butter and tea and had to perform task work of chopping wood in the workhouse yard. In this respect the Crusade benefited from the work of previous hunger marches which had forced workhouse masters to waive 'casual ward regulations' for marchers.[58] When interviewed for the documentary series *People's Century*, Crusader Billy MacShane touchingly sang the local folk ditty 'Oh how I miss my relief'. The song vividly captured the fear of the workhouse in popular imagination.

Oh how I miss my relief,
Now that they've stopped my dole,
A wife and three kiddies to keep,
And not a shovel of coal,
The landlord is coming tonight,
He's coming to chuck us all out,
There's no hesitating,
The workhouse is waiting,
Old pal, how I miss my relief.[59]

***

Despite his trenchant anti-communism, Herbert Morrison, leader of the London Labour Party, met with Metropolitan police chiefs to organise the Hyde Park demonstration to oppose the new UAB regulations. This demonstration would also receive the National Hunger March, giving an unprecedented – though not outright – degree of official Labour Party support to a hunger march. Even this begrudging support was not extended to the Jarrow Crusade. Morrison had known Ellen Wilkinson since her early days in politics in the Fabian Society. For some years they had had a relationship and she had recently courted controversy by supporting Morrison for Labour Party leader against Attlee despite the fact that Morrison was more to the right of the Party than either herself or the incumbent leader. Her personal attachment and political sponsorship of the right-wing Morrison is a puzzling aspect of her political complexion demonstrating that at times she weighed character, class background and capability above similarity of political outlook. Though she never married because she didn't see why she should give up her career for a man, Ellen Wilkinson had a number of close male companions notably Walton Newbold MP, John Jagger MP, Frank Horrabin MP, Harry Pollitt and Herbert Morrison MP.[60]

On 7 October, the Labour Party conference was debating communist affiliation to the Party. Will Lawther, Vice-President of the Miners' Federation of Great Britain, from the 'little Moscow' of Chopwell, County Durham, whose brother Clifford died in Spain within four months of this conference, spoke in favour of the motion. Despite the miners' union backing, the motion was lost heavily,

592,000 to 1,728,000.[61] Within the Labour Party views were highly polarised on this question, Ellen Wilkinson described the CP as 'bone of our bone, flesh of our flesh', but the NCL's *British Labour and Communism* pamphlet branded the communist-led NUWM a 'force for antagonism, dissent and disruption'.[62]

In the afternoon, two Spanish socialists, Jiménez de Asúa and Isabel Oyarzabal de Palencia, addressed the conference. Jiménez de Asúa attacked the policy of non-intervention, whereby the major powers prevented the Spanish Government from buying weapons thus:

> In the papers this morning you will have read that there has been a terrible air bombardment by heavy bombers of the villages around Madrid. We could not stop that bombardment. Why? Because we had not the fighting aircraft to do it, because the Pact of Non-Intervention has prevented us from getting them. What does it mean, the Pact of Non-Intervention? On the legal side - I am a lawyer; I speak as a lawyer - on the legal side the Pact of Non-Intervention is a monstrosity. It has become the most powerful intervention against the Spanish Government.[63]

In Spain that day, state confiscation of the land of rebels was decreed. In the Basque Country, Aguirre was sworn in as President of the Basques in their ancient capital, Guernica, which became infamous on 26 April 1937, when it was destroyed by German bombers; an event depicted by Picasso for the International Exhibition in Paris later that year. As the Spanish Civil War intensified, twenty child refugees from Guernica and other parts of the Basque country found a home on Tyneside.[64]

Thursday 8 October: 'Hungry Ill-Clad Men'
Darlington to Northallerton (pop. 4,794), 16 miles

Defying his 74 years, Councillor Pearson Harrison accompanied the Crusade on its first five miles out of Darlington. Along the route villagers brought baskets of apples and pears from their orchards to present as tribute to the marchers. At Great Smeaton, the cooks, Con Shiels and Cuddy Errington, had busied themselves preparing Irish stew. The marchers departed the village on the second leg of their journey to the small agricultural town of Northallerton at 2 pm. For the first time, showers punctuated their progress with only the odd sunny interlude and the temperature barely crept above 10°C.

There was no official reception in Northallerton, with not a single member of the council greeting them, though the Crusaders were welcomed by locals and the churches. The congregational minister, Reverend Thomas, underlined the religious character of the march:

> I don't think the decision of the council not to welcome the marchers can be taken as representative of the people of Northallerton. This march is the finest organised I have ever seen. It is, in my opinion a religious matter, as the provision of comfort for one's fellow men is the main basis of our Christian religion. It is our duty as individuals to spare no effort to help our unfortunate comrades and I do think that the churches of this country should have led the march and taken it right to London as an appeal not only to the Government but also to the common humanity in man.

The Reverend T. Sykes, a travelling evangelist, also blessed the marchers. David Riley was 'heartily pleased' with the cheering welcome from the north Yorkshire folk of Northallerton who would have normally considered those from County Durham as strangers; instead they treated the marchers 'like our own people'.[65] Claude Robinson, the Jarrow headmaster who visited the Crusade at weekends, was told the reception in Northallerton was 'at least, not very enthusiastic'.[66] The *Northern Dispatch* (Darlington) reported that the men 'groused' about their reception and David Riley said, 'Thank God we found decent clergy in Northallerton'.[67] Members of the Methodist congregation funded a tea of ham and salmon sandwiches. Tommy Corr, the leader of the mouth organ band that had formed on the march, led a sing-song at the piano of the North

End Methodist Hall. Because the North Riding County Council refused the use of schools, sleeping quarters were the Zion Church Hall, the Drill Hall and the South End Methodist Hall. Those in the Drill Hall had drawn the short straw of a cold uncomfortable night.

Labour Party conference debated a motion on Palestine which supported the creation of a Jewish homeland and regretted ethnic violence that had broken out between Arab and Jew. The motion fell. Conference failed to mention let alone support the Palestinian general strike taking place at the time. Three motions on unemployment, malnutrition and the Special Areas followed. Ellen Wilkinson spoke to one of these motions. She outlined the tragic situation in which a child born in Jarrow was twice as likely to die before its first birthday than elsewhere in Britain.[68] She refused to be fobbed off with reports and investigations, she wanted the Party to act which it thus far had failed to do. She condemned the black circulars that instructed local Labour Parties to reject appeals for help from hunger marchers under the pretext that some of them might be communists. The use of communist involvement as a recurrent excuse for refusing to work with the NUWM or mobilise a mass campaign against unemployment or fascism angered Ellen Wilkinson and many on the Labour left. She scornfully hoped, 'when Sir Walter Citrine [General Secretary of the TUC] gets to the pearly gates, St. Peter will be able to reassure him there is no communist inside'. She also revealed that the National Executive had not allowed a collection for the Jarrow marchers among the delegates.[69] Criticism of the Party drew Lucy Middleton, parliamentary candidate and wife of the National Secretary, into the debate condemning Ellen Wilkinson for 'sending hungry and ill-clad men on a march to London'. Her husband, Jim Middleton, had turned down Deputy Mayor Rennie's request for a collection in support of the march at the conference. This was not the hostility of the Middleton family but, as Ellen Wilkinson explained in *The Town that Was Murdered* 'an attitude of official disapproval. The Trades Union Congress had frowned on the marches, and the Labour Party Executive followed the lead'. Ellen Wilkinson did not let Lucy Middleton's accusation go unchallenged at the conference, denouncing it as a lie and a personal attack. In what was to become the classic account of the Crusade, published by the Left Book Club, Ellen Wilkinson registered her surprise because their march was '100% respectable' and she had gone to Edinburgh 'to put a word in for the other marches as well as get general backing for our protest movement'.[70] Despite the Labour Party's repeated claim to the heritage of the Crusade, this betrayal has been remembered. Claude Robinson, writing in *Tribune* at the time of the People's March for Jobs in 1983, described Middleton and the NEC for whom she spoke as 'another enemy more insidious and unexpected'.[71] Given the way that Labour Party leaders – Michael Foot, Neil Kinnock and Tony Blair – have associated themselves with the Crusade, one might assume that the party had supported the march. Historians have on occasion made the same mistake.[72] The re-invention of Labour's relationship with the Jarrow Crusade began in earnest with the 1950 election campaign when the Jarrow Crusade was a prominent theme of election speeches and featured on one of Labour's election posters.[73] Such associations have created a myth of Labour support for the Crusade.[74]

The counter-current of memory serves to recall the reality of Labour's record. Peter Flannery's serialised drama for television *Our Friends in the North* (1996) examined, to wide critical acclaim, the political history of the North East since the 1960s.[75] It connected personal stories with grand political events: the American civil rights movement, the Wilson Government, T. Dan Smith, Thatcher and the miners' strike. Amongst these looms the memory of the Jarrow Crusade. *Our Friends in the North* did not present us with the consensual image of the Crusade but a complex subject of political, personal and intergenerational conflict. The march was personified in Felix, Nicky's father. Unlike Labour Party member Eddie Wells, Nicky's early mentor, Felix was disillusioned with Labour and politics. We encounter Felix in brief flashes but he stands as an important political yardstick. Felix, the cynical former Crusader, mocks his son for electioneering for Labour as it had 'denounced the Jarrow Crusade before it got to Durham'. That Peter Flannery's grandfather was on the march confers an insider's authority to this challenge to the legend. This is important because of the connection between the Crusade legend and local, regional and national identities and it is highly significant that such authentic voices as Peter Flannery and Con Whalen questioned the Crusade's myths.

The outcome of the debate at the Edinburgh conference was a party investigation into the Special Areas overseen by Hugh Dalton, though Ellen Wilkinson could not see the utility of another report 'when the pore of every unemployed man was indexed by this time'. She later admitted that it was a good report, revealing the utter distress of areas like Jarrow. The Distressed Areas Commission, which was set up to compile the report, visited Jarrow on 14 January 1937.[76] The conclusion that one might reasonably have drawn was that the Party should have mounted a protest against these conditions. Of course by then it was too late.

The North East Area Guardians met in Jarrow to determine the relief of the dependants. The Unemployed Assistance Board, run by the Ministry of Labour, had turned down their application. Hargreaves, the assistant district officer of the UAB, officiously declared:

> We are bound to take the view that except in special circumstances, men who are engaged on an organised march do not come within the Act. That is, though fit and able, they are not available for work.[77]

Claude Robinson remembered that the Area Officer of the UAB, Ivery, was 'in the eyes of the people of Jarrow ... little less than a monster'. When the means test officer would call people would pass their household goods over the wall to neighbours until he left.[78] It was therefore up to the locally administered Public Assistance Committee to relieve the wives and children of the Crusaders. Councillor Hey observed that the refusal of the UAB and Ministry of Labour was the Government's 'first kick' against the Crusade.[79] PAC paid the lowest rates of benefit which were known as 'the pineapple' in Jarrow. Fifty years on, at the age of 76, Martha MacNulty still remembered the shock of receiving the letter telling her that the benefit would be stopped as her husband marched to London.[80] The situation of the march leaders was even

43

worse because as members of the PAC they could not claim its relief. The difficulties of Crusaders' families in getting relief was a running saga throughout the march and was not finally settled until Ellen Wilkinson came to a dead end in her questioning of the minister in the House of Commons. She raised the refusal of the UAB to grant benefits to marchers in the House of Commons on 12 and 19 November.[81] She wanted to know why, when every effort had been made to maintain communication with Jarrow and Hebburn Labour Exchange, the men were deemed unavailable for work. She found the Ministry of Labour's reply 'idiotic'.

The people of Jarrow were squeezed between the means test officers and the landlords. For example, estate agents Joseph Dobson Ltd collected from hundreds of properties across Tyneside, including from five of the marchers (McCauley, Thornton, Dobson, Miller and McGuckin). Each week Dobson's agent would check off the names in his grubby black rent book as they paid up.[82] Harry Clarke remembered the 'rent man' as a figure who was nearly as hated as the 'means test man' and Con Shiels recalled how the landlords and their agents were popularly thought of as 'bloodsuckers ... not very well liked at all'.[83] You paid in cash and you could forget about repairs. Weekly rents typically ranged from six to ten shillings and because times were so hard most of Jarrow's tenants owed back rent, many with several pounds worth of arrears. Jimmy McCauley's household owed £11 13s and 9d but Andrew McGuckin, another Crusader, only owed 7 s 3d. The landlords typically owned many houses. For instance, Llewellyn Evans had ten tenants on the Crusade and 181 properties in Jarrow. George L. Young had nine Crusaders paying him rent along with 213 other households and his family owned a total of 408 properties in Jarrow. The housing situation in Jarrow was a major contributor to ill health. Some progress was made during the interwar period in terms of slum clearance through the Housing Acts but at the time of the Crusade 6,664 people or 17.4% of Jarrow's population lived in overcrowded conditions.[84] There was very little council housing in Jarrow in the 1930s, although the Primose estate was under construction. Owner occupation was largely restricted to the 'posh' end of Jarrow around Bede Burn Road, Wansbeck Road and their surrounding area. There was also a political significance to the relationship between tenant and landlord. The names of major families of landlords – the Reavleys, the Patties, the O'Connors, the Crumbleys, the Pearsons – were synonymous with the local Conservative Party, its councillors and even the former MP.[85] One of the leading Conservatives on the council, Charles Reavley, owned 58 houses rented to the impoverished folk of Jarrow but with Edward, Norman, Janet and John Reavley, the family owned 135 properties.

Friday 9 October: Stab in the Back
Northallerton to Ripon (pop. 8,576), 17 miles

After breakfast of jam and bread, the Crusaders readied themselves to set out as news of the debate at the Labour Party conference arrived. David Riley, the march marshal, addressed the men in the Market Hall of Northallerton saying it was a 'stab in the back'. The audience of marchers cheered when he said that they would be sending a telegram in protest at the conference's position. It read: 'We the sons of England's most famous town, resent the unsympathetic attack on our members and the deliberate attempt to pauperise our Crusaders'.[86] During the morning's marching, a downpour dampened spirits and it remained cold throughout the day.

Ellen Wilkinson had a long record of opposition to the scourge of unemployment. Her father, a Lancashire cotton mill worker and an insurance salesman, had known his share of unemployment. In the House of Commons, she complained of the effects of mass unemployment in Middlesbrough which was her first constituency. She was a regular contributor to debates on this question. She exposed the iniquitous and phony hunt for idlers on unemployment benefits that took the shape of the infamous 'genuinely seeking work' clause. Outside parliament, she established a long association with protest over unemployment.

The Crusaders had to face rain for much of the journey but cars stopped to make a donation. Regular contributions to march funds were an index of support for the Crusade. Donations came from passing motorists, from the audience at the Crusade's daily public meeting, from workplace collections and private individuals. In total the Jarrow Crusade raised £1,567 0s 5d, of which the general public donated £680 16s 11d. The money was principally spent on clothing, allowances to marchers, return train fares and the wages of helpers. At the end of the march, the Mayor's Boot Fund received the surplus of £26 8s 8d. A finance committee oversaw this aspect of the Crusade and the sterling work of council employee Sam Rowan ensured a day-to-day attention to detail.[87] In all there were four committees organising the march: finance, publicity, roads and food, and health.

Right Reverend Geoffrey Charles Lester Lunt, the Bishop of Ripon (1935-46), welcomed the Jarrow marchers and tried to stir enthusiasm for them in the quiet cathedral town. By chance the Bishop's son-in-law, Reverend S. Harvie Clark, was the Rector of Jarrow, so the bishop had been regularly updated with the difficulties of the town. The bishop had only limited success. Ripon had largely escaped the scourge of unemployment and, with only 150 unemployed in the town, the local Social Services Committee had disbanded itself at its annual meeting the week before.[88] The *Evening Chronicle* reported that the folk of Ripon had eyed the marchers 'askance', their local response was 'unsympathetic' and there had even been 'titters' from the younger onlookers. The bishop was able to offer the men a service in the Cathedral for which he asked for a show of hands. Nearly all hands lifted in the air. He also extended an invitation to the men of a tour of the palace grounds. The bishop had assembled the Reverend W.L. Hann, of the Coldsgate Methodist Church, the Very Reverend Canon E. Levick of the Catholic Church, the Deputy-Mayor of Ripon, Alderman J.I. McHenry and Captain E. Hartley of Ripon Labour Party to greet the men. The lukewarm reception in Ripon may in part have been due to the ambiguous attitude of even the Bishop of Ripon's son-in-law who had conducted the church service in Christ Church at the beginning of the march but privately disapproved of the enterprise. The Rector of Jarrow told the Bishop of Durham on 15 October that the clergymen of Jarrow and the 'reasonable people in Jarrow itself ... were opposed to it'.[89] With Clark, public actions and private comments did not add up. For their evening meal, marchers ate two boiled eggs and bread and butter. In other places, local sympathisers had provided food for the Crusade but in Ripon march funds had to sustain the men. If this precedent continued their finances would quickly drain away.

In other events that day, the British Broadcasting Corporation announced that it would begin a regular television transmission on 2 November. The BBC was to develop a deep infatuation with the Jarrow Crusade. With its keen eye for heritage, it commissioned important works on the Jarrow Crusade.[90] The reason for this is the kind of history that the BBC prefers and the values that it embodies. Apart from its less mainstream arenas, it seeks to present a national consensus and avoid controversy. The Jarrow Crusade's constitutionalism and its respectability make it more convenient subject matter than the other hunger marches. This is not to say that all of this work is entirely uncritical but the overall effect is undoubted. For similar reasons, the national curriculum and our schools concentrate on the Crusade to the near exclusion of other marches. Like Harry Clarke, the fictional nine-year-old Clogger, in *The Road to London: a Tale of the Jarrow March*, a story written for the national curriculum in history, tailed the Crusade to Chester-le-Street where he was returned home by a friendly policeman.[91] *The Road to London* exemplifies the widespread use of the Jarrow Crusade within the national curriculum for history in British schools.[92] Here the key institutions of the British state – the public broadcaster and the education system – have reshaped the contours of the history of the 1930s and contributed to the process of myth-making. Having witnessed the role that the BBC played during the General Strike, Ellen Wilkinson was in no doubt about its function as 'a great propaganda machine, to be used openly against the workers in time of crisis, and more subtly in "normal" periods'.[93] Surely an example of this more subtle use can be recognised with the Jarrow Crusade. Here we witness the institutional dimension of the myth of the Jarrow Crusade's universal support at work.

It was the final day of the Labour Party conference, which debated the coalmining industry, the united front, and Spain. On the last of these issues, Clement Attlee, with the Labour leadership feeling the impatience of their Spanish guests and of much of conference with non-intervention, called for an investigation by the non-fascist Non-Intervention Committee members into the breaches of the agreement by the fascists. Ellen Wilkinson interjected, asking how long that would take. Despite the apparent contradiction between Labour Party policy and their Spanish guests' views on non-intervention, Clement Attlee later in the week proposed that the Party reproduce these two speeches as a party pamphlet.

Saturday 10 October: The Trial
Ripon

Uncertainty surrounds events at Ripon. According to the *Shields Gazette* at the time, for their amusement the Crusaders held a mock trial of David Riley with Eddie Fitzpatrick donning the judge's robes. Marshal Riley was sentenced to fatigue duty and 'cat bully beef' for the rest of his life. Flannery was also sentenced for tripping the judge on the march. Sixty years later, the *Evening Chronicle* reported the trial differently which was not of Riley but of a marcher who had broken the strict instructions not to get drunk.[94] Eddie Fitzpatrick was the 'judge' and John McGeary the 'court clerk' in this account, although both had forgotten what happened to the defendant. The implication of the later version was that news of the disciplinary action had leaked out and the story of the mock trial limited potential damage in the press.

The medical students, Mr Cargill and Miss Blake, reported that the men were in good health and that tending to blistered feet was the principal preoccupation. One of the men had suffered from exhaustion but the bus had come to his rescue. The dog had also needed the bus as respite from the pavement-pounding but had recovered by the arrival of the Crusade in Ripon. With the oldest man in his early sixties and the youngest 18, the *Ripon Gazette and Observer* reported the majority of the men were between 20 and 25 years old.[95] This was not evident from the *Shields Gazette* article on 2 October when the younger men were admonished for not coming forward or Ellen Wilkinson claim that 62% were veterans of the Great War. It is quite possible that the youthfulness of the Crusade was stressed to allay criticisms about the health of the marchers.

In the market square Alderman Dixon, the Mayor of Ripon, opened the public meeting saying that after initial doubts he had been convinced of the wisdom of the march because it was a well organised crusade that woke the conscience of those beyond the depressed areas. This must have been music to the march leaders. The mayor had internalised those arguments that the advance party of the Crusade, Jarrow's Conservative and Labour electoral agents, had to put. Ripon's newspaper reported that he offered a remedy for their plight, that, while suggested by the religious symbolism of the Crusade, must have seemed impractical and metaphysical but not out of place:

> He knew of only one remedy for the crises in which we were placed and that was to bring into all our relationships, industrial, municipal, national and international, the standards set by Christ [Hear, hear]. Christianity taught by Christ had not yet been tried.[96]

The Mayor of Jarrow articulated a this-worldly faith in public opinion. His moving speech described Jarrow's lost prosperity and prodigal malnutrition.

> In every town and city and village on our way to London we are going to put before the people of this country the plight of our depressed town, so that public opinion, which is the greatest factor in this country, may make itself felt. ...We don't want our people to be fed always by charity. It is alright for six or 12 months for people to receive unemployment benefit, but when it comes to 10 or 15 years things begin to tell. We feel that after 15 years of hardship, while the rest of the country may be progressing, we at the northeastern corner are left entirely on our own. We feel as the nation needed our services in 1914-18, we need its services now. Jarrow has been termed the most depressed town in the country, but we are here on behalf of all the towns in similar position to our own. All we are asking is that our unemployed men

shall be allowed to work and earn sufficient money to keep their wives and children.[97]

David Riley illustrated the human price of Jarrow's fate. For every one still-born child in Ripon there were two in Jarrow and for every one TB victim there were two in Jarrow. Jock Hanlon and R.J. Hall, Ripon's prospective Labour parliamentary candidate, also addressed the audience before the Mayor of Ripon closed the meeting. Hanlon, a plater at the Mercantile Dry Dock when in work, died in 1972 the day before he was to receive the honour of being Freeman of the Borough for his services to the town as mayor and as one of the leaders of the Crusade.[98] At the conclusion of the meeting, the Mayor of Ripon proposed a resolution, which was unanimously endorsed, in support of the Crusade. The Ripon Conservative Association donated two guineas to the march funds.[99]

In South Shields that night 4,000 demonstrated against the Means Test. Local miners' lodges, Harton and Marsden, were at the forefront of the protest.[100] The North East witnessed a number of major demonstrations over unemployment in the 1930s.[101]

In the evening of 10 October there was a show in the Palladium Cinema for the marchers where local performers treated them to a rendition of 'The Blaydon Races'. Marchers also acquired a drum that they put to good use on the rest of the journey as accompaniment to the mouth organs. During their three night stay in Ripon, they lodged in the Coltsgate Hill School. This accommodation was relatively comfortable and warm as Crusader James Hamilton, an unemployed seafaring fire stoker, attended to the school boiler ably employing his skills. The unfortunate John McCourt spent the weekend in Ripon Cottage Hospital with enteritis. The 22-year-old Frank Coyne had to return to Jarrow because of the death of his grandfather. He returned in Jarrow headmaster Claude Robinson's car on Friday.[102] In an effort to undermine the Crusade, the Labour Exchange enquired as to whether Samuel Anderson was available for work at Palmer's Hebburn site.

Sunday 11 October: In the Cathedral
Ripon

The Bishop of Ripon held a special service for the Crusaders in Ripon Cathedral which the Mayors of Jarrow and Ripon attended. Other Jarrow folk – Thompson and Rennie, the mayor and his deputy, Councillor Mrs Scott, Mr McCabe, Councillor Crumbley, Mr W. Gordon JP, Paddy Scullion's mother as well as other relatives and friends – made the day trip and attended the service.[103] March organisers must have been delighted with the legitimacy that this, after the Bishop of Jarrow's blessing, bestowed on their Crusade.

The medical students advised James Guy to return home from Ripon due to illness. There were now three Crusaders missing: Guy, McCourt and Coyne. After the Crusade's return, Guy felt obliged to write to the *Gazette* to refute local rumours that he had spread gossip that the marchers 'were half-starved'.[104] Because of the widespread nature of the tittle-tattle and the belief that Guy was its source, he had been challenged on several occasions and he wanted to clear his name. The theme of the good health and the hearty nourishment of the marchers was therefore in part to diffuse this hearsay circulating back in Jarrow.

It was a good job that the school boilers were fired as Sunday night witnessed freezing temperatures. With the weekend to ponder the lukewarm reception in Ripon, the prospect of prosperous and Conservative Harrogate must have caused some anxiety amongst march leaders and the men. Much of the rest of their route would be through such prosperous parts of England very different from their own. Local papers along the route naturally tended to play up the local generosity displayed to the Crusade. Whilst the *Shields Gazette* and *Evening Chronicle* worried about the drain on finances incurred in Ripon, the *Ripon Gazette and Observer* detailed the local contributions suggesting that this would cover the £18 cost of food for the weekend.[105]

After Ferryhill until they reached Wakefield, the Jarrow Crusade was in Conservative territory. Partly because of the Crusade, it is commonplace to think of Jarrow as a Labour town but this was not so before 1935. The Jarrow constituency was only formed in 1885 and included Hebburn, Wardley and Felling. It was a Liberal stronghold for the town's major employer Charles Palmer (MP from 1885 to 1907) and then his son Geoffrey (1910-18), with a brief Labour interlude (Pete Curran, 1907-10, on a Labour and Irish nationalist ticket). When R.J. Wilson won the seat for Labour in 1922, the Liberals were eclipsed. With the collapse of the second Labour Government in 1931 and the general election that returned the National Government, there was a nine percent drop in Labour's vote in Jarrow and the Conservative W.G. Pearson secured the seat. Ellen Wilkinson only recaptured the seat narrowly in 1935 for Labour.[106] The political tradition of Jarrow was therefore distinct from that of most other parts of County Durham where the pattern was a transition from Lib-Labism to Labour stronghold under the influence of the Durham Miners' Association. Instead, in Jarrow, Liberal hegemony was based on employer paternalism rather than trade union Liberalism and a protracted period of contested transition took place in which the Conservatives were players.[107] This may explain the involvement in Jarrow of national Conservative figures who were concerned to keep a blue foothold in the North East.

Week Two: Ripon to Chesterfield

Monday 12 October: Rolls Royces, Red Flags, Bad Eggs
Ripon to Harrogate (pop. 34,440), 11 miles

With Jarrow's Mayor Billy Thompson at the head of the procession, the Crusade left Ripon at 9.20 am and accompanied the marchers all the way to Harrogate. Ripon's deputy mayor bade them farewell. Fine and mild weather complemented good spirits after a well-deserved weekend's rest. The band played 'Tipperary' as they embarked on the shortest and least arduous leg of their journey thus far through agricultural north Yorkshire. They passed the small villages of Wormald Green, South Stainley, Ripley and Killinghall, crossing the River Nidd. Despite a chilly night, the Crusade enjoyed its warmest temperatures – up to 14^{0}C – in a cloudy but mainly dry day. Newspapers reported that Rolls Royces stopped, wound down their windows and handed five pound notes to the procession of out-of-work men.[1]

That afternoon, a demonstrator who had come to greet the marchers was asked to take down his banner, 'because he was a communist'.[2] The *North Mail* reported that the offending banner, which proclaimed 'Harrogate workers welcome Jarrow workers', had first been unfurled two miles outside Harrogate to cheers from the Crusaders.[3] Journalistic sensation transformed this trivial event into a 'communist banner waving incident' headline. Anti-communism was to become a recurrent theme for the press, a topic that the marshal of the march encouraged in order to underline the non-political character of the march and to assure local Conservative associations on whose support the Crusade depended. An anti-communist organisation that was responsible for many a trade union activist being put on an employer's blacklist, the Economic League, even supported the Crusade while listing the communist participants on the National Hunger March in an effort to discredit it.[4]

The march leaders also sought to prevent any religious controversy as they allowed a 'town missioner', Mr G.H. Govier, to distribute the gospel of St. John on condition that it contained no sectarian material.[5] Because of the large proportion of Irish and Scots immigrants in Jarrow, there had been a history of sectarian organisation, parades and conflict in the area.[6] Jarrow's immigrant population had grown with the shipyard, although over time those tensions declined. In the 1920s, the Catholic population transferred its political allegiances. Most Catholics used to vote as Father Mackin prescribed but now looked to Labour. The Catholic socialists who were responsible for this political shift – Symonds, Riley and Scullion – were the same people who led the march.[7] That the march leaders adopted a rhetoric of the 'sons of England's most famous town' in their desire for respectability belied the ethnic diversity of the marchers, creating a myth of Englishness. The Bishop of Sheffield believed that they were doing a 'very English' thing. This myth has made the Crusade attractive to those who seek to repackage history as narrowly defined identity or heritage. Jarrow was a Geordie melting pot. The Crusade's marshal was an Irish Catholic and probably between half and two thirds of the marchers were first, second or third generation Scots or Irish.[8] Over time, Jarrow's fourth and fifth generation have forgotten their identification with Scotland and Ireland and this has reinforced the myth of Englishness.[9]

Support was invited from all denominations, but the Church of England carried the greatest establishment prestige given its constitutional status as the church of state. Paradoxically a 'crusade' led by Catholic socialists made great play of the respectability that the Church of England conferred at church services and with clerical welcomes. According to the memory of participants, some of the Catholic marchers even worried about excommunication for attending Anglican services.

If the Crusaders were slightly anxious about their reception in the spa town of Harrogate because of its Tory complexion and affluent character, then they must have been relieved when the crowds of well-wishers were so dense that they caused a town centre traffic jam. The reception, according to Jarrow headmaster Claude Robinson, 'passed all expectations'.[10] Some of the Crusaders sampled the free supply of Harrogate waters at the pump room. One joked, 'It's for invalids. That means I'm entitled to a spot. I've got sore feet.' Others grimaced as they tasted it. 'Bad eggs', another remarked. The Crusaders were invited to the Harrogate Toc H to relax but because the council was in session, there was no official reception.[11] The Crusaders were then fed as the guests of the Harrogate Rotary Club at the Territorial Army Drill Hall, where they spent the night and which was, luckily, centrally heated.

The march leaders, the Mayor of Jarrow and Ellen Wilkinson (having returned from Edinburgh) went to the Winter Gardens for the public meeting. G.A. Spenceley, the Deputy Mayor of Harrogate, welcomed the packed room and Rev J.H. Bodgener chaired. Councillor Newsome of Harrogate spoke next, declaring:

> Harrogate was in a comfortable position, though it had its own unemployment problem, but what must conditions be like in a depressed area like Jarrow, where people were workless and dying of starvation? Surely in those circumstances every human sympathy was bound to go out to the affected and every effort made to assist them. There must be something sadly wrong in the country when crowds of men were unable to get employment and the means of livelihood.[12]

After Newsome, Mayor Thompson, formerly a woodworker at Palmer's, addressed the assembly. He again recalled the yard's indispensable contribution to the war effort:

> From 1914 to 1918 Jarrow was one of the most prosperous towns in the British Isles, and we feel that as the nation needed our services then, we need its services

now. Jarrow has been termed the most depressed town in the country, but we are here on behalf of all towns in a similar position to our own. All we are asking is that our unemployed men shall be allowed to work and earn sufficient money to keep their wives and children.

After the mayor, the four march leaders and Ellen Wilkinson spoke. Sam Rowan remembered the effect of Paddy Scullion's speech that night:

Well at Harrogate, when he got on about the infant mortality rate, you know, compared to Harrogate you see, and told the tale of the midwife who had gone into a house to deliver a child and she had to put her own penny in the gas. … By the time Paddy Scully had finished that night the women were in tears. They were shedding buckets of tears in their fur coats, I can tell you, down in Harrogate.[13]

Ellen Wilkinson said, 'I know that the authorities are getting very tired of Jarrow. They are going to be even more tired of the name before we have finished'.[14] She continued:

We say that if this area in the north east is suffering as a result of these policies, they ought not to be left to bear alone the burdens which should be shared by the whole nation. Jarrow, one of the most efficient shipyards in the country, has been closed in order to suit a Stock Exchange speculation, but there comes a time when the national interests have to be considered before the gambling speculations of the Stock Exchange (applause).[15]

The 'Wednesday gossip' column in the *Harrogate Herald* enthused about her speech:

The piece de resistance of the evening, however, came at it is conclusion, when Miss Ellen Wilkinson, MP for Jarrow, addressed the meeting. A petite figure, with a wealth of bronze hair, spoke fearlessly from the heart, and as she warmed to her subject she fired the audience to frequent bursts of acclamation. I can quite understand Miss Wilkinson's popularity in political circles, and in her the Jarrow crusaders have a marching companion whose efforts in the Parliamentary sphere will not slacken until the fate of her constituency has received deeper consideration than it has to date. As I listened I was reminded somehow of Joan of Arc.[16]

The size of the public meeting surprised most people in Harrogate and was more than the marchers anticipated. The whip-round at the end raised a magnificent £13 8s 4d which was the largest sum thus far. Less happily, unemployed labourer James Quennan was sent home on the advice of the Crusade's medical students. There were now four marchers missing due to ill health or other personal problems.

Forty-two blind marchers of the National League of the Blind trekked from Wakefield to Barnsley that day. Amongst their number was Newcastle Councillor J. Clydesdale, who had lost his sight in a factory accident before the war, as was Robert Hanlon, of Fenham (Newcastle), brother of the Jarrow Crusader and Councillor James 'Jock' Hanlon. They were marching on behalf of the 67,534 registered blind persons in England and Wales.[17] Despite the inclusion of the demands of the blind in the King's speech, legislation did not pass in that sitting of parliament but did ultimately result in the Blind Persons' Act of 1938. This reduced the age at which blind people could draw a blind person's pension from 50 to 40 years, affecting about 8,000; though the extension of these pension rights to all over 16 years would have added only an extra 9,500 to the figure.[18]

Back in the North East, a range of methods was being used to tackle unemployment. In Sunderland, Mayor Thomas Summerbell opened the Southwick Occupational Centre for the Unemployed. Summerbell was Sunderland's first Labour mayor (1935-7) just as his father had been the town's first Labour MP (1908-10). Unemployment had been one of the father's concerns having written a pamphlet in 1908 – *Afforestation: the Unemployed and the Land.*[19] As part of the efforts of the Commissioner for the Special Areas of England and Wales, work started two days later on the Team Valley Trading Estate in Gateshead which was intended to bring work to the area and over which the Angel of the North now keeps a stoical eye.

Tuesday 13 October: Royal Treatment: Beer or Tea, Sir?
Harrogate to Leeds (pop. 473,400), 15 miles

Harrogate shopkeepers provided a tasty breakfast of ham and paste sandwiches and the deputy mayor addressed the men as they left the town,

> I don't think we have let you down here. The meeting at the Winter Gardens last night was the finest I have seen in that Hall in the past thirty years. It was representative of all sections of Harrogate society. That is saying a great deal because Harrogate people are difficult people to get to turn out at night. I hope that by this united crusade you will be able to make such an impression on the Government that they will feel they are bound to move and do something to bring about better conditions in Jarrow.[20]

Harrogate RSPCA bought a licence for Paddy the dog which had followed the marchers from Jarrow. However, when the RSPCA arrived at the drill hall, the Crusaders had already left. The day was dull and not at all warm. Six-and-a-half miles from Harrogate, after passing through Dunkeswick and crossing the River Wharfe, a police inspector and half a dozen constables suddenly appeared before the marchers. If the Crusaders were initially puzzled, then the sight of Harewood House should have explained all. The 29,700 acre estate belonged to Henry George Charles Lascelles, 6th Earl of Harewood (1882-1947), and the Princess Royal (1897-1965).[21] The police presence betrayed the secret anxiety of the royal family about the unemployed and their own future.[22]

In the nineteenth century Leeds had developed as the wealthy capital of the wool trade. The Crusaders marched up to the great symbol of that wealth, the Town Hall, which Asa Briggs described as 'a magnificent case study in Victorian civic pride'.[23] As they did a contingent of greenshirts (the Social Credit Party of Great Britain) with banners and drums tried to join in the procession but were rebuffed by the Crusade's police escort.[24] Inside, in the crypt of the Town Hall, Sir William Nicholson – a former Lord Mayor (1911-12), President of Leeds Conservative Party, a member of the exclusive London Carlton Club and proprietor of W. Nicolson and Son – provided a sumptuous meal for the Crusaders with full waiter service and white table cloths. The Conservatives held a large majority on the council, but reflecting the non-partisan character of the event, officials of the Leeds trades union movement were also present.[25] R.C. Davies, the Chairman of the Leeds Conservatives, welcomed the marchers. His speech included these guarded words:

> We recognise that you are marching as representatives of your borough to call attention to the urgent necessity for employment to the stricken town you have left behind you. The wisdom of placing the strain of so long a march upon untrained men is not for us to judge, but it would be a poor day for this country if the time arrived when a constitutional and orderly appeal such as yours is to any section of the people failed to impress those who are at the head of the Government of our land. We cannot pretend to know full details of your cause, but we do know and appreciate the great difficulties you have undergone, and we would be poor citizens if we did not sympathise with you in your quest for work.[26]

The speech revealed the mindset of Conservative supporters of the march. They disagreed with their fellow Tories who argued that the march was unconstitutional, they hinted that they did not think such marches wise, or that they would not normally support them, but here was an exception. The hospitality offered to marchers was also first and foremost a matter of civic pride. This no doubt repeated the arguments that the Conservative emissary from Jarrow had put to them.

'Beer or tea, sir?' inquired waiters in dinner dress and waitresses in white aprons brought the plates and tidied the tables. 'If we get another meal like this' commented one of the Jarrow lads, 'we will be able to march to Canada'. One newspaper reflected that it was a meal the marchers would never forget, and they didn't. Bob Maugham, who had only worked a month in ten years, reminisced about this meal six decades on: 'It was a bit of a holiday. We got a grand meal in Leeds. Roast beef (we hadn't had that for a long time). Yorkshire pudding, and a bottle of pale ale. Even in the Tory places we were well looked after'.[27] Con Shiels noted in a letter to his son:

> Con, we have just come in to Leeds and my we had a time. I have had a good dinner in my time but I do not think I can beat this one ....[28]

One marcher kept his serviette as a memento of the meal asking Ellen Wilkinson to sign it. She obliged using her lipstick to write the autograph.[29] Even the Crusade's mascot, the black dog, was treated like royalty, eating out of a silver tureen.[30] In what was the largest public meeting of the journey, 1,000 turned out to hear Jarrow's tale in the Town Hall. The collection provided £7 5s 1d for march funds. In Leeds, the bi-partisan approach worked as efficiently as the town's wool mills. Whereas the Conservatives fed the marchers, the Leeds Trades Council provided the night's shelter in the Harehills Labour Club. There Leeds Toc H entertained the marchers.

Back in the North East, the Labour Lord Mayor of Newcastle, Alderman W. Locke, provided breakfast in the Newcastle Socialist Hall for 50 hunger marchers. Amongst their number were 18 men from Blyth and Ashington including Councillor R.S. Elliott. Elected to Croft Ward in 1931, Bob Elliott was one of two communist councillors in Blyth. As an unemployed miner and NUWM member, he had developed some skill at representing and advising the unemployed at the Courts of Referees and Public Assistance

Committees. Shortly after the march, Bob volunteered for Spain and died at the Battle of Brunete in July 1937. A block of sheltered housing in Blyth bears his name.[31] All told, around 90 joined the International Brigades from the North East. 23 died. The death of Wilfred Jobling from Gateshead in the Spanish Civil War caused a minor controversy in Jarrow. Jobling died fighting for the republicans in Madrid in March 1937.[32] He had been a member of the National Administrative Council of the National Unemployed Workers' Movement and secretary of the local Communist Party branch.[33] He took part in the 1936 march and chaired the meeting in the Blaydon Miners' Welfare to celebrate the marchers' return on 22 November.[34] Before joining the fray, he had written a letter offering the support of his organisation to the Jarrow march. Scullion moved a motion sending condolences and mentioned the letter of support on hearing of Jobling's death. Although the council resolved to send condolences to the family, the *Shields Gazette* reported a rebuke from the mayor:

> The Mayor said it was true that a letter was received from Mr Jobling prior to the march offering his services but beyond that he knew nothing of him. He thought there would be no harm in sending a letter to the widow but he considered Counc. Scullion had taken advantage of the opportunity allowed him in introducing matters which did not come into question.[35]

Ellen Wilkinson honoured Wilf Jobling in a *Tribune* article.[36] With Jobling's photograph adorning the publicity, she also spoke at a rally on 15 January 1939 commemorating those from Tyneside who died in Spain. Jobling's participation in the Spanish Civil War has been celebrated in Jack Lindsay's poem 'Requiem Mass for the Englishmen fallen in the International Brigades'.[37]

On this day the front page of the *Shields Gazette* bore a photograph of the dozen or so strong South Shields contingent of the National Hunger March.[38] A month later, Steve Cooling and Steve Codling (who also died in Spain) wrote from their lodgings at the London County Council Centre of their arrival in London. They recalled the generous welcome in such places as Selby, Doncaster, Lincoln and Peterborough, as well as the warm handshake and sympathy of Chuter Ede, their MP, on their visit to the House of Commons.

Boldon Miners' Lodge, Boldon Labour Party and Co-op Party provided the dinner for the north-east contingent of the National Hunger March. On arriving in Sunderland, the marchers were entertained at the Wearmouth Miners' Hall and slept at Highfield workhouse. Tom Money of Northumberland, Councillor J. Ancrum of Felling Urban District Council and Councillor T.A. Richardson of Houghton-le-Spring U.D.C. were the march leaders. Their oldest marcher was a 64-year-old Boer War veteran Alec Vetters from Blyth and the youngest a 16-year-old from Sunderland, Paddy Durkin.[39] The north-east contingent would follow a different route to London and arrive a week later than the Crusade meeting up with contingents from East and West Scotland; South Wales; Lancashire and Merseyside; Yorkshire, Nottinghamshire and Derbyshire; and a women's contingent.[40] Organisers maximised the geographical impact of the march as each contingent took different routes and overall they stayed overnight in 132 different places compared to 21 for the Crusade.

Ellen Wilkinson must have been thrilled at the news that the Asturian miners whom she had visited in defeat two years previously had captured their capital Oviedo. During the Asturian insurrection, they had held the city between 6 and 11 October 1934.[41] In April 1937, she met the widow of Asturian miner, inspirational orator and member of the Spanish Communist Party Central Committee, Dolores Ibárruri, 'La Pasionara' (the passion flower) in Valencia. It was La Pasionara who had coined the anti-fascist clarion call, 'no pasarán', 'they shall not pass'. One of Ellen Wilkinson's many nicknames was the 'pocket pasionara'.

The blind marchers with concertina and drum accompaniment entered Barnsley on Tuesday afternoon after staying in Wakefield the previous night. A.B.N. Forbes, local blind organiser of the Joint Blind Welfare Committee, met the marchers. Robert Hanlon, on the National Marching Committee, told the local paper 'the men were receiving the most courteous treatment each place they stopped in and they were particularly grateful to the police for their assistance in patrolling the streets and keeping the route clear'.[42] Men had come from Aberdeen, Dundee, Hull, Tynemouth, Newcastle, Sunderland, North Shields and Bradford. They held an open-air meeting on Market Hill which Forbes chaired and at which Clydesdale spoke. They spend the night in Baths Hall and ate buttered teacakes, tea and beef sandwiches.

Wednesday 14 October: The Cabinet Condemns Wee Ellen and Paddy the Dog
Leeds to Wakefield (pop. 54,626), 9 miles

In Leeds, women Labour Party members repaired tattered garments and brought gifts of boots and clothes for the marchers. The Crusaders breakfasted in the Hudson Road works canteen of Montague Burton Ltd on porridge followed by bacon, sausage and tomato. There Councillor D. Beavers, an employee at the tailoring works, handed over a magnificent collection from the factory employees of £31 14s 6d. The stay in Leeds scotched anxieties over finances, more than compensating for the deficit incurred at Ripon. They received a marvellous send off from a huge crowd of workers. Favourable weather conditions eased the day's marching with the mildest temperatures so far.

Leeds officials of the RSPCA inspected the male black dog that had accompanied the marchers from the start and gave him a clean bill of health. Symptomatic, depending on your view, of the 'human interest' or trivialised reporting of the Crusade, the newspapers latched onto any possible story about the Crusade's canine companion. One indicator of the popularity of this story was that the Crusade received many offers to buy the dog. With such interest, accuracy was not particularly important as the papers seemed to be confused about his name and breed. According to different reports, his name was Jarrow, Paddy, Peter, and he was a mongrel, a Labrador and less plausibly a retriever or even a terrier! When the confusion about his name was commented on, the reporter admitted that he answered to none of the aforementioned names. Eric Forster writing for the *Evening Chronicle* fifty years on claimed that the marchers discovered that Peter, his real name, belonged to a lady in Hebburn and that this was kept from the press at the time.[43] When this was discovered David Riley asked Councillor W. Crumbley, the chair of the social committee of the Crusade, to ask the woman if she would allow her dog to continue on the rest of the march. Ellen Wilkinson wrote that Paddy was 'more photographed than the proudest dog at Crufts'. The Leeds officials of the RSPCA issued an owner's licence to Samuel Needham, the marcher who had befriended the stray. Several newspapers carried this story. Paddy has become integral to the cultural legacy of the Crusade. Rose Reeve's musical *Crusader* celebrated him in song:

> We are the Jarrow lads, we're marching for our cause
> With a second-hand bus and a black stray dog with blisters
> on his paws.[44]

In a nice touch of surreal humour, an actor on all-fours played Paddy in the musical *Cuddy's Miles* and even got a punch-line towards the end of the play. The dog is featured in several of the most used photographs of the march, and alongside the banners, Ellen, capes and the mouth organs constitute the essential iconography of the Crusade. In one frequently used photograph of the Crusade the dog is nearly pulling Ellen Wilkinson off her tiny feet. The dog illustrates the unique relationship between the Crusade and its 'embedded' journalists. This relationship rendered the Crusade more story-like, more fabulous and a more attractive muse to authors and artists.

The newspapers seized on the story of Ellen Wilkinson's fatigue. Such copy fitted with the press' male chauvinist assumption of Ellen Wilkinson's feminine frailty. Whole articles were devoted to a litany of such stories: the rather shocking idea of a woman leading a hunger march; how she disliked walking; how she was walking with the aid of a stick; was too tired to go on; was near collapse; was now feeling better. To understand her conviction politics, one has to appreciate her dual battle against ill health and dispirited exhaustion. In her novel *The Clash* (1929), we first encounter the heroine Joan, a union organiser in the Yorkshire coalfield, who is a thinly disguised Ellen Wilkinson, 'having one of her crises'. Joan says, 'I'm tired. I can't go on doing this work every day. You can't go on handing out bits of yourself to people who don't want to be bothered. Anyway I can't … I just can't.'[45] The novel is set during the General Strike. We witness how addressing a public meeting of miners in 'Shireport' drains her physically and a few minutes after the meeting's end she is slumped asleep. In some ways, travelling the length of the country for difficult negotiations and speaking engagements, Joan's intensive work schedule paralleled Ellen Wilkinson's during the Crusade. Ellen, 'the fiery atom', 'Miss Perky' was notorious for her indefatigable commitment and tireless convictions but in Joan, Ellen Wilkinson allows us to see the strain of having to live up to this reputation. Even the indefatigable fatigue and the tireless tire. She struggled with asthma, pneumonia and over-work which underscored the cycle of energetic commitment and sapping despair. She ultimately lost this battle on 6 February 1947 after overdosing on the drugs she used to control these afflictions. Her biographer Betty Vernon angrily rejected the suggestion that she had taken her own life.[46] Legends need heroes and villains; history is not so simple in its requirements.

Opening at 11 am, Prime Minister Stanley Baldwin presided over the weekly meeting of the cabinet. The Crusade and the other marches were of direct concern to several cabinet members. For the people of Jarrow, here was a real rogue's gallery. At the Home Office, all possible threats to public order were Sir John Simon's prerogative but the clashes between fascists and anti-fascists were the top of his (and the cabinet's) agenda. Ramsay MacDonald, Prime Minister until June 1935, was now Lord President of the Council. He had achieved notoriety for the 'great betrayal' – abandoning the Labour Party and forming the cross-party National Government with Liberals and Tories because members of his cabinet could not stomach cutting the dole by 10% as high finance wished. Ellen Wilkinson had organised a march from Jarrow to his Seaham constituency on 17 January 1934 when he pompously told her that she should be preaching socialism.[47] But she had certainly made an impression. In an internal Treasury report the following month, the National Government was very cautious about openly showing a special interest in Jarrow after this protest because they believed that it would make Ellen Wilkinson's return in the election a certainty.[48] The nation's next Prime Minister, Neville Chamberlain who replaced Baldwin in 1937, was at this time Chancellor of the Exchequer, of whom Ellen Wilkinson observed in 1930:

> His small head on a long neck sits well on a spare athletic body. It seems as though he could draw that head inside his wide collar and retire into his shell like a tortoise. Spiritually, I imagine, he is always doing that.[49]

Then there was Sir Samuel Hoare, the First Lord of the Admiralty, in whose order books the Jarrow Conservatives forlornly hoped to find the town's rescue. In February 1933 this strategy floundered as the Admiralty and the Committee on Trade and Employment blocked the Minister of Labour's request to waive the rules on tendering and award Palmer's a contract that would have saved the yard.[50] Sir Samuel was also an advocate of appeasement and had had to resign as Foreign Secretary because of the public outcry at his over-accommodating attitude to Mussolini's invasion of Abyssinia. Sir Kingsley Wood, the Minister of Health, and Ernest Brown, the Minister of Labour, obviously had the Special Areas as one of their concerns. Finally, of course, there was Sir Walter Runciman, the President of the Board of Trade, who had told Jarrow of the failure of the steelworks scheme.[51] In a full order of business dealing with such matters as Spain and the King's Speech at the opening of parliament, the first two items for discussion were public order and the National Hunger March under which the Jarrow Crusade was subsumed. The cabinet resolved to issue the following statement:

> Ministers have had under consideration the fact that a number of 'marches' on London are in progress or in contemplation. In the opinion of HM Government such marches can do no good to the causes for which they are represented to be undertaken, are liable to cause

unnecessary hardship for those taking part in them, and are altogether undesirable. In this country governed by a parliamentary system, where every adult has a vote and every area has its representative in the House of Commons to put forward grievances and suggest remedies, processions to London cannot claim to have any constitutional influence on policy. Ministers have therefore decided that encouragement cannot be given to such marches, whatever their particular purpose, and Ministers cannot consent to receive any deputation of 'marchers', although, of course, they are always prepared to meet members of Parliament.[52]

That very day MI5 provided the Home Office with disconcerting news that could potentially undo the strategy that this statement embodied in a highly embarrassing manner.[53] The National Hunger March was planning to send a delegation directly to the King who had cultivated a reputation for sympathy for the working class.

Two days later the Chief Constable of the Metropolitan Police reported that communist leaders believed it possible that the King would ignore the Government's advice not to grant an audience with the marchers and this would prove 'a severe rebuff to the National Government'.[54] On 21 October, Major Alec Hardinge, the King's Private Secretary, reassured Hutchinson at the Home Office that such a visit would 'naturally ... not [be] entertained for a second, except on Ministerial advice' though he may have been expressing his own understanding of protocol rather than the King's view as Hardinge was a key opponent of the King's marriage to Wallis Simpson.[55] Not only was it possible that the National Hunger March might be embroiled in a constitutional crisis, a sympathiser of the Crusade had advised that it too should circumvent the Government by a direct appeal to the King who had visited Jarrow as the Prince of Wales.[56]

The National Hunger March was still entertaining the notion of an audience with the King on 12 November but in a surprising last minute climbdown by the Government a delegation was allowed to see Ernest Brown the Minister of Labour. This contradicted the cabinet's statement of 14 October, which was reiterated on 5 November in the House of Commons.[57] 12 November was also the date that the new UAB scales were to be implemented but were postponed. This curious royal connection with the hunger march continued as the London Reception Committee met after the hunger march to consider another march during coronation week if there was any new threat to the benefit rates for the unemployed.[58]

Given that Edward's supporters were pressing him to oppose Baldwin and reject abdication, and that he broke protocol on his visit to the depression-hit Rhondda and Monmouth valleys on 18-19 November by implying criticism of the Government over the issue of unemployment, the possibility that this was the reason why the National Hunger Marchers received a ministerial hearing is not as fanciful as it might seem.[59] The tour of South Wales was to be his last official trip. As the King listened to his unemployed subjects, in the presence of the Ministers of Labour and Health, he remarked 'Terrible! Terrible!', which must have made the cabinet members feel distinctly uncomfortable. Ernest Brown was booed at points during the visit. In the shadow of the derelict Dowlais steelworks on 18 November, amongst the crowds who had come to see the King was a delegation of the Welsh hunger marchers carrying a banner which pleaded 'Hunger marchers ask the King to abolish the Means Test'. The marchers also addressed an open letter to him which was distributed in the streets of Pontypool. The King asked A.H. Holder, the Chairman of the local council in Blaenavon to see the letter, and said, 'I have followed everything I have seen in South Wales with the deepest interest. Something will be done about unemployment'.[60] The significance of such a statement was that it was widely interpreted as a challenge to the Prime Minister's authority and the phrase 'something must be done' became a refrain of criticism for Baldwin. Indeed, during the visit the King had dined in the royal train with Sir Malcolm Stewart, who had resigned from his post as Commissioner for the Special Areas and supported the Jarrow Crusaders, along with the Ministers. According to one report, Edward was seen through the window banging on the table.[61] All this added to the pressure upon the Government to act on the question of the Special Areas and made them more uneasy about the abdication crisis. Ramsay MacDonald – after dining with Sir George Gillett, Stewart's replacement as Commissioner for the Special Areas in England and Wales – wrote in his diary on 21 November that the King's visit had 'aroused expectations … [which] will embarrass the Government. These escapades should be limited. They are an invasion into the field of politics and should be watched constitutionally. Besides he might easily use this method for cloaking the other troubles in which he plunges at present.'[62]

The Crusaders were as yet unaware of the Government's ill-judged attempt to discredit and dishearten the marches. As on other days, passing motorists stopped to donate to march funds. The total was £2 13s ½d between Leeds and Wakefield. Alderman A. Charlesworth, the Labour Mayor of Wakefield, welcomed the Crusade with the support of local Conservative and Labour Parties as well as Canon Noel Hopkins, the Provost of Wakefield on behalf of the Bishop of Wakefield. Reverend M. Bain extended a welcome from Wakefield's nonconformist churches. A public meeting was held in the Music Saloon.

The marchers were somewhat disappointed with their reception at Wakefield after their extravagant welcome in Leeds. They sat down to potted meat sandwiches and tea for their evening meal to be followed by fried sausage and bread and butter for their breakfast. Frank McGuckin, one of the marchers, returned home because of the sickness of one of his children.[63]

Salem Street Church, which had been closed for the past three years, provided their overnight accommodation. Referring to the adjacent cemetery, the *Evening Chronicle* ran the ghoulish headline, 'Jarrow Marchers R.I.P. in Ancient Wakefield City'. David Ramshaw wrote in his diary:

> Left for Wakefield. Civic reception: Menu, sandwiches
> and tea. Slept in pulpit of condemned church. Received
> 1s donation from funds.[64]

Crusaders had to improvise in the dusty disused church. John McNulty slept on a gravestone. Rising as ever at 6 am, the Crusader who dossed down in the pulpit addressed his impromptu congregation with a sermon of mock piety. Con Shiels stoically confided to his son that the reception in Wakefield had not measured up to that of the previous days 'but never mind we have to take the bad with the good'.[65]

Thursday 15 October: The Goodwill of All and the Jarrow Riot
Wakefield to Barnsley (pop. 71,000), 10 miles

Both Ellen Wilkinson and Mayor Thompson made public statements that the Crusade would continue. Ellen Wilkinson saw only hypocrisy and 'crocodile tears' in the Government's humanitarian concern for the marchers:

> I think that for ministers to have left these men unemployed all these years and continually increased the screw in the unemployment regulations to talk about the men being hungry and ill-clad now when they are better fed than ever in their lives, is, to say the least of it, unwise.

The mayor also countered strongly in his statement to the press:

> The march is going on unless the Government gives us an assurance that industry will be started in Jarrow. We have not yet asked the Government to receive a deputation and have no intention of interviewing cabinet ministers or the Government. The Government cannot refuse to receive the petition which will be presented in the House of Commons on 4 November by Miss Ellen Wilkinson, our Member. I object to the reference in the Government statement about hardship, so far as the Jarrow March is concerned ... This march is different from any other march ever organised: it is non-political and has the goodwill of all.[66]

David Riley informed the Crusaders of the cabinet's statement. He asked if the Government were going to intimidate them, to which they answered with a resounding 'no!' He drafted a telegram to the Mayor of Jarrow, which read as follows:

> We, the Jarrow Crusaders, are determined to continue on our mission to London, also to continue to put our case before the people of our country en route, thereby making no departure from the original object of our undertaking.[67]

In contrast to the Crusade leaders who denied that they wished to have a ministerial hearing after the infamous cabinet statement, Pat Devine, secretary of the London Reception Committee of the National Hunger March, publicly demanded just such an audience.

The cabinet's statement backfired because it drew much greater media attention to the marches. Amongst the well wishers as they left Wakefield was Lady Mabel Smith of the Labour Party National Executive. John McCourt rejoined the Crusade by train after his spell in Ripon Hospital with enteritis. Andrew Kelly, aged 40 years, was taken to St. Helen's Municipal Hospital with influenza. On route they sang:

> Tramp, tramp, tramp, the men of Jarrow,
> Marching on to London every day,
> We are only seeking work,
> and you'll find that we'll not shirk,
> If you start us building right away.[68]

Later they themselves would be celebrated in poetry, painting and song.

Despite the prominent coverage of the support that churches gave the Crusade, behind the scenes Herbert Hensley Henson, the Bishop of Durham, was doing his best to undermine the march. He wrote to Cosmo Gordon Lang, the Archbishop of Canterbury, on 15 October to this effect. He had read the report in *The Times* about the Bishop of Jarrow's blessing of the Crusade with consternation. Henson had spoken to the Bishop of Jarrow about the matter the week prior to the Crusade and the latter had assured him that he would take no part in the event, showing his superior his letter declining the council's invitation. The Bishop of Durham believed that the Bishop of Jarrow had lacked the 'courage to stand up to a spate of local sentiment'.[69] He upbraided his 'too-complaisant' Suffragan on Thursday 8 October for his error, remarking in his diary:

> Assuredly, and quite reasonably, his blessing would be taken to imply his approbation. So gravely do I estimate the potential mischeifs (sic) of these fatuous demonstrations, which are mainly designed in the interest, not of the Unemployed, but of the Labour party, which is 'fishing in troubled waters', that I must needs regret this public association of my colleague with the demonstration.[70]

It might seem that the bishop had nothing to gain from a public stance that invited widespread condemnation even from within the Church. The reason for the bishop's great determination in opposing the Crusade was not only his paranoid fear of communism and his hostility to Labour but because, as his letter to the Marquis of Londonderry revealed, his battle to keep Church of England clergy out of politics, too many of whom were openly sympathetic to the Labour Party.[71]

***

Thirty from Sunderland joined the north-east contingent of the National Hunger March which left Sunderland for West Hartlepool. On their behalf, Durham County Councillor T.A. Richardson also responded to the cabinet statement:

> Our reply to the Government is that we rely not only on the march itself but upon the workers left behind in the various towns, villages and hamlets. We believe that these people and these marchers will compel the Government to receive a deputation. It was such demonstrations as

these which compelled the government to retreat in February last year when they had to restore cuts and pay unemployed on the means test back-pay. The leaders are determined that the Government will receive them.[72]

He was referring to the Standstill Act of early 1935 when the Government suspended the cuts in benefit that resulted from the introduction of the Unemployment Assistance Board scales. The UAB scales had provoked some of the largest protests of the interwar period and rioting in Sheffield that forced the Government to suspend the new benefits rates. This is far from the tranquil image that the Jarrow Crusade projects and is one of the reasons for its popularity with the mainstream politicians and historians who stress the constitutionalism and stability of Britain in the 1930s. Dismissing the inner city riots of 1981, Norman Tebbit infamously implied that such things did not happen in the 1930s, 'My father was unemployed in the 1930s and he did not riot. He got on his bike and looked for work'. But riots did occur, not only in Sheffield, but also elsewhere, such as Birkenhead, West Ham, North Shields and Belfast.

Even in Jarrow, on 13 May 1939, a pub brawl escalated into 'the Jarrow riot' because of heavy-handed policing.[73] At around 10pm, PCs Jackson and Curry tried to arrest Wilfred Page as he and another were fighting outside a pub in Walter Street. A large hostile crowd surrounded and followed the officers as Page struggled against arrest, biting the finger of one officer according to the police. Police charged with their truncheons to disperse the estimated 500 who gathered. When the cinemas closed the numbers swelled to 1,000 and around Monckton Road and Grange Road they threw dustbin lids and half-bricks at the police who had drawn in reinforcements from Hebburn, Felling and Boldon. Windows were smashed and the car that the police used to take Page to the station was damaged in the fray. The crowd then went to the police station and the face-off lasted for a further two hours, with the police repeatedly baton charging at the people.[74] Three people with minor injuries were taken to Palmer's Hospital. With a crowded gallery looking on and a hundred gathered outside, sixteen appeared before magistrates on charges of being drunk and disorderly, assault on a police constable, obstruction and wilful damage. Three received custodial sentences. The court handed Martin Derrick, a 28-year-old, the heaviest punishment, six months imprisonment, for hitting Sergeant Dent on the head with a half-brick, obstruction and wilful damage (valued at £45). Derrick professed his innocence and said he was not a 'criminal or gangster'.[75] Magistrates fined the rest between 6 shillings and 80 shillings each depending on their charges; only one case was dismissed. The *Shields Gazette* worried about the dent that the riot made to Jarrow's reputation contrasting so dramatically as it did with the Crusade. Such sentiments overlooked the accumulated bitterness towards the police and the likelihood that the neighbours, relatives and even Crusaders themselves took part in the riot; indeed, four of the sixteen charged shared a surname with a marcher. In contrast to the *Gazette's* reaction, Ellen Wilkinson asked for the Home Secretary to investigate the police's role that night.[76] As the trials were then pending, the Home Secretary declined. By the time the House of Commons was due to return after the summer recess the country was at war and the Jarrow riot was forgotten; it has largely remained forgotten ever since.

After a day of spells of sun, rain and cloud, Joseph Jones, Mayor of Barnsley, President of the Miners' Federation of Great Britain and General Secretary of the Yorkshire Miners' Federation, welcomed the Crusaders on their arrival in his pit town. The local newspaper pictured him 'making friends with Paddy' alongside Ellen Wilkinson and Joe Symonds in front of the men.[77] He congratulated them upon the broad support they had received from all sections of the community. 'These troubles', he declared:

> proved it was now realised that the actual purpose of the march was absolutely guileless of any political intent as was first implied. The march had been expressly designed to exert pressure in the proper quarter, so that steps might be taken not merely to bring temporary relief and succour to a depressed and oppressed community, but that a course should be followed whereby Jarrow's languishing industries were permanently revived and the normal

industrial and commercial pulse-beats at last restored. Jarrow, as a locality, was besieged – held captive in the paralysing grip of economic adversity. The Government was the rightful custodian of the welfare of the people, and they could see to it that Jarrow was relieved from its social and economic distress.[78]

That year Joe Jones also wrote a book putting the case for nationalisation, *The Coal Scuttle*. Jones had played an important role in the 'miners' two bob' campaign in July 1935 and against company unionism. Miners' militancy and confidence were reviving after the defeat of the lock out and General Strike of 1926.[79] Having said that, the miners' union leadership did not want to lose control to rank-and-file militancy and opposed the stay-down strikes that were being adopted in some pits. A public meeting was held in the Miners' Hall which the Rector of Barnsley, Reverend Canon H.E. Hone, chaired and at which John Potts, the local MP, spoke. Ellen Wilkinson told of conditions on Tyneside and sympathised that many of these hardships were shared by the people of Barnsley:

> Jarrow's problem was not only that of the general depression – for they realised that there was a great deal of unemployment in Barnsley and it surrounding districts – but it was a problem definitely due to the Government's policy. They were asking the Government to do something towards providing a solution by removing the shipyards ban, and by lessening the monopoly pull behind the Steel Federation.[80]

Trying to counter prejudices about the 'undeserving poor', Ellen Wilkinson went out of her way to stress the proper character of the Crusaders to the *Barnsley Chronicle and South Yorkshire News*:

> ... the men were a model to all marchers; they took the greatest care to leave no litter behind them and were always cheerful. Every place through which they had passed had extended to them the warmest welcome, and Barnsley itself had shown the hospitality characteristic

of the 'county of the broad acres'. The ratepayers of Barnsley were exceedingly generous in their treatment and she felt sure the marchers were deeply appreciative.[81]

During the meeting, the marchers were guests of the management at the Theatre Royal, or Empire, Alhambra and Pavilion picture houses. Most nights the Crusaders went to the cinema and, after the exertions of the day, many would fall asleep.[82] After the performance that evening, the Baths Hall provided the Crusaders with a meat and potato pie supper and sleeping accommodation. One Crusader, unemployed miner Alec Sewell, was left behind in Barnsley Hospital because he had tonsillitis and a temperature. Barnsley as a coal town knew the harsh effects of the Depression and it also knew the pain following the terrible pit accident of 6 August 1936 when 57 had been killed. The Jarrow marchers were not the only celebrities to visit the town that month. On Sunday 18 October, George Formby visited Barnsley for the benefit of the Wharncliffe Woodmoor Disaster Fund.[83]

In other news, Malcolm Stewart, the Commissioner of the Special Areas in England and Wales, announced his resignation for 'personal reasons and with great reluctance'. His post established under the Special Areas Act, he had been appointed on 14 November 1934. He published reports on the Special Areas in July 1935 and February 1936. Ellen Wilkinson was amongst the MPs to pay tribute to Stewart, an honest man in an impossible situation, describing his 'impossible job of trying to save the face of a government that intends to do nothing for the Special Areas'. His last report as commissioner published in November, his association with the Crusade and his meeting with Edward VIII on the South Wales trip suggests that Ellen Wilkinson was right. On 14 November, Sir George Gillett, MP for Finsbury 1923-35, took over.[84]

Friday 16 October: Sheffield Steel
Barnsley to Sheffield (pop. 523,300), 13 miles

On Friday morning, after their breakfast of porridge, sausage, mashed potatoes and bread and butter washed down with tea, Canon Hope officially bade the marchers farewell, commending their 'very gallant' act. He apologised for the mayor's absence as he had gone to London. 'He's not walking there', quipped the Canon to the amusement of the men. The marchers set off later than usual after a trip to the baths thanks to the hospitality of the mayor. Ellen Wilkinson remembered:

> how we blessed him! [He] had the municipal baths all heated ready for the men, and where I had the muscle-easing luxury of the women's municipal foam bath.[85]

Though the weather was fine, a strong wind meant that it was impossible to display the banners.[86] The *North Mail* noted the eventfulness of Friday's march: the Crusaders got lost temporarily and managed, unintentionally, to give their police escort the slip.[87]

Sam Rowan had the daily task of collecting the Crusade's mail from the nearest post office. Friends and relatives, like Con Shiels's son, kept in regular touch, addressing their letters to the 'Jarrow Crusade'. As the Post Office knew the march itinerary, the mail would be waiting for Sam in the town where the marchers were spending the night. In Sheffield, Sam presented his credentials and asked for the Crusade's mail. The counter clerk refused, saying that each individual must collect his own mail. Sam calmly asked to see the postmaster. The clerk brought a colleague. Sam asked if he was the postmaster. He wasn't. Sam insisted on seeing the postmaster. The third official who arrived admitted that he too was not the postmaster. Sam stuck to his guns and eventually the postmaster appeared. He, like the three others who were still watching, refused to hand over the mail. So Sam asked what time the office closed that night. At 7 o'clock, he was informed. 'Alright,' said Sam, 'I'll march 200 men in here at five to seven to see if there's any post'. Preferring to get home on time, they handed over the mail straightaway.[88]

For George Orwell in *The Road to Wigan Pier* (1937) Sheffield epitomised the way industry scarred the English landscape:

Sheffield, I suppose, could justifiably claim to be the ugliest town in the Old World: its inhabitants, who want to be pre-eminent in everything, very likely do make that claim for it. It has a population of half a million and it contains fewer decent buildings than the average East Anglian village of five hundred. And the stench![89]

J.B. Priestley described his entry into Sheffield as like running along the edge of a smouldering volcano then descending through a 'murky canopy' into thick smoke which appeared to be the 'steaming bowels of the earth' itself.[90] Sheffield's working class knew its share of hardship. During the winter of 1931-2 nearly one-fifth of Sheffield's working-class families were living on or below the poverty line.[91] Between 5,000 and 10,000 new houses were needed to eliminate overcrowding and in June 1932 unemployment was estimated at 65,000. On arrival in Sheffield, either because they had taken the wrong route or because many of Sheffield's population were still at work, there was only a modest reception for the weary marchers. Indeed, one woman who had mistaken them for fascists shouted abuse at them, though she apologised when she realised her error. One familiar face greeted them though. George Fettes, who had been born in Jarrow had lived in Sheffield, for 15 years. He pulled at the sleeve of Benjamin Stevenson asking, 'Recognise me?' The marcher, who had not seen his pal since 30 May 1915 on a battlefield in France, replied 'Great Scott. It's Geordie Fettes. I thought you were dead!'[92]

Dr. Leonard Hedley Burrows, the Bishop of Sheffield and member of the House of Lords, provided a more official greeting. Despite being on friendly terms with the Bishop of Sheffield, the Bishop of Durham complained about his 'strong belief in slogans and platitudes' with 'great power of public work, greater perhaps than his powers of thought or knowledge'. The Bishop of Durham also criticised Burrows as a 'complaisant servitor' of Church centralisation and a 'forcible echo' of the Archbishops.[93] After blessing the men, Burrows stated that they were doing a very English, very constitutional thing and donated £5. 'All governments are like wheelbarrows', he mused, 'useful instruments but they need to be pushed'.[94] Reverend E. Benson Perkins of the Sheffield Methodist Mission also welcomed the Crusaders. Jarrow's mayor joined the marchers in Sheffield having travelled from the North East by train. His Sheffield counterpart, Alderman Frank Theaves CBE, JP, secretary of the Sheffield branch of the T&GWU, was cheered as he welcomed his 'comrades' from Jarrow. He told them:

> You represent to me a tremendous tragedy. The tragedy of unemployment. ... There is a certain section of people who regard the unemployment problem as something to be forgotten. They do not want to think about it. It is uncomfortable. But there are also those who do think of you and I hope that as a result of your march the public conscience will be awakened. When you return home to Jarrow I hope you will have the satisfaction of knowing that you have done your job well.[95]

Lending ecclesiastical respectability to the event, the Bishop of Sheffield and 20 clergymen graced the platform of the public meeting held in the (Methodist) Victoria Hall. This act of solidarity from the Bishop of Sheffield and so many churchmen could not be dismissed, as the Bishop of Durham did in his diary, as merely 'parsons eagerly welcoming them on their way'.[96] After the meeting, Sheffield Corporation provided accommodation and food in six classrooms of Pomona Street School.

There, a group of Scottish ex-servicemen who were marching to London to call for higher war pensions also stayed the night.[97] These marchers, who had started out five weeks before with fifty from Inverness, arrived at 3 o'clock in the morning, their ranks thinned to 16. The *Shields Gazette's* reporter related the terrible hardship they had endured. Amongst other woes they were lost for some considerable time on the moors. He continued:

> The people of Sheffield this morning commented upon the difference between the two marches, the one failing through disorganisation and the other, the Jarrow Crusade, marching on from triumph to triumph as an example of efficient arrangements.[98]

These ghost-like figures entered the room of sleeping Crusaders in Alex Glasgow's play *Whistling at the Milestones*. They told of their shocking lack of organisation to an audience of sympathetic Crusaders who had a whip-round for the unfortunate Scots.[99] As the Special Branch report noted, this was not part of the National Hunger March but a group of veterans calling themselves the British Campaigners' Association who had set out independently of the other marchers.[100] Only 13 of the original 40 or 50 arrived in London and only 100 spectators listened to John Fagan, their leader, at Hyde Park's speaker's corner on 8 November.[101] Unlike this unfortunate affair, the National Hunger March was organised by people with years of experience of such events who lent careful advice to Ellen Wilkinson about the necessary preparations for a successful march.[102]

Misinterpretation of this episode has fuelled the myth that the Crusade's organisation contrasted with the organisational shambles of all other marches. This misconception sowed the dragon's tooth of myth about the Crusade. For those on the Crusade, including its accompanying journalists, this confusion was understandable at the time. This was their only encounter with another march up to this point. When they did meet up with another march – the National League of the Blind march – they could make no such complaints and the same would have been true of the National Hunger March. Indeed, the *Mansfield and North Notts Advertiser* remarked that the blind march 'surprised many who saw them by the ability they displayed in keeping in perfect formation and, by use of their leader's signals, avoiding sundry obstacles on the road'.[103]

Three marches – the National Hunger March, the National League of the Blind March and the Jarrow Crusade – appealed the Sheffield's labour movement for support. The reaction to each march differed. The blind march received the earliest, most sustained and systematic support with the establishment of a sub-committee of the Sheffield Trades and Labour Council (STLC) which reported regularly to the executive over close to a three-month period. It organised accommodation, speakers for the demonstration (two Labour councillors and a Co-operative Party member), and funds.

The first discussion of the Crusade on the Labour and Trades Council weekly executive meeting came three weeks after the first discussion of the blind march; they had received a letter from the Mayor of Jarrow. Support for the Crusade was established at the monthly delegates' meeting on 29 September and on 15 October Stoddart, Labour agent for Jarrow, addressed the executive meeting. There was no sub-committee but the STLC did collect £9 17s 0d (a similar figure was collected for the blind march) and provided stewards for the Crusade's public meeting.

The attitude to the National Hunger March was quite different and confused by the black circulars policy of the national leadership of the Labour Party and Trades Union Congress, which instructed their organisations to shun such campaigns. Sheffield's Labour City Council refused to support the hunger marchers.[104] But the march seriously divided opinion within the local movement. The issue of the new Unemployed Assistance Board regulations, the object of the National Hunger March, overshadowed all other marches. The Sheffield Trades and Labour Council (STLC) condemned these regulations on 28 July and organised a demonstration on 20 September at the Fair Ground which attracted 5,000 people. The collection, which was for Spain, amounted to over £12. At a delegate meeting on 29 September a motion was moved for the executive to set up a sub-committee to organise a Sheffield contingent of the march. The next executive meeting resolved to ascertain who was organising the march. At the following executive meeting the secretary said that the TUC had instructed them not to support the march. A vote was taken to support the march nonetheless which was lost 5 to 22. The following week at the full delegate meeting, support for the march was more narrowly defeated by 46 to 34. Two days before, however, Sheffield Hallam Division of the Labour Party, which Darvill, the President of the STLC attended, voted to support the march.[105] After the end of the march, perhaps to resolve the disputes, Sheffield Trades and Labour Council sought clarification from the Labour Party National Executive Council about the official position on the hunger march. The Labour Party NEC resolved to send them a 'friendly letter ... intimating that the NEC had not been consulted regarding the march and could therefore accept no responsibility'.[106]

Whilst the blind march and the Jarrow Crusade received support from the labour movement in Sheffield, they were soon forgotten, neither even featuring in the annual report of the Trades and Labour Council.[107] In contrast, Spain and the campaign against the UAB were prominently mentioned.

If the Jarrow Crusade could count on the support of the local Labour movement in Sheffield, it also drew support from local capitalists. In response to the cabinet's condemnation of the marches, Allan John Grant, local industrialist and chair of the Northeast Derbyshire Conservative and Unionist Association (1934-45) complained:

> This is no time to discuss the principle of these marches now that the deputation from Jarrow has reached Derbyshire. The one point that concerns us is that 200 of our countrymen who have endured a severe spell of unemployment are staying for a day's rest in Chesterfield and it is our privilege and right to do all we can for their comfort. Here in the Chesterfield and Sheffield area we have enjoyed a steady return to prosperity in the last few years and hope and believe that the time has come when the depressed area of Jarrow will follow the rest of our country into the coming era of industrial improvement and security.[108]

With figures like Grant, the Crusade had some very surprising admirers indeed. Grant was one of the barons of the Sheffield steel industry. He was the managing director at the Atlas Works of Thomas Firth and John Brown Limited and chairman and director of Firth Vickers Stainless Steel Limited (1934-1944).[109] Allan Grant's support for Crusade reflected some of the divisions that existed within the British Iron and Steel Federation. Another prominent figure in the Sheffield industry, Sir William Firth, had supported Jarrow's case for a steel works whereas the strongest opposition came from Middlesbrough steel interests.[110] The Atlas

Work supplied stainless steel to shipbuilders and the firm had long had a relationship with Clydebank shipbuilding interests.[111] To glance at the newspaper report of Grant's endorsement, the Crusade had wooed another notable supporter but the reality was that Jarrow's cause had become the unwitting object of a family squabble of powerful strangers, the British steel industry.

Like Grant, Major E.G. Whitaker, the Conservative agent for Sheffield, supported the Crusaders. As well as providing each with a pack of cigarettes, he bluffly referred to the attitude of officialdom. Of the refusal to meet the Crusaders, he said:

> We are told that you won't be seen by the Government. To the devil with that. Your march is a good thing, and whether my Head Office likes it or not I don't care. Good luck.[112]

Robert Winship, aged 42, was left behind in Sheffield General Hospital having collapsed with recurring malaria in the school; his condition was satisfactory. The Crusade had now lost six of its original members: Winship, Queenan, Guy, McGuckin, Coyne, and Kelly.

***

Events in India held a significance for both Ellen Wilkinson and Government. Underlying the other difficulties of the cabinet was a protracted crisis of imperial overstretch, with revolts of dissatisfied colonial subjects in such places as Palestine and India as well as political instability in Iraq, where a coup took place during the Jarrow Crusade. Ellen Wilkinson's championing of the oppressed led her to support the cause of Indian independence. That Friday, 35 were killed in Hindu-Muslim communal riots in Bombay. Ellen Wilkinson had visited India four years earlier at the time of the Congress Party's third civil disobedience campaign and counted Nehru and Gandhi among her friends and acquaintances. She was a principled opponent of imperialism. From 17 August to 7 November 1932, Ellen Wilkinson was part of a delegation of the India League, a body sympathetic to Indian independence together with Monica Whatley, Leonard W. Matters and V.K. Krishna Menon.

Their 534-page report detailed the brutalities of British rule in India and the contradictions of the Government's dual policy of reform and repression.[113] They travelled to Bengal, Assam, Gujerat and the Afghan border region as well as Bombay and Delhi. They catalogued the repressive government ordinances that suspended civil liberties and examined the methods of police rule, even used against women and children, which included shooting on unarmed demonstrations or charging with *lathis*, mass arrests and awful prison conditions.[114] The report exposed the mendacity of the Government's position and the widespread support that existed across different social classes and religious communities for self-rule and the Congress Party.

Ellen Wilkinson's attitude to India was part of her wider world view. Edward Conze recalled telling her of the bombardments of the Royal Navy along the Ygantze River. She was moved to tears and impressed Conze with her passionate internationalism: 'to me the problems of the millgirls of Shanghai are as important as the millgirls of Manchester'.[115]

Saturday 17 October: His Holiness the Bishop
Sheffield to Chesterfield (pop. 65,800), 12 miles

After a breakfast of porridge, ham and bread and butter, the marchers faced the worst weather conditions up to this point with gale force winds and bitterly cold showers. Ellen Wilkinson left the Crusade for engagements in Glasgow. Reporting on Saturday's events, several newspapers carried tales of attempts at communist infiltration of the Crusade. Some communists from South Normanton (a pit village ten miles south of Chesterfield) held an open air meeting in Chesterfield's market square. One of the speakers announced that they had collected £20 for the Crusade by the sale of flags and distributed pamphlets about the hunger marches from Scotland and Jarrow. Allen Moorhouse complained to the march marshal because this, the Conservative official believed, contravened the non-political character of the march. On hearing the news, David Riley said he would 'refuse to accept it [the money]' and they had 'collected without authority'. Chesterfield's Conservative agent condemned the communists, saying 'I think that it is a vile trick to attempt to exploit the Jarrow marchers in this way'.[116] In part presumably to reassure his benefactors, the Chesterfield Conservatives, David Riley commented to another journalist:

> This is the fourth time the communists have tried to gatecrash. They are not going to get in as easily as they think. We are determined at all costs to preserve the non-political character of this Crusade, and we shall defend ourselves strenuously against any attempt at interference. If necessary we shall call the authorities to assist us. They have already been notified, and are aware of our difficulty, but so far we have not made any definite appeal for intervention.[117]

In the same article that reported the 'exploitation' by the Chesterfield communists, the *Evening Chronicle* inadvertently revealed a double-standard at work. Whilst the Mansfield Conservative Association offered a substantial donation, there was no similar dramatic refusal from the march leaders.[118] In fact, anti-communism was the necessary companion of Conservative support, thus undermining the claim that the march was non-political. In effect, the organisers chose between political allies, rejecting NUWM or communist advances in favour of the Tories. That is not to deny a certain persistence on part of the Communist Party, which was certainly determined to support and unite with the Jarrow Crusade in line with its policy of the Popular Front against fascism, which Stalin hoped would predispose France and Britain towards an alliance with him against German expansion.

The Crusade fell victim to another act of treachery. Saturday's edition of *The Times* carried a letter from the Bishop of Jarrow, who had blessed the march as it left Jarrow. 'I entirely agree with the official announcement from 10 Downing Street', he coldly stated, referring to the statement made three days before. He concluded, 'The problem for Jarrow is an industrial one ... we clergy are not qualified to judge'.[119] Though not a constitutional lawyer, the bishop summoned enough expertise to proclaim that the march was 'eminently undesirable and inconsistent with the principles of our Parliamentary system'. Perhaps his superior, the Bishop of Durham, who specialised and published in the field of early constitutional history, had advised him.[120] The Bishop of Jarrow indicated how he had turned down the mayor's invitation to participate in the Crusade or speak at its public meeting in London. In *The Town That Was Murdered*, Ellen Wilkinson forgave Bishop Gordon for this letter because she firmly believed that the Bishop of Durham, had pressured him into writing it.[121] Her suspicions were right. On Thursday, the Bishop of Durham 'told [the Bishop of] Jarrow to read the statements in the Times, and consider whether it did not require from him some kind of disclaimer'.[122] When this disclaimer appeared the Bishop of Durham was pleased, smugly divulging to his diary that the letter was 'well-written, effective, and sufficient for the purpose'.[123] Perhaps Ellen Wilkinson's later generosity towards Bishop Gordon reflected the fact that he had recently died. It also cast an unfavourable light on Henson. This betrayal was not forgotten in the folk memory. North-east folk band Lindisfarne recalled in the song *Marshal Riley's Army* (1978):

> While his holiness the Bishop, with his infinite
> Christian wisdom
> Like Peter when the cock crew, had denied them.

Ellen Wilkinson was busy tackling other enemies of the Crusade. The *Worcester Evening News* reported Ellen Wilkinson describing Sir Walter Runciman, the President of the Board of Trade, as a 'block of ice'. The contrast in lifestyle between humble marchers and the minister could not have been greater. The Runcimans' vast wealth derived from ship-owning and they were part of the north-east plutocracy. Even the Bishop of Durham had to concede:

> Great economic resources contrast painfully in the minefields with mean and even squalid social conditions. The wealth of industrial magnates stands out luridly and dangerously against the background of Tyneside slums and many of the older pit villages.[124]

Another north-east plutocrat, the largest and most established of the Durham mine owners and close friend of the Bishop of Durham, Lord Londonderry, was one of Hitler's most ardent English admirers.[125] Despite his reservations, the Bishop of Durham went that November to Londonderry's Wynyard Hall where Ribbentrop, Hitler's ambassador in London, was guest of honour.[126] Appeasement and fascist sympathies amongst members of the British ruling class are other aspects of the late 1930s many would prefer to bury in the nostalgia for the Jarrow Crusade.

Sunday 18 October: Conservatives Come to Our Rescue
Chesterfield

On Sunday morning, the Mayor of Chesterfield, Councillor H.P. Short, ignored the decision of his council to shun the Crusaders and visited them at breakfast to lend his support. In Chesterfield, the black circulars had done their mischief and it was the Conservatives and business folk who came to the aid of the Crusade in this Labour town. The Conservative agent Allen Moorhouse explained to the local press how Mr J. Bishop and others had worked like Trojans to support the marchers. £19 13s had been raised as well as gifts of food and clothes and the loan of blankets. The Victoria Café laid on five meals over the weekend. Mr Bishop told how 'Business people in the town had assisted most willingly and generously. Not one person or firm who had been asked to help refused'. Moorhouse could not resist an understated reference to the local Labour Party's failure: 'he did not criticise Chesterfield Town Council for refusing the marchers' request for assistance: that was their business'.[127] David Riley thanked the Conservatives 'for coming to their rescue'.

The spiritual needs of both major denominations were catered for this Sunday. In the morning, a mass was celebrated at the Roman Catholic Church of the Annunciation, Spencer Street, for Catholic marchers, and at 3.30 pm, Archdeacon the Venerable T. Dilworth-Harris held a service for the Crusaders in Chesterfield Parish Church with its famous twisted spire. As for their physical needs, J. Cornelius and J.D. Blake replaced T. Gibbons and R. Doll, the two medical students who were accompanying the marchers and had to return to their studies. The latter pair had taken over from Cargill and Blake. In the evening, marchers attended a concert put on by local entertainers. Jarrow's mayor, who had spent the weekend with the marchers, returned to Jarrow on Sunday evening. During the weekend, the marchers were Rector E.W. Platt's guests at the Trinity Institute in Chesterfield. R.M. Carruthers, the caretaker, was such an attentive host that the men clubbed together to buy him a pipe in gratitude. The advance party of Jarrow's two political agents had arrived in Chesterfield on Wednesday and had made these arrangements with the assistance of the Chesterfield Conservative agent, Allen Moorhouse. The Labour council had taken a decision not to support the Crusade, in line with official party policy.

Week Three: Chesterfield to Northampton

Monday 19 October: Red Ellen, Jarrow Royalty and Prior Engagements
Chesterfield to Mansfield (pop. 47,000), 12 miles

Another Chesterfield councillor, J.W. Thompson, broke ranks with his Labour colleagues to give his guarded support to the Crusade early on Monday. Addressing the marchers after breakfast, he 'deprecated marches on London, but theirs was an exception'.[1] Walking through the coalmining and agricultural landscapes of north Derbyshire and Nottinghamshire, the Crusaders faced a heavy downpour and strong winds and several got colds as a result.

One coal company, John Bowes and Partners, is particularly significant to the story of the Crusade. From its inception it brought together the Palmer family and the Bowes family of old aristocratic lineage who resided at Glamis Castle, Scotland, Streatlam Castle and Gibside, a few miles from Jarrow.[2] By the interwar period, Patrick Bowes-Lyon the eldest son of Claude George Bowes-Lyon (the fourteenth Earl of Strathmore and Kinghorne) became chairman of the company. The link with the Palmer family continued as Major G.M. Palmer was its managing director in 1933.[3] The Bowes coal barons provided a royal connection with Jarrow. The youngest sister of Patrick Bowes-Lyon was Elizabeth Angela Marguerite Bowes-Lyon, who on her marriage in 1923, became the Duchess of York, and then Queen in 1937. As Duchess of York, she had visited Jarrow on 28 July 1928 to launch the *York* from Palmer's. Harry Clarke, the youth who skipped school to walk alongside the Crusade for a few miles on the day of its departure, vividly remembered another visit when she opened the Bowes coal docks. The party arrived in a Rolls Royce 'like gods, come down from Mars' and old 'bolshie' fitter George Craigs said at the corner of the street where people gathered, 'the beggars never worked in their lives'. As the family had owned pits before the laws that banned child labour, he continued, they'd 'made a fortune out of bairns'. The contrast between their wealth and Harry's own life left a deep political impact on him and Geordie Craigs's words stuck with him. Harry lived in the downstairs of a terrace with two rooms for a family of 15, no running water, and an outdoor toilet shared with the upstairs family.[4]

After the publicity of the Crusade and reading Priestley's *English Journey*, Bill Brandt, the internationally renowned photographer, immortalised scenes from Jarrow in the late 1930s: a man on a bicycle returning from the slagheap, a scrawny ill-fed cat in the foreground of washing lines on cobbled backstreets, an impoverished child's jam-smeared face peering inertly into camera and, perhaps most famously, its coal searchers – three slouching figures clambering across a slagheap scavenging for small fragments of coal without which they would freeze that night.[5] Brandt captured how life on the dole was reduced to a struggle to keep warm and fed. Con Shiels remembered going to the dumps of coal dust in South Shields with a bucket and using water to fashion them it into balls, drying them by the fire before they could be used for fuel.[6] He would also go to the butcher's shop late on Saturday evening to get the best price for cheap cuts of meat that would not keep until Monday.

Mansfield, like Chesterfield, had a Labour council but did not shun the Crusade as the latter had done. The Deputy Mayor J.A. Beth, on behalf of the mayor, Alderman G. Abbott, greeted the marchers in front of the Town Hall. After a visit to the corporation baths, they had tea in the Parochial Hall and then enjoyed a free cinema trip.[7] The public meeting in the Co-operative Hall had Ellen Wilkinson as the major speaker who had just returned from Glasgow. Marchers slept in the buildings of Broomhill Lane School.

The marchers were pleased to see the return of their MP and her oratory was as always impassioned and impressive. In the fullest exposition of her ideas, *Why Fascism?* (1934) which she co-authored with Conze, Ellen Wilkinson identified herself as a revolutionary socialist:

> "Revolutionary" as an adjective applied to politics is an ambiguous term. It can mean civil war, which in Britain can be ruled out of consideration. Equally it can mean radical change. Using the term in this sense, we suggest that a "revolutionary Socialist Party" offers the only constructive alternative which is able to generate sufficient steam at a time of crisis to prevent Fascism achieving the popular strength which in other countries has generated its success.[8]

She was highly critical of Labour Party leadership's approach to socialism. 'Reform or "Gradual Socialism"' that is the 'gradual attaining of the control of the means of production' was 'impossible':

> Socialism cannot be presented to the nation as a gift from the Parliamentary Labour Party. It cannot be built down from above, with only the passive consent of the citizens as expressed from time to time by their votes. It must come from the active participation and eagerness of the masses of the people.[9]

Ellen Wilkinson was a determined advocate of women's rights. As a full-time suffrage campaigner, a woman's trade union organiser, a woman Labour MP, she connected the issues of class and gender. Her novel *The Clash* provides useful insights into her views. The middle-class birth control campaigners anger Joan, the heroine, because of their patronising attitude to the realities of working-class women's lives. *The Clash* returned time and again to the gulf between Joan's Bloomsbury feminist friend Maud Meddows and the coalfield where Joan's deepest political loyalties lay and from where she saw the hope for social change coming. The novel also addresses a woman's dilemma of career or marriage when Tony Dacre asks Joan to give up her life in politics for him. She refuses.

In the collective memory of an ageing generation of Jarrow folk, Ellen is 'revered'.[10] She encapsulates the socialist and activist element of the British working-class movement. People in Jarrow still remember her inspiring street meetings on the steps of the railway station. Accused of neglecting her constituents by local Tories after visits to the US and Spain, Ellen Wilkinson pointed out that she regularly spoke at the public meeting in her constituency, something that her Conservative predecessor did not do once. It was by these methods of street meetings and campaigning that Independent Labour Party activists had initially won the North East for the Labour Party in the early years of the century. As Paddy Scullion, former mayor of Jarrow, told the *Sunday Times Magazine* in 1975, she was, 'a small red-haired woman, but by God, a fighter'.[11] Or, as one of her obituaries suggested, 'Five foot of dynamite' (though this posthumously adds two inches to her height).

Tuesday 20 October: Underwear in Nottingham
Mansfield to Nottingham (pop. 265,000), 14 miles

On the way to Nottingham the Crusaders got lost because the Mansfield police had given such poor directions. March leaders disagreed over whether to retrace their steps and go the shorter route to Nottingham or carry on a road they had taken that would take them through more industrial areas. Ultimately, Riley won out for the shorter option because 'the men come first'. Between Mansfield and Nottingham, they were without Ellen Wilkinson because she had a prior appointment to present prizes at a hospital in Dewsbury.

If George Orwell found Sheffield ugly, novelist D.H. Lawrence extended this judgment to his native Nottinghamshire coalfield which the Crusaders were passing through. In 1929, he wrote:

> The real tragedy of England, as I see it, is the tragedy
> of ugliness. The country is so lovely: the man-made
> England is so vile. I know that the ordinary collier,
> when I was a boy, had a peculiar sense of beauty, coming

from his intuitive and instinctive consciousness, which was awakened down pit. ...

Now though perhaps nobody knew it, it was ugliness which betrayed the spirit of man, in the nineteenth century. The great crime which the moneyed classes and promoters of industry committed in the palmy Victorian days was the condemning of the workers to ugliness, ugliness, ugliness: meanness and formless and ugly surroundings, ugly ideals, ugly religion, ugly hope, ugly love, ugly clothes, ugly furniture, ugly houses, ugly relationship between workers and employers. The human soul needs actual beauty even more than bread.[12]

Unknown to the Crusaders, the prospective constitutional crisis worsened that morning. Baldwin met the King to ask him to get Mrs Simpson to delay her divorce. The King refused to interfere in her business. There were potential compromises – a morganatic marriage (whereby Wallis would not assume the royal titles) or a legal challenge to delay the divorce – but failure to pursue these led the King and Prime Minister towards a constitutional crisis.

On arrival in Nottingham, crowds showered 'cascading coins' at the feet of the marchers and the Corporation, which had a small Conservative majority, provided a meal in the Co-operative Hall.[13] Alderman Sir Albert Ball, Lord Mayor of Nottingham, welcomed the marchers to the town. There were several examples of East Midlands generosity in Nottingham. In a city known for its hosiery and textiles, especially lace, two Nottingham firms presented the Crusaders with 200 sets of underwear and a local manufacturing chemists gave a large amount of medical supplies. As elsewhere the co-operative movement provided substantial support to the march, the Nottingham Co-operative Society donating 32 pairs of boots and 12 pairs of trousers and socks. In total, the co-operative societies accounted for a fifth of all march funds, three times that from the trade unions and five times that from all political parties. Music hall comedian Sandy Powell sent his accordion band to cheer up the exhausted marchers and donated £5 to their funds. David

Cummings' short story about a guest lecture given by David Riley to a group of university students dramatised and embroidered this event. In this version, Sam Rowan finds Sandy who took the entire cast in taxis to where the marchers were staying and performed the whole show for them.[14]

But there were limits to the official sympathy in the lace town. There was no public meeting in Nottingham. This was implausibly because there were no available venues as well as because the council had banned open air meetings and they could not make an exception. Despite the failure of the Crusade to find a venue, Arthur Greenwood, deputy leader of the Labour Party, was speaking in Nottingham that night on the issue of the marches and several Crusaders attended. Newspaper headlines quoted Greenwood describing the Crusade as 'no credit'. Without departing from the Labour leadership's position at the Edinburgh conference, Greenwood gave an anti-government spin to his remarks:

> Their tragic march is a terrific indictment of the National Government. To think that blind men should have to tap their way to London to ask for justice is no credit to the sense of decency of the people of this country and less to this Government. To think that a dying city like Jarrow should with the unanimous approval of its people, irrespective of party, have to send down by road, tramping day by day, representatives of that town to appeal to the Government is again no credit to the people and less to the National Government.[15]

If Middleton's speech had been, as David Riley put it, a 'stab in the back' from the Labour Party leadership, Greenwood failed to redeem the situation with his cautious and ambiguous comments.

***

This equivocation anticipated another leader of the Labour Party in another great social conflict. Neil Kinnock unveiled Vince Rea's sculpture of the Crusade in Jarrow metro station (paid for by the Tyne and Wear Passenger Transport Executive) on 28 April 1984 during the first weeks of the miners' strike. He was within three miles of Boldon Colliery. This event was one of the infamous 'prior engagements' that kept Kinnock from visiting the miners' picket lines for so long. Those advising the Labour leader carefully selected the potent but safe symbol of the Jarrow Crusade. Patricia Hewitt, Neil Kinnock's press officer, wrote a memo about the trip to this effect. This advice, however, was leaked to the press:

> Factory gate meetings are not good from the TV point of view. Visits to pubs and clubs can be ruined by a single drunk, better avoided. Visits to workplaces on the point of closure or derelict sites should be avoided.[16]

The event was nearly an embarrassment but a quick repaint obscured 'obscenities daubed with felt-tip pen'.[17] The Labour Party leader's efforts to follow Patricia Hewitt's recommendations failed as Kinnock was pictured in the press with a *Socialist Worker* placard saying 'Victory to the miners' behind him. Six original Crusaders watched the ceremony as the Labour leader treated them to his famed rhetoric:

> Until dignity and liberty have been restored we will not be able to say that the Jarrow marchers have truly come home. These marchers were striking a blow for dignity. In 1984 their memory is still relevant. The need for us to live and work with that memory is still with us. We must make sure future generations do not have to march.[18]

The relationship between the history of the miners and the history of the Jarrow Crusade is a significant one. The memory of the TUC General Council's abandonment of the miners when they called off the General Strike of 1926 is a bitter one and one with a powerful cultural legacy in the North East. Jarrow had itself been a pit village before Palmer arrived and it was surrounded by mining villages. The great strikes of 1831 and 1832 were part of its history and the last man to be gibbeted in this country, Will Jobling, was a Jarrow miner accused of murder during the 1832 strike. Artist and curator Vince Rea sought to commemorate the gibbeting of Will Jobling in the Bede Gallery, as did Jarrow-born Alan Plater in the play *Close the Coalhouse Door* (1968). This play takes the form of a discussion of local working-class history and threads together miners' struggles (of 1831, 1832, 1844, 1872 and 1926) with the unemployed protests of the 1930s and with Ellen Wilkinson. This is done in such a way as to leave open whether the Crusade or other hunger marches were being referred to. The play incorporates the songs of Alex Glasgow, one of which poignantly reflects on the return to mass unemployment as many are 'standing at the door, at the same bloody door, waiting for the payment as my father did before.'[19] Alex Ferguson's *A Woman's Walk*, a play about the wives' experience of the Jarrow Crusade, also threw the memory of the General Strike in the face of the trade union bureaucracy. Jess, struggling to feed her kids while her husband is marching to London, chastises union official Patrick McGovern for the TUC's constitutionalism in 1926 and during the Crusade:

> Like you did with the National Strike? How much did you change then when you surrendered without a shot being fired? Leaving pitmen like my father to fight your battles for you? Twenty long weeks, remember? Oh, yes, you did, you left the miners to their fate. I was ashamed of you then and I'm ashamed of you now.

Ellen Wilkinson herself pointed the finger at the trade union leadership for the suffering of the starving miners and victimised engineers in her novel *The Clash* and in her contribution to a history of the strike.[20] These very institutions of trade union officialdom have been responsible for establishing the Crusade in the collective memory through commemorations, banners and official histories. For example, the banner of the Northern Region Transport and General Workers' Union bears an image of the Crusade, the TUC was integral to several of the repeat marches (in 1981 and 1986) and the Crusade is prominently featured in the TUC's official history, all encouraging the myth of TUC support.[21]

English national mythology and crusade symbolism have also formed an intimate liaison. Saint George's flag derived from the crusades. The sign of the cross was of course one of the defining characteristics of the crusades and English knights adopted the red cross of Saint George. The cult of Saint George spread amongst crusaders in several parts of Europe. There is little English about the historical George who acts as patron saint to a cosmopolitan array of towns, nationalities, professions and (especially skin) diseases. Thus the term 'crusade' suggests an association with Englishness. Another important English myth, associated with Nottingham, that of Robin Hood, also has strong connections with the crusades. In some versions of the legend (including the 1938 Errol Flynn Hollywood version) good King Richard returns from the crusades to restore justice within the kingdom. The Robin Hood legend like that of Jarrow has been reshaped for different purposes. Later romantic writers appropriated the legend for the aristocracy by making the hero a dispossessed lord – Robin of Locksley or the Earl of Huntingdon.[22] Of late, local historians and heritage industries have battled over whether Robin truly belonged to Derbyshire, Nottingham or Yorkshire. Each retelling of the Jarrow legend has its own villain, its own Sheriff of Nottingham, be it Runciman, Londonderry, the Bishop of Durham, Lithgow, Duncan or Norman. Whilst heroes and villains are part of the narrative requirements of a legend, they simplify the historical reality. The historical investigation of the Robin Hood myth bears crucial insights for the legend of the Jarrow Crusade. Historian J.R. Maddicott noted how the Robin Hood story, kept alive in the spoken word just as the Jarrow Crusade was, 'can undergo more than one mutation during its life … reworked to suit the taste of each generation'. Holt noted that Robin Hood was 'becoming all things to all men' and warned against the fable becoming progressively 'adulterated'.[23] These processes are well underway with the Jarrow Crusade but in this case it is taking place through the most modern cultural forms as well as the oral dimension.

While marchers slept in Sneinton House, Nottingham's 'municipal hostel' (a journalistic nicety for the squalor of the workhouse), Alderman Ball retired to the splendour of Stansted

House in Wollaton Park where he resided as Lord of the Manor of Bunny, Bradmore and Tollerton.[24] With mansions for some and workhouses for others, housing was just one indicator of the depth of class divisions in Britain at the time. The press, with its regular updates about the careful medical care of the men, reported that 28-year-old Thomas Melia had been taken to hospital with a temperature and unemployed labourer William Cameron had to return to Jarrow to have all his teeth removed. These were the days before NHS dentistry and rotten teeth were a sign of generalised malnourishment.[25] With these two losses, the Crusade was now eight short of its full complement.

Wednesday 21 October: Migrant Tynesiders
Nottingham to Loughborough (pop. 27,500), 15 miles

As in Chesterfield and elsewhere, the work of Bob Suddick, the Conservative agent for Jarrow, brought results. Nottingham Conservative Association provided breakfast for the Jarrow marchers before they set out. The morning was cloudy but mild. Ellen Wilkinson rejoined them at Bunny, halfway to Loughborough. The comings and goings of marchers continued because one marcher returned home to enter hospital for 'recurring malaria'.[26]

The cabinet convened at 11 am but unlike the previous week did not discuss the hunger marches or Jarrow. Instead the most pressing items were foreign affairs with the upcoming five power conference and of course Spain. Consideration of other matters followed: imperial concerns in Palestine, the King's Speech and the legislative programme for 1936-7.[27] This was because, whilst it did get considerable press coverage especially in the provincial newspapers along the route, the Jarrow Crusade was not front page news in the nationals. There were more urgent concerns. Ultimately the Government were hoping the issue would go away.

Time and again on the route down to London, the Crusaders came across natives of their home town who had left to seek new employment years before. One such case was a broken down motorist, Hugh Morris, who had lived in Jarrow for 25 years, and for whom the driver of Jarrow's supplies and equipment bus had stopped to help. Migration touched many families in Jarrow. Crusader Dennis Cox's family illustrates the scattering of families in the search for work. He was the only one of five brothers to stay in Jarrow; Eddie, Billy and Thomas had gone 'down south' for work and Jimmy had gone to sea.[28] Migration was of course much easier for the young and unattached but not so easy for skilled shipyard or steel workers with wives and children. The scale of migration was such that, in net terms, Tyneside had lost 92,158 of its population due to this cause between 1926 and 1938 and London and the Home Counties had gained 1,076,235 in the same period.[29]

On their arrival in Loughborough, the Mayor, F.G. Fleeman, greeted the 196 marchers. Loughborough council donated £50 to march funds and workplace collections were made to provide a meat and potato pie meal and the cost of lodging on the floor of the Drill Hall (the blind marchers had slept there only the night before). Lawrence Kimball, the local Conservative MP, gave two guineas to the fund.[30] S.K. Lewis, President of the Loughborough Rotary Club, procured cinema tickets for the Crusaders.[31]

***

Back in County Durham a controversy had broken out over the Unemployment Assistance Board. Professor H.M. Hallsworth, a member of the UAB, had addressed the Junior Imperial League and described the UAB as 'the finest piece of social legislation on the statute book in a generation', stating that payments were 'extremely generous' to children and that there were even 'excessive payments'. When reports of this reached the Durham Miners' Federation, Sam Watson and Will Lawther, two of its leaders, complained in the strongest terms about the complacency and the politicking of the academic.[32]

On her travels that day, Ellen Wilkinson met a contingent of national hunger marchers between Wakefield and Barnsley, amongst them Harry McShane and Wal Hannington, the NUWM leaders.[33] The three of them, along with Clydeside ILPers Jimmy Maxton and John McGovern, had formed the delegation of the 1934 hunger march which Ramsay MacDonald had refused to see.[34] Ellen

Wilkinson was a long-time sympathiser of the NUWM and was on the Hunger March Reception Committee in 1936.[35] At the local level, Ellen Wilkinson spoke at numerous NUWM events including one in Newcastle on 25 January 1937 and in Hebburn on 15 September 1937. She was to join the north-east contingent of the 1936 National Hunger March at Romford, marching with them to their East Ham digs on 12 November.[36] In *Why Fascism?* (1934) she and Edward Conze berated the Labour Party's attitude to campaigns like the hunger march:

> The British leaders of labour to-day, forgetting the tradition of incessant propaganda out of which their whole movement was brought to birth, tend to disapprove of hearty, popular movements like the Hunger March which carried the protest against the Unemployment Bill into the villages and valleys. They objected to the "Communist inspiration" of this particular effort, but have made no attempt at any other protest than the procedure provided by Parliament. Dignified conferences and mass meetings, attended almost exclusively by the converted, cannot stand up against tempestuous, popular movements like Fascism has become in every country where it has achieved power.[37]

To ignore the other hunger marches, as some historians do who favour the Jarrow Crusade, is therefore to neglect an important dimension of Ellen Wilkinson's activism.

Thursday 22 October: The Last Crusader, the Relics of the Cross and the Living Dead
Loughborough to Leicester (pop. 243,143), 11 miles

Andrew Kelly, who had been in hospital in Barnsley with malaria, rejoined the Crusade in Loughborough.[38] Marchers were in good spirits and Ellen Wilkinson announced that she would march the rest of the route. Of the marchers she said 'They are a strong lot and have withstood the ordeal splendidly'.[39] The *Leicester Daily*

Mercury, as did other newspapers, spotlighted Ellen Wilkinson's participation. Even describing the Crusade as 'Miss Wilkinson's march' , the paper discussed the comfortable blue suede shoes that she was marching in after discarding heavier footwear and how she had failed to rendezvous with an old friend, journalist Hannen Swaffer who was also in Leicester on that day.[40] 'Swaff' famously observed 'Freedom of the press in Britain means freedom to print such of the proprietor's prejudices as the advertisers don't object to'. This is particular apt for the Crusade. Some historians seem to accept, uncritically, the idea of contemporary publicity as the criterion of success but publicity was a means to an end not an end in itself. This supposition also downplays the extent to which the press had its own agenda and that a part of the press remained indifferent or hostile. As Ellen Wilkinson's heroine put it in her novel *The Clash*, press freedom in Britain meant the 'right for Lord Rothermere to say what he likes'.[41] Journalists looked for stories that conformed to their own assumptions, or more accurately those of their editors or newspaper proprietors. Given the structure of British press ownership at the time there is an unsurprising degree of uniformity about the stories, comment and style of the coverage of the march.[42] This was the age of the press barons and ownership of national and provincial papers was predominately in the hands of Lords Beaverbrook, Rothermere, Camrose and Kemsley. For example, by 1928, Lord Camrose owned two national dailies, 14 provincial dailies (including the *Evening Chronicle*) and eight provincial weeklies as well as over a hundred other periodicals.

A cross-party committee of five councillors (Scullion, Patterson, Suddick, Trainor and Rose) was set up to deal with publicity for the march. If the organisers desired a non-political march, then they failed to recognise the ideological content of the press coverage. Either the march organisers consciously sought to develop such themes because they thought that they would receive the most favourable press or they accepted the agenda of the largely right-wing press. Either way, each of these themes provided the journalists with an image of the Crusade that they wanted, an image that has subsequently been generally adopted even by historians. The 'last Crusader', Con Whalen, who outlived all his companions, was outspoken about the role of the press. In an interview, he stated: 'They manufactured it. Everything to do with it were manufactured by the press.'[43] He reiterated the point each time journalists sought the last authentic voice of a marcher.[44] It is out of the press coverage that the key themes of the legend of the Jarrow Crusade were conjured. Reflecting on the reaction to the Crusade, historian of the press James Curran observed that in effect, the press barons and their more or less subservient editors were policing 'the boundaries of legitimate dissent'.[45]

***

Legend and false memory joined the Crusade and St. Mark's Church (Leicester) in a metaphysical embrace. Parishioners believed that the marchers had slept in the church and had had their feet washed in a religious ceremony. In return for this, the marchers supposedly left a cross as a token of their gratitude. Some parishioners, tricked by the idiosyncrasies of human memory, even asserted that they were present at the presentation of the 'Cross of Jarrow'. There was no reference to St. Mark's in the newspaper accounts of the Crusade's passage through Leicester. Two local historians who have researched the church's past found no connection with the Crusade, and, instead, found that according to Parish records, the 1934 hunger marchers donated the cross.[46] 52 years after the Jarrow Crusade, the Mayor of Leicester 'returned' the cross which is inscribed with 'inasmuch' to Jarrow. Posing for local newspapers, Danny Maidment, Mayor of South Tyneside, and Don Dixon, the MP, officially received the cross.[47] At the time, 100 visitors came to see the artefact including six Crusaders amongst whom was Jimmy Foggon, who said, 'I don't remember it very well but its part of the march and that's all there is to it'.[48] But as with the relics of the true cross during the medieval crusades, popular belief in Jarrow reciprocates those in the East Midlands. According to the local folklore, the cross, like the petition box, was fashioned out of wood from Jarrow.[49]

Three decades earlier, in 1905, while Jarrow prospered, Leicester had suffered from the scourge of mass unemployment with both hosiery and shoemaking in a commercial slump. Prominent

Christian Socialist Canon Donaldson, Amos Sheriff and Stuart Gray led a hunger march from Leicester to London. A painting in St. Mark's Church recorded this hunger march.[50] In 1905, the Labour (at that time Labour Representation Committee) leadership, as in 1936 was initially hostile. Ramsay MacDonald complained 'these disorganised bodies of unemployed ... would seriously damage the chances of securing a rational and sympathetic consideration of the Unemployment Problem'. On 4 June 1905, 440 unemployed men from Leicester, many of them army veterans (37%), set out with a crowd of 20,000 bidding them farewell. Like later marchers, they relied on local support on the route to London, on this occasion in the main from the Independent Labour Party. In its quasi-military discipline and organisation and its religious appeal it bore strong similarities to its successor from Jarrow.[51] They arrived in London on Friday 6 June, held a demonstration and marched from Embankment to Hyde Park on the Saturday. Having revised his earlier position, Ramsay MacDonald, the leader of the ILP, spoke, as did Donaldson, Sheriff and the Reverend Russell Wakefield, the Mayor of Marylebone. On Sunday after attending a service at Westminster Abbey they held a meeting in Trafalgar Square which attracted, according to police, 3,000 people. The meeting began with the singing of two hymns. Taking up the issue of unemployment in 1905 and again in the interwar period was an important part of the process of the implantation of the Labour Party. The right-to-work campaign of 1905-6 was a crucial part of the establishment of the Labour Party as a political force which would address working-class issues, just as the hunger marches and the Jarrow Crusade were in another formative period of the Party's history. The 1905 march lingered in the memory. The *Daily Herald* and the *Reynolds Illustrated News* remarked on the similarities between the Jarrow Crusade and the Leicester march of 1905.[52]

The Crusaders followed the same route through Leicestershire that the 123 blind marchers took the day before. The Crusade then held a public meeting in Association Hall with Ellen Wilkinson speaking and Councillor R. Hallam, the Conservative Lord Mayor of Leicester, in the chair. Dr Cyril Bardsley, the Bishop of Leicester, lent more Anglican support donating £5 to march funds. The

Crusaders slept that night in Swain Street Institution, some in uncomfortable stone cubicles.[53] In the post bag, Thomas Rumford received some surprising news from Jarrow. The story had circulated around South Shields that he had died and was to be buried on Monday. A woman had called at his house asking if she could attend his funeral. 'I feel alive anyway but to make sure I went to see one of our doctors,' he told the *Gazette* reporter, 'He agrees with me that at any rate I do appear to be still living.'[54]

Friday 23 October: Working till Dawn
Leicester to Market Harborough (pop. 9,000), 14 miles

Leicester was a relatively prosperous factory town that specialised in worsted hosiery and knitted goods. But areas like Leicester also had unemployment. In *Men without Work*, the Pilgrim Trust surveyed unemployment in six towns at roughly the same time as the Jarrow Crusade. Leicester was chosen because it claimed to be the 'most prosperous city in England' and typical of the thriving towns based on light industry in the Midlands. The Trust's social investigators sought to 'look below the surface of this prosperity and discover what was the unemployment that it concealed'. According to their calculations, in these Midlands towns – Birmingham, Northampton, Coventry, Nottingham and Leicester – there were over 5,000 workers who had not found three days work in the last year. These long-term unemployed were typically semi-skilled factory workers who were victims of technological change. *Men without Work* used the example of a skilled shoe worker who cut the leather of the upper shoe, or a 'clicker' as he would be known. This particular clicker had worked at the same firm for 40 years but had been laid off in 1932. Because the shoe firm would not take on clickers over 50 years of age he had no chance of finding work. The investigators believed that the situation of such people was in some respects worse than the long-term unemployed in the Special Areas because they were more isolated and a greater stigma was attached to unemployment in a 'prosperous' big town.[55]

When J.B. Priestley travelled through Leicester two years before the Crusade, he did not notice unemployment. But he did discover the new world of work inside the rationalised modern hosiery factory of the Wolsey Company. This world would be just as alien to the skilled shipyard workers of Jarrow as to the middle-class author. The shopfloor were:

> really much further from the controlling centre of things, the heart and brain of the industry, than their grandparents were, for they cannot know what happened to the material they are working with half an hour before it reached them or what will happen to it half an hour after they have let it go. Their outlook must necessarily be restricted to their one endless tiny task. They are not bullied or even nagged at; …but between the time when they 'clock in' and 'clock out' their central human dignity, which entitles them under our democratic system to a vote as good as anybody else's, has no real existence, except in that dream of life which occupies their minds as their fingers fly to do their one mysterious little task.[56]

In contrast to this study in modern alienation, Ellen Wilkinson encountered a very different type of labour in the East Midlands town. Leicester Co-operative Society boot repairers had worked into the night for free to repair the marchers' boots. She recalled visiting them at 2 o'clock in the morning before going to bed:

> There was such a gay enthusiasm for this unusual bit of help, that it was fun to be among the men. One boot-repairer, pulling to pieces an appalling piece of footwear remarked, "It seems sort of queer doing your own job, just because you want to do it, and for something you want to help, instead of doing it because you'd starve if you didn't. I wonder if that's how the chaps in Russia feel about it, now they are running their own show."[57]

Russian workers, of course, did not run their own show, but at the time workers in Barcelona, as George Orwell described in *Homage to Catalonia*, did, and this would have provided a closer analogy for the boot-makers' night of unalienated toil. One day later, the revolutionary government in Barcelona passed the Catalan collectivisation decree. In the Catalan capital, a social revolution accompanied the civil war with workers collectivising their workplaces. In parts of Catalonia and Aragon, the land was collectivised. The anecdote says much about Ellen Wilkinson's political illusions of the Soviet Union as a workers' state. She was certainly not alone in this. The Webbs' *Soviet Communism – A New Civilisation?* (1935) showed how even those from the right-wing of the Labour Party, who shared with Ellen Wilkinson a Fabian background, could be deluded by the equation between nationalisation and workers' control.[58] This did not mean that she was an uncritical supporter of Russia or a naïve fellow-traveller of the Communist Party. Reflecting on the catastrophe of Germany in 1933, she was highly scathing of the German Communist Party for its subservience to Moscow because this had robbed it of its revolutionary character that she deemed necessary. In an article in *New Dawn*, she criticised the sectarianism of the Communist Party, the subservience of the Comintern to Russian interests and how its anti-democratic rhetoric soured British workers to it. Her vision of socialism was based on a grass-roots democracy built on workplace democracy and workers' councils (soviets).[59] Ellen Wilkinson's view of Russia was, however, like that of so many of her generation, a fateful weakness to be cruelly exposed in the Big Brother atmosphere of the Cold War. There is a degree of uncertainty about the evolution of her ideas on this question. Towards the end of her life she did not have the time or the inclination to clarify her views theoretically as she had done in *Why Fascism*. The political career which placed her in high office consumed more of her time and energy. There was only a little time for journalism in the breach, let alone serious writing. Also, because Ellen Wilkinson was underestimated as a thinker and her personal papers were destroyed after her death, we do not know her attitude to the small anti-Stalinist Marxist left. The time of her death, the moment of the drawing of the iron curtain, was a great moment of truth for the generation of leftists of the 1930s. Many who had nursed direct or indirect affiliations with Stalinism publicly recanted. If the Webbs' *Soviet Communism* epitomised the infatuation of the left with Russia in the 1930s, *The*

God that Failed, in which celebrated figures such as André Gide and Richard Wright renounced their political pasts, summed up the late 1940s. That Ellen Wilkinson died in early 1947 means that this riddle of her politics is left unanswered. It is one of the reasons why she remains a complex and enigmatic figure.

In reality Ellen Wilkinson's politics underwent a complex evolution on this and other matters. With the degeneration of the Russian Revolution, she left the Communist Party in 1923 and flirted at the turn of the decade with Trotskyism. She campaigned for Trotsky's right to asylum in Britain and corresponded with Stalin's exiled enemy.[60] During the 1930s, because of her activist commitment she was involved in a number of campaigns set up by or in close association with the communists – the Reception Committees of the Hunger Marches, the India League, the Relief Committee for the Victims of German Fascism, the Legal Commission of Inquiry into the Burning of the Reichstag and the Left Book Club. But she was also critical of the communists for subservience to Moscow and described the show trials as 'idiotic'.

During the Spanish Civil War, however, unlike Orwell, she supported communist positions that the revolution must take second place to the war effort. She blamed the anarchists and the POUM for the May days in Barcelona and welcomed the governmental reshuffle whereby Largo Caballero was replaced with the right of the Socialist Party and greater communist participation.[61] Attacking appeasement, her perspective on international relations at this time was that the Soviet Union did not want war and that the democracies should form an alliance to stop Hitler. She was one of the strongest proponents within the Labour Party of the Popular Front and pushed this view with her Labour Party colleagues.[62] On these questions then she was closer to the Stalinist position than the revolutionary one. Nevertheless she did not go so far as some on the Labour left in her illusions about the Soviet Union and resigned from the editorial committee of *Tribune* over the Soviet invasion of Finland in 1940.

***

At 5 pm on Friday 23 October, J.J. Willis, the Assistant Bishop of Leicester welcomed the Crusaders. Ellen Wilkinson was 'hardly able to speak' and in a 'state of collapse' when she arrived in Market Harborough. Sam Rowan recalled the mixed feelings of the men to Ellen Wilkinson's pace-setting at the head of the march, 'They loved the little woman, like, but they cursed her for holding them back'. Every photograph testified to the deep affection that the Crusaders had for her and the relaxed relationship between the MP and her constituents. In one photograph, she accompanied the mouth organ band on a drum and in another she sat her head tossed back in laughter at a joke amongst the marchers at lunchtime. She spent the night as guest of the Assistant Bishop of Leicester. That night, from 7.30 pm, Canon E.B. Redlich chaired the public meeting that was held in the County Cinema. Describing the Crusade as a 'pilgrim's progress', he hoped that 'the men will find their promised land'.[63] Their handbill proclaimed:

> The 'Crusade for Work' has been organised by the Jarrow Town Council on strictly NON-POLITICAL lines and has the support of Political Organisations in the Town. This meeting is held for the express purpose of presenting 'Jarrow's Case' to the citizens of Market Harborough.[64]

Market Harborough was less than a third of the size of Jarrow and could not have been more different. It was a market town without industry, prosperous, but not like Leicester with its low unemployment and good wages. Market Harborough prospered in the style of the commercial middle class and the rural well-to-do. Its infant mortality rate was 33 whilst Jarrow's was 104.[65] P.A. Dormer, the Medical Officer of Health for Jarrow, who had inspected the men before their departure, reflected in his annual report on the conditions that led to Jarrow's high figures for infant mortality. He recorded:

> Overcrowding and poor housing conditions contribute largely to the deaths under all three headings [gastroenteritis, premature birth, pneumonia], while malnutrition and ill health in the mothers are

contributory causes in those being classified as being due to premature birth.[66]

For J.B. Priestley, Market Harborough epitomised fox and hounds country. His views give some clue to the audience of the public meeting:

> Men and women whose whole lives are organised in order that they may ride in pursuit of stray foxes two or three days a week, who risk their necks for a vermin's brush, who will deny themselves this and that to spend money on packs of hounds, who spare no pains to turn themselves into twelfth-century oafs, are past my comprehension. All I ask is that they should not pretend to be solemnly doing their duty when in reality they are indulging and enjoying themselves. The fox-hunter who begins mumbling excuses, who tells you that he hunts to rid the countryside of foxes, that hunting is valuable because it improves the breed of horses (i.e. hunters), is a contemptible fellow.[67]

In his *English Journey*, J.B. Priestley mused about several locations on the route of the Jarrow Crusade namely Wakefield, Sheffield, Chesterfield, Nottingham, Leicester. He had visited Jarrow itself and intended sympathy rather than condescension:

> There is no escape anywhere in Jarrow from its prevailing misery, for it is entirely a working-class town. One little street may be rather more wretched than another, but to the outsider they all look alike. One out of every two shops appeared to be permanently closed. Wherever we went there were men hanging about, not scores of them but hundreds and thousands of them. The whole town looked as if it had entered a perpetual penniless bleak Sabbath. The men wore the drawn masks of prisoners of war.[68]

Priestley's literary interest in Jarrow did not stop with his famed travelogue. It was also exercised in his novel *Wonder Hero* (1933). This is the story of Charlie Habble who receives a substantial monetary reward from a newspaper for an act of bravery at work. The narrative follows him from his native Midlands to the glitzy West End of London to 'Slakeby' a fictional town based on Jarrow. (Undoubtedly Priestley's research for *English Journey* served a double purpose.) Charlie goes to the shipbuilding town to visit his malnourished and seriously ailing aunt Nellie. When Charlie first arrives in the town he is struck by its dereliction:

> This wasn't an industrial town any longer: it was a graveyard, with grass growing over it and with its cold mill chimneys as monuments.

As his uncle shows him around Slakeby and tells him of the demise of the shipyard:

> They looked again at the melancholy river, which robbed of its trade, but not its filth, like Slakeby itself, which still looked as dirty as it did when every big chimney was spouting black fumes. ... The streets were filled with them [the unemployed], just hanging about, no money in their pockets, not enough food in their bellies or blood in their veins, seeing little hope anywhere.[69]

Indeed, Priestley observed 'the reality of Jarrow is far worse than anything I imagined for Slakeby'.[70]

Combining social commentary and travel writing, Priestley's *English Journey* was certainly full of wit and impressionistic observation but he also sought to go beyond this to make a more telling analysis of English society in the 1930s. In autumn 1933, he encountered not one but three Englands: 'Old England', nineteenth-century England and new England. Old England was a country of 'cathedrals and minsters and manor houses and inns, of Parson and Squire'. Nineteenth-century England was that which the industrial revolution had transformed into 'a cynically devastated countryside, sooty dismal little towns, and still sootier fortress-like cities'. Modern, post-war England had according to Priestley its origins in America. It was a country of 'arterial and by-pass roads, of filling stations and factories that look like exhibition buildings, of giant cinemas and dance-halls and cafes, bungalows with tiny garages, cocktail bars, Woolworths, motor-coaches, wireless, hiking, factory girls looking like actresses, greyhound racing and dirt tracks, swimming pools, and everything given away for cigarette coupons'. Market Harborough belonged to the old England of parson and squire. The marchers certainly came across the other two Englands. Indeed, the Crusade united this divided nation: powerful and prostrate, rich and poor, north and south but this unity was superficial and fleeting. When the Crusade and the show of unity had passed old division returned. The real experiences of, for example, their wealthy hosts or opponents were worlds apart.[71]

***

Crusaders slept on the stone floor in the unfinished casual block of Harborough Institute. The men complained of being cold and damp. Not a single member of Market Harborough Urban District Council visited the men or wished them well. Of course, the *Market Harborough Advertiser and Midland Mail* objected to the dent on the town's reputation:

> Reports in the London press were liable to leave the impression that the men endured great hardship by sleeping on brick floors in the new block of the institution. Actually the men were very comfortable. The master and matron spared no effort in giving them a warm welcome.[72]

Saturday 24 October: Tentacles of the Octopus
Market Harborough to Northampton (pop. 93,930), 17 miles

The *Evening Chronicle* reported beautiful weather on Saturday morning: 'brilliant sun shone as we stepped out for Northampton on a road carpeted with leaves'.[73] Just eight miles to the east of Market Harborough stood the newly constructed Corby steelworks. Stewart and Lloyds, the Scottish iron and steel concern, had acquired the small ore fields and blast furnace at Corby. In 1930 the Chicago consultants C.A. Brassert and Co. recommended a large integrated iron and steel works using the Bessemer process, like Jarrow's proposed steelworks, for the Midlands market. The Bank of England had also commissioned Brassert to develop rationalisation plans for the steel industry as a whole when bankers acquired a large stake in the industry and these consultants were also used by the Government to consider Jarrow's case in 1936. Stewart and Lloyds' plans for the steelworks in Corby were shelved because of the Depression but when the Government abandoned free trade and used tariffs to protect British industry in 1932 the scheme was revived.

Corby steelworks had achieved an annual output of 350,000 tons. Much greater demand existed for such steel because huge quantities were being imported largely from Germany. The British Iron and Steel Federation (BISF), and in particular Teesside members South Durham and Cargo Fleet, sought to limit competition and were responsible for the failure of the steel plan for Jarrow. Sir Malcolm Stewart and Sir John Jarvis commissioned Brasserts to produce a report that established Jarrow's suitability as a site for Bessemer steel production. Then having consulted his north-east members Sir Andrew Duncan commissioned a second Brassert report to consider the best location for such a plant and whether it would take work from other BISF members. The BISF had secured considerable privileges from the National Government in both setting tariffs most beneficial to its interests and in assisting the Government in the formation of an international cartel which included Europe's biggest steel producers, including Nazi Germany (together with France, Belgium, Luxemburg and Poland). Understandably there was considerable anger that the economic appeasement of a fascist power should lead to misery in Jarrow. Claude Robinson pointed to the close relationship between Montague Norman, the Governor of the Bank of England, and Hjalmar Schacht, Hitler's economics minister, believing that Jarrow was a victim of the strategy of strengthening Germany as a counter-weight to the Soviet Union.[74] Even *The Economist* excoriated the Federation for its monopolistic practices and the Government for facilitating this.[75] In March 1935, the BISF had persuaded the Government to impose a tariff of 50% against imported steel.

When Jarrow town council asked the President of the Board of Trade to intervene to help the project of a steelworks for Jarrow in July 1936, all he could offer was a general inquiry by the Import Duties Advisory Committee, thus definitively killing the Lord Aberdare scheme first mooted in October 1934.[76] It was after the failure of the town's deputation to the President of the Board of Trade on 14 July that the council decided to launch the Crusade.

In mid-June it became apparent that the opposition of one Teesside firm had jeopardised BISF approval and the plan was now dead. In cold and tortuous language, Runciman announced the death of the project to the House of Commons – 'it is considered very unlikely that the scheme will be proceeded with'.[77] Under pressure to account for its actions, the BISF's official statement tried to justify its position. It stated that the capital expenditure was greater than foreseen, that its members had objected and that new plants should supplement rather than displace existing production.[78] It is hard to imagine the rollercoaster of hope and despair that the people of Jarrow had boarded through no choice of their own. They were victims not only of conspiracy but also of cock-up for Jarrow should not have been given hope when objections to the plant had not been resolved.

***

On 24 October 1936, Ellen Wilkinson convalesced for part of the day, catching up with marchers on route to Northampton. She then spent the weekend in London making arrangements for the presentation of the petition to parliament and for the Crusaders' stay in London. Robert Mogie dropped out of the march before arriving in Northampton and saw a doctor there; he then rejoined the march. Crusaders were welcomed by the Mayor of Northampton, Councillor S. Perkins, and Commander John Williamson, the Chief Constable of Northampton, who was also a generous contributor to the march funds, which now stood at over £1,000. Crusaders slept on straw in St. James School in blankets provided by Northampton Public Assistance Committee. The prosperity of the south contrasted with that of the north and Crusaders received offers for work from a trader in Leicester and from a confectioner in Northampton. These jobs were however poorly adapted to the skills of steelworkers and shipbuilders of Jarrow. But some Jarrovians who had migrated to Bedford to find work met up with friends on the Crusade in Northampton. Blind marchers also arrived in Northampton on this day. Brothers on different marches, James and Robert Hanlon, were able to meet up here.

In the evening, the Crusade staged a public meeting in the largest venue available, the Town Hall. The Conservative Mayor of Northampton chaired the meeting and the four councillors appealed to the citizens of the shoe-making town. There was no Ellen Wilkinson, but Claude Robinson, the headmaster at the Jarrow secondary school, having travelled down in his car for the weekend, filled in:

> I spoke and ... my address was the most shatteringly effective to this audience because the figures I was able to quote were given by the Headmaster of the Secondary School, in which type of school such social conditions, inconceivable in any circumstances, were to them quite irreconcilable.[79]

South Wales National Hunger March contingent, numbering 370 marchers, rallied in Cardiff city centre. Four Labour MPs, S.O. Davies of Merthyr, George Hall of Aberdare, Edward Williams of Ogmore, and James Griffiths of Llanelly, addressed them.[80] The South Wales Miners' Federation formed a Council of Action with the Welsh Labour Party and the Welsh TUC to organise and support the Welsh hunger marchers. At the 4,000 strong send-off demonstration in Newport, the leader of the Labour group on the council and three MPs spoke.[81]

Sunday 25 October: Mixed Blessings: the Bishop and the Opera
Northampton

Another Jarrovian, Albert Potts, was taken to hospital in Northampton. He was not strictly speaking a Crusader as he was accompanying the men on his bicycle. He needed hospital treatment because he had fallen from his bike on Friday.

The connection between the Jarrow Crusade and Northampton was renewed some six decades later. The Northampton Bach Choir commissioned Will Todd to write an opera to commemorate the 60th anniversary of the Crusade and *Burning Road* was first performed at the Derngate Centre, Northampton, in November 1996.[82]

Ben Dunwell's libretto used as its central metaphor Jarrow and the cycle of life, where the marchers were born and would die just as they would march away and return. Both the libretto and the music stress the pain and endurance of the men on the 'burning road'. As such the listener is struck by the Christian notion of suffering and agony of Christ on the cross. It pays tribute to the Crusaders, reeling off the names of all the marchers in song. Unlike the original crusades which were accompanied by revivalist preaching, the invocation of religious sanctity was not a sign of religious fervour on the part of the marchers but more the attempt to gain respectability from church leaders as one aspect of the British establishment. Because the opera takes the religious associations of the Crusade at face value it reconstructs the event as a solemn, almost pious, event and would perhaps not be recognisable to the marchers themselves who relied on a rough and ready humour and comradeship to keep their spirits up. Crusader John 'Smiler' Harney's evocation is probably closer to the mood the marchers:

> From dawn to dusk we marched along, with smiles upon
> our faces,
> We had our smokes and cracked our jokes, in scores of
> different places.[83]

In another of the ironies of the Crusade's history, Durham Cathedral, whose bishop had denounced the march in 1936, hosted the *Burning Road's* second performance in May 1997. Vince Rea introduced the music, which was performed in the presence of the then two remaining Crusaders (Jimmy McCauley and Con Whalen). On this occasion, Jimmy McCauley, unhelpfully for those seeking to enjoy the nostalgia of the event, undermined the myth of the Crusade's success:

> It's nice that this was written for the marchers, but I cannot understand it in some ways, because the march was not really a success. It didn't bring jobs back to the town – only the war did that.

He also commented that the Bishop of Durham would have hanged them all.[84] Memories can be stubbornly impervious to myth. The Bishop of Durham's letter published in *The Times* condemned the Crusade as 'a revolutionary policy'.[85] He continued, 'It substitutes for the provisions of the constitution the method of organised mob pressure', threatening 'before the winter is out … grave public confusion and danger'. Ellen Wilkinson's reply was printed on Monday 26 October. She pointed out that the much-vaunted constitutional methods proposed by the bishop had been 'tried over and over again to no avail'. She alluded to the bishop's lax attitude, implicit in his condemnation of the peaceful petitioning of parliament, to the very political freedoms that had disappeared in much of Europe:

> Nothing now remains for us but to place our case before the citizens of our country. For the Bishop of Durham to stigmatise as 'revolutionary' the quiet exercise of our constitutional right to offer a petition to parliament is dangerous in these days. When constitutional rights are threatened on every side, democrats should watch vigilantly rights that have been struggled for and won through centuries of British history. … If this is 'organised mob pressure' so is every quiet exercise of the right of free speech.[86]

Sculpture in Jarrow Metro Station

Plaque for Vince Rae's Sculpture in Jarrow Metro Station

A View of Ellen Court, Wilkinson Court and the Jarrow Crusaders
Public House

Jarrow Crusaders Public House

Statue of Sir Charles Mark Palmer, Formerly in Jarrow Town Centre

Labour Party 1950 Jarrow March Poster
By Permission People's History Museum

The Spirit of Jarrow in Morrison's Car Park, Jarrow

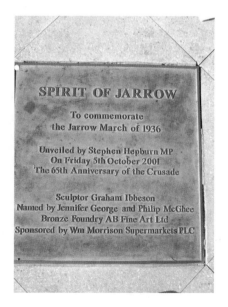

Plaque for Spirit of Jarrow

Even that weathervane of free-market business opinion, *The Economist*, disputed the bishop's and Government's logic and pointed out the irony involved in the situation where the Government was giving 'unparalleled statutory powers' to the ironmasters and dragging the country in the direction of a 'corporative state'.

> There is certainly a rich attitude of those who repudiate as 'unconstitutional' the march of 200 unemployed to lay a petition before Parliament, while accepting as apparently hallowed by constitutional precedent the action – avowed and undisputed – of certain interests within the Iron and Steel Federation in using semi-official powers to suppress the Jarrow scheme on admittedly sectional grounds.[87]

The Bishop of Durham had written to *The Times* once before regarding unemployment. The letter, which appeared on 13 December 1932, revealed the results of a questionnaire he had sent to parish priests in his diocese. In keeping with his mendacious attitude towards the Crusade, the questionnaire was a sop to some of his vicars who wanted the bishop to organise a general campaign to raise money for those in need. A conference of 17 vicars from the most needy parts of County Durham had pressed the bishop to act. Instead he circulated a questionnaire and then sent the letter to *The Times* which made a very guarded request for funds to buy boots and shoes. This provided £5,000 which the bishop admitted was not enough to cover the considerable hardship. His objections to a proper fundraising effort exposed a residue of Victorian attitudes to the relief of unemployment. His principal reason was the difficulty in discriminating between the deserving and the undeserving and the lack of reward for thrift. It was scarcely realistic, in the conditions of mass unemployment that the bishop witnessed everyday, that any amount of thrift on the part of a working-class household could insulate against the Depression. Similarly, it was perverse to propose that a greater problem than the relief of hardship was that of the malingerer.[88]

The bishop and Ellen Wilkinson could not be more dissimilar, separated by class, politics and morality. She was not the kind of example that he would have approved of: he found women who smoked abhorrent, she was unmarried and had had several affairs.[89] His conservatism is illustrated by an encounter that he found shocking with a frank young married woman who asked why unmarried women 'should wither miserably into old maids'.[90] Ellen Wilkinson shared this view and once famously demanded why a woman should marry when there were so many good careers open to her today. The bishop's qualified objection to birth control betrayed his elitism and eugenicism. As he told one correspondent: 'The sterility of the best classes is probably more socially disastrous than the fecundity of the worst; and if, in seeking to reduce the latter, you increase the former, the rest of your propaganda will be gravely ill.'[91] He must have found Ellen Wilkinson's politics disconcerting too. He was hostile to collectivism of any sort but saw 'mechanised collectivism' – that is public ownership plus motorcycles and cars – as 'only fit for a nightmare'.[92] He viewed the growing attachment of the working class to the idea of nationalisation as 'class vanity' and ignorance.[93] He had enraged miners so much in 1925 when he wrote an article for the *Evening Standard* condemning their stance in negotiations that only the intervention of police prevented miners ducking the Dean of Durham, Bishop Welldon, into the River Wear on the day of the Durham Miners' Gala. The miner MP J. Ritson denounced Bishop Henson for 'galloping...loose' in the press while 'drawing such huge surpluses in royalties' from the pits of County Durham.[94] The bishop saw communism rather hysterically as a threat to Christian civilisation and compared it to Islam:

> Both movements command the sympathy of the oppressed "lower" classes of the civilised world, and are able to count on their more or less open co-operation. In the earlier instance, the movement became militant, and swept like a conflagration over the Eastern world. Will Bolshevism do for the West what Mohammedanism did for the East? It is a disquieting speculation.[95]

On all these counts, the bishop must have quietly disapproved of, and even disliked, Ellen Wilkinson. Her association with the Crusade probably weighed heavily in his decision to condemn the march. More than that he honestly believed that the clergy should not take political stances, though he saw no contradiction between this and his public opinions on a range of political matters or his seat in Parliament. Thus in a letter to one of his vicars, he warned against the clergy involving themselves in 'an ardent and often unwise and ill-informed advocacy of popular causes'.[96] This, in his eyes, was precisely what Bishop Gordon had done on the day of the Crusade's departure.

But for all his elitism and hostility to the left, the bishop was not, as Ellen Wilkinson indirectly hinted in her angry response to *The Times*, a sympathiser with fascism. Indeed, Henson wrote a pamphlet against Mussolini's criminal invasion of Abyssinia denouncing it as an imperialist adventure to divert domestic attention from the growing unpopularity of his regime. He condemned Mussolini's contempt for the League of Nations and international law and the systematic use of poison gas.[97] He also, like Ellen Wilkinson, exposed Nazi terror in Germany and aggression abroad in print.

The Mayor of Jarrow, as 'a member of the Church of England, a church warden', also issued a press statement rejecting the bishop's sensational claim that the march was unconstitutional. The Bishop of Durham was clearly out of step with many of his colleagues. Although the *Church of England Newspaper* applauded the Bishop of Jarrow for distancing himself from the Crusade, which it considered of 'doubtful' use and wisdom, it 'regretted' that the Bishop of Durham referred to 'these unfortunate people from his own diocese as revolutionaries'.[98] The polemics between Church of England clergy about the Crusade in 1936 contrast with the Church's subsequent approval of the event and this contributes to the impression of institutional and universal sympathy for the Crusade, and thus a mark of its success.

Week Four: Northampton to London

Monday 26 October: Forgotten Town, Missing Marchers
Northampton to Bedford (pop. 40,727), 21 miles

Bitterly cold winds and intermittent showers accompanied the longest leg of the journey. Returning from London, Ellen Wilkinson met the Crusaders eleven miles from Bedford and walked with them the rest of the day. Conservative Alderman H.R. Neate welcomed the Crusaders to Bedford as did H.W. Liddle, headmaster of Bedford Modern School. The schoolmaster was a native of Tyne Dock, so knew Jarrow well, and was the chairman of the Northumberland and Durham Association in Bedford, which donated £4 2s 6d to the marchers.[1] Liddle and the Bedford Rotary Club had 'adopted' Eden Pit, a workless County Durham village. As part of these efforts 20 people had been found work in Bedford and the association was intended to prevent the northerners feeling homesick. There were 60 such adoption schemes between the prosperous and the distressed areas but the most substantial was the County of Surrey Scheme that Sir John Jarvis, then High Sheriff of Surrey, had established for Jarrow.[2] Their voluntary efforts were a poor substitute for adequate welfare provision. The spirit of employer paternalism ran through the scheme and as such it offered a patrician solution that expected a dutiful quiescence from the workforce that it engaged. Unemployment could be counted on, as Karl Marx put it, to 'weigh down' on those in a job and hold their 'pretensions in check'.[3] Every foreman or employer knew that they could say that there were a dozen people waiting to take your job. During the Crusade, one episode at Thomas Ward's ship-breaking operation attracted to

Jarrow by Jarvis reveal the authoritarian side of such paternalism. Wages were little more than the dole and five workers were victimised for asking for a half-penny an hour rise. Cowed by unemployment, their colleagues did not back them up. Having been sacked, the unfortunate men were ineligible for unemployment benefit.[4]

That evening a public meeting for the 'Forgotten Town' was held in the Town Hall. Each marcher received cigarettes and tobacco from the local Rotary Club and the Toc H club staged an evening concert for their entertainment. As in every town, the cinemas gave the marchers free tickets. The Reverend A. St. G. Colthurst, Vicar of St. Paul's, blessed the marchers. Their overnight accommodation was in the Workingmen's Institute where they were tightly packed and cold. The Poor Law authorities provided blankets but there was only cold water for washing and shaving.

The Crusaders' numbers were now reduced to 195 with two back in Jarrow and three in hospital. A more serious number of Crusaders has been lost over time as only 185 of the original marchers are listed in the historical record.[5] There is also a discrepancy between the total of 200 marchers given by the organisers and the 207 mentioned in Special Branch reports. That means either that there are at least 15 and possibly 22 'missing' Crusaders, or, less likely, that the numbers were artificially rounded up to 200. Not only is there the problem of the missing Crusaders, little is known of most Crusaders even in Jarrow. When the Jarrow and Hebburn Local History group hosted an exhibition of photographs in an effort to identify the marchers in 2001, they were disappointed with the numbers of relatives who came forward.[6] All told, 65 out of 185 of the list of Crusaders were identified, as were, significantly, a further six unlisted Crusaders. Generally the information available about the Crusaders is poor and much of it has unfortunately been lost. A few Crusaders did register their views through oral history or television and radio interviews. The march leaders were most often interviewed, speaking as they did in 1936 on behalf of the Crusade. Much more information is available about contingents of the National Hunger March which the authorities took much more seriously. The Chief Constable of Glamorgan, for example, sent the

Home Office photographs and ridiculously elaborate detail about marchers. Names, addresses, heights, complexions, hair and eye colours, build, convictions, politics, dress and other particulars were sent to the Home Office. Some were marked down as 'dangerous agitators', one as a potential informant, others as respectable. The Home Office knew who had three toes missing, who walked with a stoop, who spoke with a stammer. One entry even recorded that the 42-year-old Labour-voting William Harris, of Treherbert, with a fresh complexion, light brown hair, grey eyes, of stout build, five foot two inches, had a 'good baritone voice'.[7]

Meanwhile, the replies to the Bishop of Durham appeared in the letters page of *The Times*. A. Charlton Curry, the former MP for Bishop Auckland, rejected the idea that the march was revolutionary and alluded approvingly to Sir John Jarvis's new industries – ship-breaking and furniture-making – that were bringing new hope to Jarrow.[8] The ructions within the Church of England over the Crusade continued. Canon L.S. Hunter, chair of Tyneside Council of Social Services, wrote to *The Times* to disagree with the Bishop of Jarrow's letter.[9] Defending himself against such public criticism, the Bishop of Jarrow sent 'a regular snorter' to the Archdeacon of Northumberland.[10] This unseemly battle of the bishops demonstrates the depth of division within the British establishment over the key issues of the day: the hunger marches, the abdication and appeasement.

Another of the forgotten episodes of the Crusade took place in Bedford. David Riley, the march marshal, sent home one Crusader on disciplinary grounds. The press did not cover the identity or reasons for this but Metropolitan Police files reveal that Fred Harris was excluded for 'communistic beliefs'.[11] Harris then went missing after arrangements had been made for him to return to Jarrow. Crusader John Kelly remembered that one marcher was 'sent home because of propaganda'.[12] Harris was allowed to rejoin the Crusaders in London after recanting.[13] March organisers threatened a second marcher, almost certainly George Cruikshank, with expulsion from the Crusade for communist views. When Con Whalen, the last survivor of the march, was asked about the attitude of the march leaders to the communists he shrugged his shoulders: 'Well, they kept them out, didn't they?'[14]

Tuesday 27 October: Leading the Blind
Rest in Bedford

The Crusaders took a day's rest after the gruelling journey to Bedford. For the support he had shown the Crusade, the Mayor of Bedford declared that he had been accused of being 'a convert to Labour, a rigid socialist, and with his hands behind his back, even a communist'.[15] Reflecting on the work of the Jarrow electoral agents, Harry Stoddart and Bob Suddick, Ellen Wilkinson described their vital role in securing local assistance and unlikely allies for the march, 'They induced mildly mystified Conservative Association Presidents to join slightly worried Labour Chairmen and their respective Mayors to welcome the men as "Crusaders" – blessed word.'[16]

In Bedford, the Crusaders again met the 100 blind marchers, who were presenting a petition to the House of Commons as well. Robert Hanlon, one of the blind marchers, visited the Crusaders in whose ranks was his brother, Councillor Jock Hanlon. The blind marchers had four goals: the amendment of the 1920 Blind Persons' Act; equal benefits with blind soldiers and sailors of the Great War; the exposure of the local authorities that had failed to make any provision for the blind since the Act and where the blind were dealt with by the Public Assistance Committees, i.e. the Poor Law; and finally that the welfare of the blind should be nationally not locally funded.[17] James A. Clydesdale described the approach of the National League of the Blind of fighting for justice not charity in its paper the *Blind Advocate*: 'no great progress can be made by a dependent or enslaved class until they move and start to aspire to better things. ... until they themselves, through their organisation, expressed their demands'.[18]

The Crusaders walked around the old town and visited nearby Stewartby, a village that had grown around a brickworks named after its patron, Malcolm Stewart, who was known to the men in his capacity as the Commissioner of the Special Areas. Malcolm Stewart had offered a grant to the Tyne Improvement Commissioners to assist in the construction of a Quay at Jarrow that would serve the proposed steel works. He made representations to the authorities for the steel works and was highly critical of the Government and the BISF in his last report about the failure of the plan.[19] Bedford Toc H laid on the entertainment that night.

The cabinet that met on 27 October had only two items on its agenda: trade negotiations with Argentina and the aero-engines affair. The latter concerned Lord Nuffield's complaint that his company, Morris Motors, had been unfairly overlooked when it came to the Government's award of aero-engine contracts.[20] A White Paper had been drawn up in response. Again despite the mounting evidence of public sympathy for the Jarrow Crusade, the cabinet imperiously ignored it.

***

The abdication crisis had begun when the marchers were on their way to Nottingham. It was then that Stanley Baldwin, the Prime Minister, challenged the King about his intention to marry divorcee Wallis Simpson. The issue was kept out of the British press but information seeped through from abroad so the crisis became an open secret. On Tuesday 27 October Mrs Simpson received a decree *nisi* judgement from Norwich assizes clearing the way for remarriage. While the Jarrow Crusade was splashed across the newspapers, they remained silent about the Simpsons' divorce. British newspaper owners and editors, including the *Daily Worker*, agreed not to carry the story which did not get into print until 3 December. With the foreign press following the story, the secret was unlikely to hold for long. There was the possibility that if Edward decided to oppose Baldwin his Government might fall. It is worth noting that Edward had supporters – such as Winston Churchill and the press baron Lord Beaverbrook – who were willing to back him against Baldwin. As things turned out Edward lost his nerve and signed his own Abdication Act on 10 December. Ritchie Calder, the *Daily Herald* journalist, recalled the reaction of the Crusaders when they overheard him and Ellen Wilkinson discussing the matter on one of the march days:

And came the midday break and we saw the people going around talking, groups were breaking up and they finally came to Ellen and to me, and said: What's it all about, the King and that woman? We tried to pass it off rather lightly, and they were absolutely furious with us, for repeating the story. Then when they began to realise that in fact it was true they were furious with him. The King believed he had the people of the country behind him. He didn't understand that the people of Jarrow had nothing, except family. This symbolically became the threat to the family, and they were very angry.[21]

The saga of the Bishop of Durham continued. A leader column in *The Times* approvingly quoted the bishop, asserting his statement had engendered 'widespread agreement with his opinion'. The bishop, always eager privately to note approval of his views, sermons or books, confided this with satisfaction to his diary.[22] This is a selective reading of the editorial. Whilst it worried about social unrest in the distressed areas (as did the bishop), it distinguished between the 'wholesome and poignant' Jarrow Crusade and other marches, and concluded with a call for concerted action from the Government to bring jobs to these areas.

Wednesday 28 October: Throwing Carrots at Goering
Bedford to Luton (pop. 61,500), 19 miles

The Crusaders left Bedford to a rousing send-off. The mayor, who presided over their departure from Bedford workhouse, regarded them as 'a very fine set of fellows'. A Luton chocolate manufacturer donated a quantity of his appetising wares to the Crusade. Before setting off, the marchers cheered the mayor, the council and the people of Bedford.

David Riley explained how, at this point, five marchers had dropped out: one with malaria, one was lost in Northampton, two were taken ill and another was 'homesick and sent home'.[23] Although Robert Winship rejoined the marchers at this stage, the Crusade lost John McCormella because of the illness of his father-in-law who was the secretary of the blast furnacemen's union in Jarrow. The weather on this leg of the journey was, as Ellen Wilkinson put it, 'awful... it rained solidly all day, and the wind drove the rain into your teeth'.[24] Labour Party member and Boer and Great War veteran, 62-year-old George Smith, the oldest marcher, told a journalist, 'I'm going strong and the rest of this walk is going to be a cakewalk'.[25] George was a Labour Party member and ran the Labour League of Youth educational classes in Jarrow.[26] The youngest Crusader, John Farndale, was 43 years his junior.

In Luton, the Crusaders were again greeted by local notables: Mayor Alderman C.C. Gillingham, members of the Guardians Committee and the Chief Constable. There was no public meeting because by coincidence the Duke of Kent had come to open Luton's new Town Hall and there was a children's firework display that evening. Bunting and crowds, Syd Sterck of the *North Mail* noted, gave the Duke and then the Crusaders a royal welcome.[27] Ellen Wilkinson left for London to make further arrangements for the Crusaders' stay there. With only a few miles to go, Bedford British Union of Fascists (BUF) asked if they could support the Crusade. David Riley firmly turned them down.[28]

The BUF should have expected short shrift given Ellen Wilkinson's record of anti-fascism. Sir Nevile Henderson, the British Ambassador to Berlin, reported that Goering had declined an invitation to Britain because 'If I came to London all your Ellen Wilkinsons would throw carrots at me'.[29] As a journalist, Ellen Wilkinson was a regular critic of Hitler and Nazi Germany. Gutter attacks being their stock in trade, the Nazi daily *Volkischer Beobachter* irrationally ranted that she was 'a half-jewess who continues to lie about Germany'. She probably took this attention from the Nazi press as a back-handed compliment.[30] More sinister though was the fact that her name was on the infamous 'Special Wanted List, GB' of those that the Nazis would round up in the event of a German invasion of Britain.[31]

Ellen Wilkinson's pamphlet *The Terror in Germany* detailed the brutality of the Nazi regime on behalf of the British section of the

International Committee for the Relief of the Victims of German Fascism, whose president was Albert Einstein. She had spent time in Nazi Germany as a journalist and was familiar with its character. The pamphlet was intended to counter the idea that the terror had ceased and to correct the misinformation coming from the regime. Great efforts were made to authenticate and document the outrages described. She was also critical of the British Government that had appeased Hitler and had created conditions that undermined Weimar democracy. She reported a German diplomat's response to a speech from Ramsay MacDonald:

> For fourteen years Republican statesmen brought back nothing but insults. Hitler has banged his mailed fist and within fourteen days your Premier is talking about Revision of the Treaties. That speech fourteen months ago might have saved German democracy.[32]

She described the counter-revolutionary terror against the working class, cataloguing routine instances of Nazi viciousness. There was nothing out of the ordinary in the case of the working-class activist from Berlin who was taken to a Nazi headquarters and beaten with rubber truncheons, repeatedly kicked in the face, flung down the cellar steps and ended up in a clinic with a broken nose, broken jaw and having lost his front teeth. In another case, Ellen Wilkinson cited a works' council who were all arrested, were forced to do military drill and sing 'Deutschland über Alles' to the point of physical collapse. Eventually, because the works' director intervened, they were released though coerced into promising they would not stand for the works' council but would support Nazi candidates. They had witnessed blood splattered walls and beatings of other prisoners with steel rods. Ellen Wilkinson reported the house-searches and floggings that took place. Alongside her narrative, a photograph recorded a worker's wrecked furniture after a visit from the Brownshirts. She revealed how doctors were ambushed and beaten for helping those that the Nazis had tortured. She spoke of the unpunished murders of Jews, communists and socialists whose corpses would appear on waste ground or in woodland. She documented the case of one victim whose relatives were courageous enough to provide the details. In other cases relatives refused to identify the corpses or go to the funerals for fear of the attention that it would bring upon themselves. She exposed the abuse and torture of women citing the example of a 26-year-old socialist woman. During an interrogation to ascertain the hiding-place of a fellow socialist, the Nazis undressed, beat and humiliated her. A signed medical certificate attested to her lacerations and festering abscesses, one the size of a fist, as a result of her treatment. Ellen Wilkinson then went on to talk of the work of the relief committee on whose behalf she so passionately penned this pamphlet. Inside Germany the committee helped the dependents of those spirited away to the prisons, SA barracks, or concentration camps, or assisted those who had been dismissed for their Jewish faith or political persuasion. Outside Germany, it tried to help the growing number of refugees from the regime. She asked readers to imagine they might be in the same boat. After all, Germany was too like England to imagine that it could not happen here and as for the belief that 'Englishmen do not do such things' she pointed to the British treatment of the Irish and Indians. She brought home the realities of the Nazi takeover:

> Imagine a group of licensed hooligans in uniform coming into your house or flat and proceeding to break everything that is in it … stealing anything of value, before proceeding to beat you with a heavy rubber truncheon or a steel reinforced whip. With blood streaming down your face, imagine yourself saying good-bye to your wife and children, not knowing if you will ever see them again, your wife knowing well that she may be called in a day or two to identify your body among others in the mortuary.[33]

In her appeal for funds she asked her readers to imagine life as a refugee:

> … you have managed to get out of the country and you are in France or Holland without a cent, not knowing

the language, not having had a meal for hours. You have the address of the Relief Committee, that is all.[34]

Ellen Wilkinson was an ideal candidate to write the committee's pamphlet not only because of her strong and consistent commitment to the cause of anti-fascism, and her journalist talents which were considerable, but because she was respected by all who met her for her honesty and integrity.

Ellen Wilkinson's anti-fascism complemented the rich history of opposition to fascism of the working class in the North East. Rennie and Stoddart, in answer to the Labour Party questionnaire on fascist public activity, noted:

> In Hebburn a crowd attacked the speaker and badly mauled him since when no further attempt has been made and in Jarrow a crowd kept up a volley of noise and compelled the speaker to desist since when no further attempt has been made. Until recently there was a branch in Felling, but now the premises have been vacated.[35]

Oswald Mosley had a hard time on the occasions he visited the North East. In early 1935, Mosley, who called for a ban on black seafarers on British ships, tried to stage a public meeting in South Shields at the Palace Cinema, provocatively near Shields's Arab community.[36] Blackshirts came from great distances to swell the numbers but they were still very much outnumbered by local anti-fascists who were able to turn Mosley's meeting into a twenty-minute shambles. Mosley had to make a hurried exit through a backdoor and escaped in a getaway car.[37]

Thursday 29 October: We Cannot Afford to Lose All the Tyneside Seats
Luton to St. Albans (pop. 25,620), 10 miles

In the morning, organisers re-equipped the march with replacement cardboard badges and two new banners as the originals had become worse for wear. The day was one of cloud and drizzle but thankfully it was mild enough.

The House of Commons reassembled after the summer recess at 3 pm. There Ellen Wilkinson quizzed Prime Minister Stanley Baldwin about Jarrow. She asked how many resolutions he had received concerning the town since July. 'A considerable number' he conceded but refused to alter his policy of not receiving marchers and said that he had nothing to add to the statement of the President of the Board of Trade on 15 July. Instead he pointed to the economic revival on the Tyne and the decline in the number of unemployed.[38] Not to be fobbed off, Ellen Wilkinson pressed the question again the following Wednesday, submitting a private notice and therefore obliging a more definite response from the Premier.[39]

The debate in the letters page of *The Times* continued. Alderman Robert Isaac Dodds, Jarrow's Conservative former mayor, added to the criticism of the Bishop of Durham and the Government and took the opportunity to praise the efforts of his fellow Conservative Sir John Jarvis. Whereas the Bishop of Durham complained that of the many plans circulating to save Jarrow none was 'sound and adequate', Alderman Dodds believed that Sir John's scheme was definitely sound and adequate. Jarvis had arrived in Jarrow two years earlier with 'energy, enthusiasm and above all a plan'. He had provided £100,000 of his own money to buy the *Olympia* for shipbreaking work in Jarrow. Dodds defended the marchers who were not 'hooligans or revolutionaries … with no less high motives than crusaders of old'. His letter also revealed a certain uneasiness with the march: 'This may not be the best way of dealing with this terrible problem, but it is the only way these men know how'. By supporting Jarvis and the Crusade at the same time, the local Conservatives had cleverly played a long-running double-game. By so doing, they distanced themselves from those in the cabinet in the hope of retaining some of their waning influence in Jarrow and the North East. As Sir John Jarvis secretly confided to the Earl of Midleton in July 1935, if it were known for a fact that the steel federation had blocked Jarrow's steelworks the political backlash against the Tories would be 'tremendous' and 'we can't afford to lose all these Tyneside seats'.[40] To the banks, Jarvis always stressed the commercial nature of his venture, to the press he talked of its humanitarian aspect, but to fellow Conservatives he privately underlined its 'political' rationale. The Jarrow Conservatives were able to identify their distinctive strategy for Jarrow and, in the shape of Sir John, a Conservative champion able to rival the political stature of Ellen Wilkinson.

Another group of weary marchers crossed the Home Counties. The contingents of blind marchers from Leeds, Manchester, Leicester and Swansea converged on Watford, where Watford Labour Party and the NUWM welcomed them. Throughout their route, with a support committee established in each rest place, they received generous support and public sympathy.[41] The next day, the blind marchers left Watford for Willesden. As they left Watford the banners of the town's Labour Party and NUWM accompanied them. In Willesden, they held a public meeting in a pub, the Jubilee Clock, where amongst the speakers was the communist Leonard Hines. The National League of the Blind had initially sought, like the Jarrow Crusade, to avoid any association with the NUWM, but were either deceived or, more likely, simply relented because of the practical support that the latter had provided.[42] It is worth noting that the National League of the Blind had instructed its delegate to the Labour Party conference, blind marcher James A. Clydesdale to support communist affiliation.[43]

In the pouring rain, Mayor Reverend B.E.F. Mitchell welcomed the Crusaders to St. Albans on the steps of the Town Hall. The Chief Constable, M.W. Thorpe, was also present. The ritual handover of the petition to the Town Clerk W.G. Marshall was then performed. Reactions in St. Albans are instructive of the way in which the slump divided Britain socially and geographically. The porter at the workhouse confided to Selwyn Waller:

> I had heard about Jarrow but quite frankly I was inclined to put the stories down to exaggerations. Now I know that what I thought could not possibly be true does in fact exist. If you can only convince everyone else of those terrible conditions, as you have convinced me. I do not think that anyone can refuse you the work you ask.[44]

An old woman originally from Jarrow, who watched the men arrive, told the journalist of the apathy of the south:

> Twenty years ago I lived in Jarrow. I came down here with my son when he got work. I have visited the old town several times in the last few years, and I have tried to tell my friends down here how terrible things are in Jarrow but its no use. They can't understand.[45]

The Conservative Hall was the venue for the public meeting, with the Deputy Mayor W. Bird in the chair. The meeting passed a motion calling on the local MP Sir Francis Freemantle to support Jarrow's petition in every possible way.[46] Sam Rowan recalled that each night the 'four laddies' (Alderman Symonds, Councillors Riley, Hanlon and Scullion) would speak and with all their practice had become word perfect. Sam would provide them with facts and figures of the town they were visiting from the town clerk and medical officer of health. By such factual comparison, the speakers could bring home the dreadful state of health, employment and council finances in Jarrow. Health statistics bore eloquent testimony to the suffering in Jarrow. Infant mortality for England and Wales was 58 per 1,000 births but in Jarrow it was 97.[47] The tuberculosis death rate for England and Wales was 702 per million, but in Jarrow it was 1,273 and in neighbouring Hebburn it was 1,592. Malnutrition among schoolchildren in Tyneside and Durham was more than two and a half times that of the South East in 1936.[48] A study published in 1940 revealed the discrepancies in local government finance between Jarrow and richer towns. A penny on the rates would yield £436 in Jarrow whereas across the Tyne, in prosperous Whitley Bay and Monkseaton, with smaller populations, the same penny rate would reap £1,091. Thus Jarrow council had less money for social services like school meals but greater need.[49] And in 1938, Newcastle council could spend £1 5s 10d per child on school medical services, meals and the like, while Jarrow could spend only 17s.[50]

Despite the common assumption that the Jarrow Crusade received universal sympathy, a part of the press remained hostile to the Crusade. Some of the press, admittedly a minority, approved of the Government's condemnation. Several newspapers, while sometimes expressing sympathy with Jarrow's plight, decried the march itself. The *Bedford Press* described the Crusade as a 'pathetic procession' and marches in general were 'ill-advised and that they serve no good purpose'.[51] The *Scots Mail* accused Ellen Wilkinson of politicising the Crusade and exploiting the hardships of her constituency.[52] *Christian World* also sounded a critical tone toward the Crusade: 'To many people, however sympathetic they may be to the marchers' cause, they merely give the impression of mass exhibitionism'.[53] Likewise the *Western Mail and South Wales News* described the Jarrow Crusade as 'cheap showmanship'.[54] The *Royal Cornish Gazette* struck a similar tone.[55]

All but 50 crusaders (who slept in the Market Hall) were lodged in the St. Albans workhouse, Oster House. The master of the workhouse laid on a special hot evening meal, one that was certainly more appetising that the workhouse's normal fare.

Friday 30 October: The Kidnap Plot and Ugly Sisters
St. Albans to Edgware, 11 miles

A curious, probably innocent, incident at St. Albans demonstrated David Riley's determination to distance the Crusade from communism. Oster House received a telephone call to the effect that two of their number – Bradley and Smith – had slept in the Barnet workhouse. This was news to Bradley and Smith who were present and as bemused as anyone by the mysterious call. The two had been taken by car the previous day for medical attention: one to a dentist to have teeth removed and the other to a doctor, with an injured hand. The men tried to guess the significance of the call. Some thought that two workhouse casuals impersonated the Crusaders to avoid workhouse regulations and task work, and perhaps even in the hope of special food rations. Others were caught up in the anxiety about political interference believing the call to be part of some elaborate scheme to insinuate outsiders into the march. David Riley repeated the tried and tested theme of political (communist) infiltration: 'If anyone attempts to "crash in" on this march, he will be met with the boot'. To compound the intrigue –

although non-plussed medical students confirmed that they had made no such request – a taxi driver arrived to take a marcher to hospital. 'It's plot to kidnap one of the lads', one of the Crusaders implausibly concluded. Others agreed. The farce was resolved when the taxi reappeared to take a female workhouse inmate to the hospital. This something-out-of-nothing provoked sensational headlines in the *Evening Chronicle*, '… "Gate-Crashing" the March – Crusaders' "Doubles" Turn Up Elsewhere – Strange Phone Call.'[56]

***

Hindsight cast a new shadow of confusion over the Crusade. In the *Squaring the Circle* exhibition, the photographic history of Trafalgar Square in the National Portrait Gallery (13 September 2003-28 March 2004), two Humphrey Spender photographs of marchers were described as Jarrow Crusaders. In fact they went nowhere near the square. The original photos appeared in a *Left Review* article entitled 'The men Baldwin would not see'. The caption for one of the photographs read, 'As the Welsh contingent halts during its march, the band rests outside Marylebone Town Hall'; hence it was neither the Jarrow Crusade nor Trafalgar Square unless this was a Welsh contingent of the Jarrow Crusade![57] Also, the catalogue of Sheffield Archives erroneously cited the diary of Joseph Albaya as that of a Jarrow Crusader.[58] Again, like the cross of St. Mark's, this confused the 1934 hunger march and the Jarrow march of two years later. A newspaper cutting about the National Hunger March's halt in Cambridge is wrongly filed in a folder on the Jarrow Crusade and the Bishop of Durham made the same mistake about Cambridge in his diary.[59]

The fallibility of memory and the suggestive attraction of the Jarrow Crusade have combined to magnify the Crusade's significance. *The Guardian* reported that the grandfather of UB40's Ali and Robert Campbell was both a Glasgow communist and Jarrow Crusader, almost certainly confusing the Jarrow march and another hunger march.[60] An article in *The Times* written during David Davis's 2005 bid for Conservative Party leadership falsely claimed that his communist grandfather led the Jarrow Crusade from York to

Aldermaston![61] Even though this was not on the route of the march, Nancy Stone recalled that the Jarrow Crusade lodged in Welwyn Friends Meeting House, in a Quaker history of the unemployment of the 1930s.[62] The oral history deposits at the National Sound Archive reveal more misappropriations. At 91 years of age, former communist William Davey from Sunderland reminisced about his participation in the Jarrow march but undoubtedly he took part in one of the national hunger marches.[63] Cabinet-maker Morris Moss told an interviewer that he had seen the Crusaders when they came to Bethnal Green.[64] Psychologists have identified the phenomenon whereby an associated memory blocks the retrieval of a correct memory. If we think about it, we have all experienced this. How many times have you had a word on the tip of your tongue only to have a similar word called to mind instead? It has been dubbed the ugly sister effect because Cinderella's ugly older sisters take her rightful place at the ball.[65] This curious trick that the mind plays on us undermines in an oblique way the claim that the Jarrow Crusade was not like the other marches. If that was so, why do so many people confuse them? Since the Crusade attracts so many innocent false claims, through such a variety of media, it cannot be dismissed as memory lapse or the simple error of archivists or curators misattributing artifacts. It has a deeper significance. This all attests to the powerful grip that the Jarrow Crusade has over the collective memory. The Crusade has potency not because of what it was but because it has been transformed into a legend. In so doing, it has eclipsed the other marches even in the memories of some of their witnesses and participants.

***

Once these diversions – the mystery call, two impersonators and the kidnap plot – had been dispensed with the serious job of marching began. Their midday halt was in Radlett where Reverend K. MacFarlane Harley and members of the Radlett Congregational Church gave them a crate of oranges. At Radlett they also met up once again with Ellen Wilkinson.[66] This was the penultimate day of the march and the one on which it reached the capital. The *Morning Post's* labour correspondent described the Crusade's arrival:

Preceded by a battery of cameras, escorted by a posse of police, pursued by a crowd of spectators, the "Jarrow Crusade" has arrived on the outskirts of London. I walked with it from beyond Elstree, stepping to the strains of several mouth organs, punctuated by a drum. Every time we approached a village, two banners were unfurled and the marchers broke into song. They were led by Miss Ellen Wilkinson, and by Paddy, the canine mascot. Scores of onlookers lined the routes, their numbers swelling into the hundreds as we neared urban areas.[67]

The *News Chronicle* reported that the Crusaders feared arrest as they passed Elstree studios because a gangster film was being made and a large number of actors were dressed as 'coppers'.[68] Perhaps this may not seem so outlandish when one considers that the Crusade had had a continuous police escort from the start and a Special Branch tail from St. Albans.

Thomas C. Dugdale's oil painting 'Arrival of the Jarrow Marchers' (1936) recorded the entry into London.[69] It shows a young well-to-do couple in their fashionable flat while through the window the Crusaders can be seen. The man sits impassively blowing smoke-rings but the woman, in a ball gown and flicking her cigarette holder, peers through the window at the spectacle. There is no great sense of sympathy because the woman's head is turned away from the viewer. The impression given is of two entirely different worlds with only a fleeting voyeuristic curiosity on the part of those from London's smart set. Currently in the possession of the Geffrye Museum where, the deputy director noted, the picture provokes strong reactions:

> Most like it, admire its composition and what could be perceived as the author's satirical comment on the class system; others vehemently dislike it, and are so overwhelmed with anger at the insolent wealthy couple that they are unable to enjoy the artist's overall achievement.[70]

Dugdale's picture is significant because it undermines the myth of universal sympathy painted as it was shortly after the Crusade, before the legend had taken root. Dugdale had apparently seen the march from the top of a London bus. The painting was shown as part of the 'Jarrow: Impressions of a Town' exhibition, which was supported by the Borough of South Tyneside and Northern Arts, on the fiftieth anniversary of the Crusade.[71]

Officialdom dealt the Crusaders another cruel blow. Several marchers received from their wives letters with news of the PAC's decision to withhold part of their allowances because the men had signed on four days before setting off and that this benefit therefore awaited them in the Labour Exchange on their return. Ritchie Calder, the *Daily Herald* journalist who covered the Crusade, told how 'smiler' John Harney's wife would only receive 4s 9d for their household of eight.[72]

On the last stage from Hendon, Thomas Dobson collapsed and was taken to Hendon Cottage Hospital.[73] Initially, the press were told that he had a skin infection and was not seriously ill. However, Bob Maugham remembered that Dobson had had a heart attack and later died.[74] Thomas Dobson, a 45-year-old labourer of 46 Stanley Street, was buried in Jarrow on 5 January 1937.[75] The coroner W.M. Patterson explained that he decided to hold an inquest 'in all fairness to officials of the march' presumably to scotch rumours and allegations about Dobson's death.[76] Dobson had had heart pains for eight months but had concealed this during his medical examination before the march because of his desire to accompany his friends on the Crusade. Joe Symonds, speaking on behalf of the organisers, told the inquest that Dobson had complained of heart troubles in the Midlands and rode along in the bus. He remained a fortnight or so in Hendon Hospital before returning to Jarrow. He died of a heart attack on New Year's Eve after a walk around the town. No doubt contributing to his anxieties, the unfortunate Dobson owed a large amount in rent (over £35) and this may explain why his name is missing and why there is the name John Downey at Dobson's address in the list of marchers, as a pseudonym to foil the UAB authorities.[77] Dobson was not the only marcher to perish.

One of the NUWM contingent, Patrick Haltin, a 36-year-old from Edinburgh, died in Pontefract from pneumonia aggravated by five years of malnourishment on the dole.[78]

The end now in sight, Crusaders began to think about their return home. One reflected:

> The first morning is what I'm afraid of. It'll be getting up and looking out of the window on the same old sight – Jarrow, knowing that there's nothing, nothing at all to do. My feet hurt terribly – but, all the same, it's been a holiday. While you're marching you don't think.[79]

Alderman A.J. Reynolds, the Mayor of Hendon, welcomed the Crusade that evening. He paid £20 from the Mayor's Fund and the Rotary Clubs of Edgware and Mill Hill provided the remaining sum for a meal of tomato soup, steak and kidney pie, with apple pie as dessert, in the White Hart Hotel, Edgware.[80] The Crusaders slept that night in the Algernon Street School. Support in Hendon was even more surprising than elsewhere as the ruling group on the council stood not as Conservatives but as 'anti-socialist' candidates.

In one indication of the impact of the march, *The Times* printed two sympathetic letters. In the first, author and journalist Sir Phillip Gibbs implored the Government to receive the marchers, who were not revolutionary as the Bishop of Durham had claimed. On his visit to Jarrow he felt ashamed that its young people were left to 'rot and waste'. The second was from the Association of Boy's Clubs after organising secretary of Durham County on the implacable character of the youth of Jarrow and County Durham and the need for work.[81] *The Spectator* also disagreed with the bishop, saying condescendingly that the Crusade was more 'pathetic than revolutionary'.[82]

***

The news from Spain brought further horror. 16 died and 60 were injured in a German bombing raid on Plaza de Colón, Madrid. Some of the dead and injured were mothers queuing for milk. The target had no military significance and was intended to strike terror among the civilian population. Ellen Wilkinson had gone to Spain earlier that year, chauffeuring Edward Conze around as he prepared his book *Spain Today*.[83] She was to visit Spain twice during the Civil War. Arriving in Valencia in April 1937, she was part of a delegation of women MPs alongside the Duchess of Atholl, Eleanor Rathbone and Dame Rachel Crowdy. Their report was a brief outline of the humanitarian conditions in republican Spain examining the refugee situation, the lack of food, the religious question, prisons and the lack of medicine. They visited Madrid and described the bombing raids that had destroyed the working-class district of Tetuán, with hundreds killed. They marvelled at the courage of the women of Madrid, three of whom had been killed in a food queue only for the queue to re-form as soon as the bodies were taken away.[84] During her second visit, Ellen Wilkinson toured Barcelona, Valencia and Madrid from 3 to 8 December 1937, with Clement Attlee MP, Philip Noel Baker MP and John Dugdale of the *Daily Herald*. She described her visit to a school in Madrid: 'Bombs have fallen on schools just like this, wrecking them completely blowing teachers and children to bits. That is how fascists bring civilisation'.[85]

Saturday 31 October: The Long, Long Trail
Edgware to Marble Arch, 8 miles

Thirty members of Bethnal Green Unemployed Association left Bethnal Green at midnight, marching through the night and arriving at Algernon Street School around 5 am to meet the Jarrow Crusade. They waited patiently outside for two hours so as not to wake the marchers. A cordon of police ensured that there could not be any fraternisation with the Crusaders. When the Crusade leaders received a delegation from their visitors, the latter asked to join the march on its final leg. Their request was politely but firmly rejected. The Crusaders tucked into a breakfast of boiled ham and tomatoes before setting off at nine o'clock on the shortest and last part of their itinerary. On this stage of the journey, Jarrow's Labour and Conservative civic notables were out in force: Alderman J.W. Thompson, the mayor, Alderman A.A. Rennie, the deputy mayor, Alderman Drummond, Councillors Mrs Scott, Mrs Soulsby, Mrs

Robinson, J. Tallach, J. Mulholland, J. Rose, R. Suddick, Stoddart, the Labour election agent and Claude Robinson, the headmaster of Jarrow Secondary School.[86]

Later on the same day, as the Crusaders filed past, communist party members attempt to join the marchers but were given the 'cold shoulder'.[87] About a hundred communists tagged on to the end of the demonstration. As the marchers entered the soup kitchen at Covent Garden, the communist contingent began to sing the 'Internationale' and the 'Red Flag'. None of the Crusaders joined in. 'Extraordinary precautions' were in place to prevent unauthorised people entering the room where food was provided by the London Co-operative Society. Con Shiels, the son of the Crusade's cook of the same name, remembered the 'very fussy' arrangements to keep outsiders from mixing with the Crusade. He had difficulty getting to see his father and it was only because he knew the march leaders that he succeeded.[88] Mayor Alderman Thompson rejoined the marchers in Hendon. For one Crusader the march had already brought dividends. John Hillcock found work as an iron moulder in London; he had been, like many of his comrades, unemployed for 15 years.[89]

Bill James looked back on the memorable last stage:

> I can remember young lasses watching us march by, all crying. They were girls from the North East who had been forced to go to London to work in service – chambermaids and the like. I think they were proud of us but it made them homesick.[90]

At Marble Arch, the 291 miles from Jarrow to London was complete. The last leg took place with large crowds looking on and plenty of photographers poised for the Sunday newspapers. The mouth organ and kettledrum band kept up spirits despite the heavy rain. The band had been formed because the two journalists had raised the money for the mouth organs from their newspaper colleagues. Amongst the favourites of the marchers were 'Roll along, Jarrow marchers, roll along', 'The Sergeant-Major', 'Tipperary', 'The

Minstrel Boy', 'Poor Old Joe', 'The Long, Long Trail', 'Annie Laurie' and 'Goodbye, old Ship, Goodbye'. According to a press report, the band was asked to make a gramophone record of the songs that they had played in the course of the march.[91] This record was never made and Tosh Corr's players disbanded on their return to Jarrow.[92]

With the march completed, it was now possible for press and participants to reflect on its achievements. These positive endorsements of the Crusade have created a myth of success. Interestingly, given Ellen Wilkinson's role, the *Sunday Sun* described the Crusade as a 'feat of physical courage notable for the manly courage that inspired it right to the end'.[93] She quipped to reporters, 'If anyone suggests a walking tour to me I'll shoot them'.[94] Her summary of the march at this point gave an insight into its organisation. She explained the key ingredients for the success of the march in the *Sunday Sun*. The support from each locality on the route – accommodation, food, entertainment, and a chance to press their case at a public meeting – that they received was essential. In particular, she praised the Conservative civic leaders who presided over most of the towns that they passed through. They were won round because of Jarrow's political truce, the joint work of the Conservative and Labour electoral agents – Suddick and Stoddart, and because Mayor Thompson personally wrote to every one of the mayors on their itinerary. The strategy of relying on the support of these men was by no means guaranteed to succeed and Ellen Wilkinson noted their initial reservations, and how these were overcome:

> Conservative mayors, hesitatingly taking the chair, nervously afraid of 'politics', and then themselves at the end of the meeting banging on the table and moving resolutions themselves to be sent to the Premier demanding that 'something must be done to bring work to Jarrow'.[95]

She observed the importance of the support of Jarrow Conservatives to the entire strategy. Even, of all places, at the Annual Leek and Vegetable Show of Jarrow Conservative Club on the Saturday before the march, Stainthorpe, the Chairman, Councillors Dodds and Suddick expressed their support for the Crusade.[96] For something to interrupt a leek show on Tyneside showed the seriousness of the matter. The truce, however, did not survive a week following the Crusade's return. The mayor's comments about Sir John Jarvis enraged local Conservatives. On Monday 9 November the Conservative Association Committee formally and acrimoniously broke the understanding. Neither side was in any mood to patch up their differences.[97]

On the organisational side of things, Ellen Wilkinson paid tribute to the work of Sam Rowan, the treasurer at the Town Hall, whose work included organising the post. Naturally, she praised David Riley, the march marshal, admitting that she and he had had several cross words before the Crusade, but that once the march was underway she deferred to his admirable leadership:

> Leadership is as important as machinery. The kindly fates gave us a hefty Irishman in Councillor Riley with an iron will and 'a way with him'. He and I had a stand-up fight or two in the early days, but out on the march I succumbed willingly to his leadership as did everyone else. A man who gets rigid obedience with a jest is a priceless possession for a show of this kind – and how he worked, and made everyone else work too![98]

A novel dimension of the Crusade was its relationship with the press. The 'embedded' journalists – Sydney Sterck of the *Chronicle* and *North Mail* and Selwyn Waller of the *Gazette* – marched the entire way, hitching lifts to the nearest telephones to provide their editors with copy. Ellen Wilkinson described the 'eager censorship' of the men as the bundles of papers were distributed with the mail. The newspaper reports were avidly digested and she told how the journalists 'got a hard time if anyone didn't like the story'.[99] Marching among the Crusaders for 300 miles brought a rough and ready journalistic accountability and probably accounts for the upbeat reporting of the Crusade not only in these papers but also others which relied on the information they provided. In addition to these factors, she underlined the strong sense of unity on the march. She believed that the humility of the march leadership and the mouth organ band cemented the sense of togetherness and high spirits. Reflecting six decades on, Bill MacShane attested to this solidarity: 'We got a good reception everywhere we went. We had good meals and a good spirit among the men – no rows. It was champion. I'd go tomorrow.'[100] Jimmy Hobbs agreed: 'There was no trouble at all. It was a crusade not a political march. We were just like a crowd of school kids.'[101] Ellen Wilkinson also thanked the clergymen (the Bishop of Jarrow notwithstanding) and the medical students from the Socialist Medical Association. Optimistic about their prospects, she told the *Sunday Chronicle*, 'we are full of confidence that our petition will meet with success.'[102]

Sunday 1 November: Hyde Park and Trafalgar Square
The Hyde Park demonstration

David Riley announced to the press that march funds totalled £1,200 and that they had a surplus of £100. With another £100 he would be able to buy a new suit for every marcher.[103] March leaders worried that if the surplus was distributed to the marchers it would be subjected to the calculations of the means test officers and would simply result in these officials subtracting the money from the marchers' benefits. In his 'Uncle Freddie' Radio 4 programme, Alex Ferguson, who at the time of the Crusade was a young child in Jarrow, described these officials as 'cockroaches in bowler hats and suits with shiny bums [who] came round to measure poverty with a cruel tape'.[104]

The national Sunday newspapers featured large photographs of the Crusade with short articles or captions. The Crusade received sympathetic coverage in *The People*, the *Sunday Pictorial* and the *Sunday Graphic*. A very short article in the *Sunday Times* sneered that 'only a small crowd was present to welcome the marchers'.[105] *The Sunday Express* pictured the drenched marchers with a caption reading 'Boots, boots, boots, boots, Kipling's poem translated into action by the marchers from Jarrow, rain dripping from their waterproof sheets as they tramped through Cricklewood'. In *Reynolds*

News, several photos were assembled together showing the men on the march, relaxing with their MP and as ever the mascot dog was prominently featured. The journalist quoted a London gent saying, 'I soon found out ... that it was emphatically not a bolshie show'. It was followed by a long article detailing their plight. In the Monday papers such as the *Northern Echo*, *Daily Sketch*, *Glasgow Bulletin*, *Edinburgh Evening News*, *North Mail*, the format of large photographs accompanied by articles covered Sunday's Hyde Park demonstration. Even Lord Rothermere's *Daily Mail*, which had red-baited the other marches, been in favoured of dole cuts and stereotyped the unemployed as scroungers, had an article entitled 'Cheers for Jarrow'.

Escorted by mounted police, and three police tenders, David Riley talked to the press of the elaborate methods that they and Scotland Yard had employed to prevent the march from becoming 'the catspaw of any political organisation'.[106] Sensitive to the criticism that they were sending 'hungry ill-clad men' and jeopardising their health, march leaders constantly reiterated the sound health of the marchers in general, detailed those who had been taken ill and the good medical care provided. Rank-and-file Crusaders in both contemporary interviews with journalists and in reminiscences return to the quality of the food they consumed on the march. It is hard to imagine the impression that a month of good food can make on men used for a decade or sometimes more to an impoverished bread and dripping diet. On their way to Hyde Park one remarked:

> There is not a man here who is not better in health for the march. We have seen food we had not seen before for nearly 12 years – good beef and ham, instead of bread and margarine.

Indeed, James Henry Walters, despite the daily exertions, gained eight pounds in the course of the Crusade.[107] At 3 pm, the Jarrow Crusade held an open-air meeting in Hyde Park. As the marchers entered Hyde Park, the mouth organ band played 'It's a long long trail' to cheers. Alderman Rennie called to the men, 'Would you come back if we could find you work?' 'Yes! Yes!', they replied.

Different accounts exist of what happened at Hyde Park. The police state that there were only 3,000 in attendance; Ritchie Calder put the figure at 50,000.[108] According to *The Times*, the London Communist Party had organised a rally to call for the lifting of the arms embargo to Spain at the same time, but in sympathy with the Crusade an organiser regretted the clash of times, abandoned the meeting and the crowd went across to Jarrow's platform.[109] The police inspector's report saw it differently:

> Every effort was made by the CP and the NUWM to get the Crusaders to co-operate with them. They even went as far as to place a vacant platform in position for them at Hyde Park, and invited them to use it; the offer was politely but firmly refused. When the Jarrow Crusaders' meeting was opened the audience at the Communist Party meeting then in progress left en masse and listened to the Crusaders.[110]

The press delighted in and exaggerated the communist infiltration story. An unauthorised souvenir brochure had been on sale for six pence outlining the case of the Crusade saying that all creeds and political persuasions had supported the marchers. Ellen Wilkinson bought one and complained to journalists that it was wrong to exploit the Crusade in this manner. It was unclear who had printed the pamphlet as there was no printer's address on it.[111] Thus the *North Mail* headlined an article on the Hyde Park demonstration 'Jarrow Men Angry: Communist Demonstrations in London, not a Peg for Propagandists'. The article misleadingly confused Ellen Wilkinson's denunciation of the sale of unofficial programmes which she described as 'exploitation' with the singing of the 'Red Flag' and communist salutes in Hyde Park. The article also suggested that the Crusaders needed a police escort as they were 'pushed and buffeted' by the crowd.[112]

However, Ellen Wilkinson's own account of the Communist Party's contribution in *The Town that was Murdered* stood in marked contrast to this. This was published for the pro-communist Left Book Club in 1939 so she was unlikely to be very critical of the communists but if it were not the case she could have simply omitted the episode. Instead her reflections basically corroborated *The Times*:

> There seemed no time to organise a Hyde Park meeting. But we hastily got permission to hold one in the park, and hoped for an audience from the crowds there. The Communist Party had gathered a big demonstration on a general unemployment protest. They generously gave way for an hour and asked their great audience to swell our Crusade meeting, which grew to enormous size when it was known the Jarrow Crusaders were there.[113]

The *Daily Herald* confirmed Ellen Wilkinson's account:

> When Miss Wilkinson began her speech she thanked the Communist Party for holding over their meeting and said that she hoped that everyone who was around her platform would go to the Communist Party's platform when the Jarrow meeting was concluded.[114]

The *Daily Worker* printed a letter of someone who had been at the Hyde Park rally saying how he believed that the CP was right to suspend their meeting in deference to the Crusade but that the repetition of the non-political character of the march was irritating. Asking for a membership form the author concluded 'To be non-political in such circumstances is surely criminal'.[115] Alex Ferguson incorporated an anecdote from the unofficial folklore of the Crusade into his play *A Woman's Walk* according to which Crusaders intervened to stop the police silencing a communist soapbox orator on the day of the Hyde Park demonstration.

David Riley used his considerable skills as an orator in front of the thousands assembled in Hyde Park. He opened with an account of the march Jarrow had made to Seaham to lobby Ramsay MacDonald, who was at that time the Prime Minister, in his County Durham constituency. There was some friendly heckling 'chuck out the Government', 'it's the fault of the Tories' and 'traitor' at the mention of 'Ramsay Mac'. Despite frowning on such political comments, Ellen Wilkinson and the march leaders must have agreed inwardly but such comments would embarrass their Conservative allies. David Riley appealed for quiet, and then spoke:

> We are doing this as non-politically as a man could do it. We cannot allow politics to walk over the empty stomachs of our women and children.[116]

> In Jarrow after 15 years of unemployment, people are collapsing from starvation and semi-starvation. We want the right to work: we do not ask for charity. Something must be done, and we shall not stop until something is done.[117]

> We believe we have had a raw deal. Conditions are such that when people are doing simple household things they collapse and at the Inquest the Coroner says it is because of starvation. We are not going to stop our efforts until something is done for us.[118]

> We had hoped, we have been promised, we have been cajoled, but nothing has happened. We have definitely determined that something has to be done, and we are not going to stop until something is done.[119]

Riley alluded to case of Lord Nuffield who owned Morris Motors, for whom, because of his complaints of injustice in relation to government contracts for aviation engines, the cabinet had commissioned a white paper:

> The cabinet listened to Lord Nuffield, who happens to be worth millions. The cabinet listened readily enough to him and promised him work.[120]

> If the cabinet are prepared to fall into line with one individual, we believe that 35,000 souls must be considered. Keep the political aspect out of this. Write to your MP, and anybody else you can write to, and insist that the people in Jarrow get a fair deal.[121]

Tales of Jarrow's bleak Christmases, where children had learned not to expect toys, moved the crowd. After the bowler-hatted marshal had spoken, Alderman Rennie addressed the crowd from the platform. He told how the life of the town was sapped as the young left for work but the old, because of their family responsibilities, had to stay to shoulder increasing distress and the growing burden of public relief. His vivid metaphor that 'once we had the finest shipyard in the country now we have the finest graveyard' caught the imagination and warmed the crowd for the next speaker, Ellen Wilkinson.[122] Jarrow's MP, her small arms outstretched, reiterated her now much-practised appeal for Jarrow. Despite its many rehearsals, her speech had lost none of its powerful poignancy:

> Jarrow as a town has been murdered. It has been murdered as a result of the arrangements of two great combines – the shipping combine on the one side and the steel combine on the other. Jarrow is an object lesson in the working of a system of society that condemns these men of ours to unemployment, and that is something we cannot get away from. What has the Government done? I do not wonder that this cabinet does not want to see us. It does not want anyone to tell the truth about these black areas in the North, in Scotland, and in South Wales that have been left to rot. These are the by-products of a system where men are thrown on slag heaps, as is the stuff that it thrown out of the furnaces. They will not be treated like slag, like things you can throw away.[123]

She moved with a spirit of passionate eloquence, placing her right hand on her hip and pointing to the sky with her left. 'There is not a wheel turning or a chimney smoking in Jarrow, when you think of slums, think of Jarrow'. Ellen Wilkinson imploringly stretched her small arms perpendicular to her body and continued:

> It has been suggested that Jarrow has been the centre of a subversive movement against the Government. It may therefore interest you to know that of the total number

of marchers 62% are old Army men who served in the war.[124]

Ellen Wilkinson paid tribute to the women of the marchers who had been forced to apply to the Public Assistance Committee in the absence of their husbands. She spoke emotionally about the high infant mortality, rickets and TB rates. 'We say these things shall not be. At least we shall not stand silent and let them be.'[125]

Paddy Scullion followed, talking about the personal toll of malnutrition in Jarrow that he witnessed as an officer of the Public Assistance Committee. In this capacity, he dealt with emaciated individuals who suffered from high rates of TB, mortality and 'mental deficiency'. Jock Hanlon described the distress of the town, saying he had been thrown out of the Houses of Parliament many times for his townsfolk.[126]

***

A week later, another rally in Hyde Park welcomed the National Hunger March. In contrast to Jarrow's humbler event, Clement Attlee, the leader of the Labour Party, Will Thorne MP, Aneurin Bevan MP, (a total of 11 Labour MPs) spoke at the demonstration.[127] The London Trades Council (LTC) described the National Hunger March Hyde Park demonstration as 'a landmark in working-class history', and with the *Daily Herald* estimating attendance at 250,000 it not hard to see why.[128] The previous Sunday, the day of Jarrow's Hyde Park demonstration, the 240-strong Lancashire contingent of the hunger march reached Redditch from Birmingham, the 500 on the South Wales contingent had reached Newbury, the 35-strong women's contingent were at Towcester, the 140 of the Yorks, Notts and Derby contingent at Market Harborough, the 140 of the Northumberland and Durham contingent at Cambridge, the 290 of the West Scottish contingent at Warwick and the 180 of the East Scottish contingent at Wolverton.[129]

A few hundred yards across London in Trafalgar Square at 1.35pm, 600 blind people, including 250 blind marchers, gathered to press the Government to amend the Blind Persons Act of 1920. The marchers had tramped from Glasgow, the West of England, Lancashire and Wales.[130] Headed by a brass band, banners arched against the wind from the South London, Greenwich, Tottenham and West London branches of the National League of the Blind; Southwark, Paddington and North Southwark Labour Party and the Paddington branch of the National Union of Railwaymen. At 2.15 pm, J.R. Pound welcomed the demonstrators and introduced an open air meeting. Amongst the speakers were three MPs – G. Hicks, Reverend R.W. Sorenson and Fred Messer – together with Ellen Wilkinson's journalist friend Hannen Swaffer, A. Wall, B. Sullivan, J. O'Keefe, T.J. Parker, W. Scringeour and Mr Brickhill. The speakers outlined how the blind deserved 'Justice not Charity' the slogan which was inscribed on the banner at the head of their march. At the time, blind workers, at the mercy of charity, were being driven to starvation. Hannen Swaffer quipped:

> Look at Nelson up there. He was blind in one eye, and they gave him a statue. If he had been blind in both eyes, they would have sent him to the workhouse.[131]

The police took a special interest in Brickhill who had founded a union of the blind in Australia as he praised the Soviet Union where the blind had secured genuine equality, where they held positions like university professorships and were recognised as human beings. He condemned the institutions for the blind in Britain where the blind were exploited as cheap labour. At 4 pm, the speeches wound up and the demonstrators dispersed.[132] The marchers took the tram to the unemployed centre in Battersea where they were staying. Unlike the Crusaders, the National League of the Blind was invited to a ministerial hearing at the Ministry of Labour on 11 November.[133]

After the Hyde Park demonstration, the Crusaders went to St. Peter's Kitchen in Garrick Street for food before going to their digs in Stepney. Dan Frankel, the MP for Mile End, welcomed the Jarrow men to the London County Council's non-residential training centre – the Smith Street Institute, Mile End Road. 'We like the East End' said one marcher, 'the people down here can understand us'.[134]

In the evening the marchers were invited to the Trinity Hall, Augusta Street, Poplar, where the Workers' Christian Fellowship provided tea and the Left Repertory Theatre staged the left-wing Australian playwright Len Fox's *Stay Down Miner*. A concert followed with a medley of Tyneside songs, with one of the march leaders – the *Evening Chronicle* did not divulge which one – treating the audience to a rendition of the 'Blaydon Races'.[135] Crusaders slept in the Mile End Institute where they were lodged until their return home. At the Institute, a police guard and identity badges ensured that no outside elements could gain access to the Crusaders. Signed identity cards were needed to get in and out of the building and London relatives of the Crusaders found it difficult to get inside.[136] That night Fred Harris, the communist who had been expelled from the Crusade, rejoined the group but returned to Jarrow the following day.

Week Five: London to Jarrow

Monday 2 November: London, Madrid, Jerusalem
Rest in London

The Crusaders had a quiet day on Monday, going to the Forum Cinema in Charing Cross at 2 pm to see special showings of *Storm over Asia* and *Congress Dances*.[1] In all likelihood, the hand of Ellen Wilkinson, who had travelled to London during the march to make the arrangements for their stay, was at work here. She was sympathetic towards Soviet Russia and a convinced anti-imperialist. The first film was an example of Soviet avant-garde silent film-making. Pudovkin's *Storm over Asia* (1928) was filmed on location in Mongolia, combining anthropology of the peoples of the Steppes and beautifully shot landscape. The film narrates the rebellion of impoverished Mongolian fur-trappers against the British occupation force in 1918. The British censors had for some time banned the film and then edited it heavily. For Ellen Wilkinson, just as the arrogance of wealthy British merchants provoked the fur-trappers, so the steel barons and the cabinet aroused the wrath of the people of Jarrow. The second film, Erich Charell's *The Congress Dances* (1931) was an operetta centred on a love triangle set during the Congress of Vienna of 1815. The Nazi regime banned it in Germany because of the Jewish members of the production staff. Ellen Wilkinson perhaps thought the film poignant, given the grand diplomacy of aristocrats redrawing the map of Europe at a time when the Non-Intervention Committee was sealing the fate of the Spanish republic and international cartels kept Jarrow's shipyard motionless. At 6.45 pm they went to a concert at Stepney Central Hall.

Individual acts of generosity towards the marchers continued. Sir Albert Levy, of Hart and Levy Ltd, provided the £100 that Riley had appealed for on the previous day to equip each marcher with a new suit.[2] The handsome sum of £13. 10s was collected in St. Jude's, Hampstead. Reverend Henry Carter of the Methodist Welfare Committee provided a three-course dinner for the Crusaders at the Stepney Central Hall, Commercial Road. Mrs Van der Elst, the notable campaigner against capital punishment, donated £50 to the march and gave them tea and a jumper each at Smith Street. The Special Branch reported that she was asked to leave after it became apparent that she was interested in self-publicity. Given the press coverage of the Crusade's wealthy backers she was, perhaps, not alone in her other-than-philanthropic motives, just less subtle.[3]

The decision that there should be a march of a non-political and religious character to respond to the failure of a deputation to get the approval for a steelworks in Jarrow had been taken at the council meeting the previous July. But it was David Riley who had originally insisted on the term Crusade. As he recalled:

> It was first intended that we should call it the Jarrow hunger march. When I was made the Marshall [sic] of the march, I said it was not a very nice name; I said Crusade would be a better title.[4]

With the acts of generosity which had been shown over the previous four weeks, the crusade metaphor came to provide an unintended parallel. The original crusading orders of knights established hospitals and relief to help the pilgrims to the Holy Land. A more contemporary example came in the shape of the encyclical of Pius XI of October 1931 who extolled the 'sacred path of a crusade of charity' against unemployment. He made known his fears about the threat to the social order that the swelling ranks of the unemployed posed and called on the 'sacred duty' of Catholics to alleviate their distress.[5]

The Pope clearly feared the social consequences of a failure to address hardship, and explicitly promoted charity in order to diffuse social conflict. But there was another connection between charity and the crusades. The original Crusades were a costly venture and the church sanctioned the sale of indulgences to raise the necessary funds. In the same way that taking the cross and venturing to the Holy Land redeemed the Crusaders of their sins (penitent remission), so the purchase of an indulgence assuaged the sins of the patron. The medieval conscience, burdened with sin and fear of the last judgement, perhaps had its modern equivalent as the comfortably-off eased their shame at the sight of malnourished northerners by putting into their collecting box. For the modern Crusader, this generosity was necessary to finance the Crusade and was not perceived as charity. Charity went against the grain of the strong working-class attachment to independence; after all, the Jarrow Crusade's goal was to restore the source of that independence and dignity: work.

The contemporary claim of Spain's General Franco to the true crusading inheritance had much greater substance than did that of Jarrow. Of course, David Riley and Billy Thompson had in mind the romantic mythology first used to mobilise soldiers and settlers for the conquest and occupation of the Holy Land, rather than the barbarous realities of the original Crusades. The first Crusade, 1095-99, began with anti-semitic pogroms, committed massacres en route, and culminated in the wholesale slaughter of the population of Jerusalem in July 1099. The resemblance to Franco's *cruzada* should have been apparent, especially given the support of the Catholic Church in Spain and Rome. The Bishop of Salamanca, Dr Enrique Pli y Daniel, sanctioned the nationalist 'Crusade' in a long pastoral letter written on 30 September 1936, Franco having approved a draft.[6] Cardinal Isidro Gomà y Tomà, the leader of the Spanish Church, had also declared the rebels' cause a crusade.[7] Even the Pope's telegram of congratulation to Franco on his final victory in the Spanish civil war in April 1939 observed that a 'heroic crusade has been fought against the enemies of religion, the fatherland and of Christian civilisation'.[8] For decades, fascist propaganda presented Franco as a Catholic Crusader, and the civil war as a latter-day equivalent of the Catholic Kings' reconquest of Spain from the Moors.

As Paul Preston, Franco's biographer, highlighted:

> The generalised portrayal of Franco as a warrior king or
> specifically as El Cid was both personally titillating to
> him and central to what passed for ideology in his
> dictatorship. In the posters and paintings, in the
> ceremonies of his regime, an impression was created of
> Franco's all-seeing omnipotence by projecting him as a
> saintly crusader entrusted with God's mission.[9]

After his brutal victory there were mass executions of around
200,000 opponents. One of the more famous of many examples of
Franco posing as a medieval crusader was the mural entitled 'Franco:
victor of the Crusade' that adorned the Military Historical Archive
in Madrid.[10] Indeed, during the Jarrow Crusade the letters page of
the *Shields Gazette* involved a lively debate about the Spanish civil
war between those who supported the republic and local Catholics
who pointed to the atrocities committed against the Spanish
Church.[11] Apart from the name, the Jarrow Crusade had nothing
in common with the reality of the original Crusades; as for the
capacity of the original crusades to generate folklore, symbols and
myth that have become integral to British history that is a different
matter, and the parallels are compelling.

Beyond intentional imitation, the analogy with the original
Crusades is rich in coincidence, ironic contrast and even insightful
comparison. The Jarrow march leaders manufactured a symbolism
which purposely drew on these earlier ventures. Whilst the religious
dimension was stressed at every opportunity, the goal was not
religious – not the capture of the Holy Land – but the most prosaic
– work. The ultimate destination was not a spiritual landmark –
the Church of the Holy Sepulchre that reputedly housed the True
Cross – but secular and political – the House of Commons. In
another act of wilful association, David Riley took the title 'marshal'
echoing the designation of the organisational leader of the crusading
order, the Knights Templar. Coincidence also connected what eight
centuries separated. A leading figure in the Second Crusade, which
was a largely male affair, was the fiercely courageous, red-headed

Eleanor of Aquitaine, reputedly the most beautiful woman in Europe. Here was a medieval predecessor for Ellen Wilkinson, whose courage was often remarked upon and, if she was not one of Europe's greatest beauties, she was certainly treated in the press as pretty and glamorous. Stella Davies recalled her courage during the suffrage campaign, speaking in the streets of Salford during a by-election:

> She was greeted with yells and cat-calls and 'go home carrots, and darn the stockings', followed by a shower of stones. As fast as they fell she picked them up and dropped them over the side of the lorry. Then as the supply gave out, she faced the unruly mob and silence fell. Her voice rang out in heavy sarcasm, 'You do well to class me with criminals and lunatics because I see you are both – and you can't aim straight, either'.[12]

Moreover, the disputed authenticity of the 'Cross of Jarrow' that officials from Leicester 'returned' to Jarrow in 1988 offers a powerful note of irony, given the contest over the True Cross. Crusaders captured this holy relic, supposedly from the crucifix of Christ, during the First Crusade. It was lost to Saladin several decades later, and then recovered. It is highly unlikely that either cross was what it purported to be. But in some sense history does repeat itself and the analogy can be considered an insightful tool in the study of the Jarrow Crusade. The power of the initial Crusades of 1095 and 1936 both inspired repeat performances.[13] Those who returned were accorded a special prestige in their communities and were able to regale family friends and neighbours with fantastic tales of their itinerary. Furthermore both Crusades developed an official legend and folklore. This is the crucial dimension of the Crusades that render them significant and memorable. Where the two events diverge is in their actual historical impact. The medieval Crusades transformed the face of Western European history, whilst the Jarrow march did not even succeed in the limited demand of securing work for a small Tyneside town.

Tuesday 3 November: A Rich Santa Claus
The Public Meeting in Memorial Hall

Tuesday was the official state opening of Parliament. Scotland Yard and march organisers had worked together so that the men could see the royal procession, and they were allocated a spot on the route on the south side of the Mall between Marlborough House, the residence of Queen Mary, and Horse Guards Parade. The five official horse-drawn carriages were to depart from Buckingham Palace at 11.20 am, pass the Crusaders at about ten minutes later and arrive at the Houses of Parliament at 11.45 am. The Crusaders got up early, washed, shaved and donned their caps. 'We've got to look tidy today of all days', one marcher told the *Chronicle* reporter before taking the underground. The papers reported a certain sympathy amongst the Jarrow marchers for King Edward VIII who had visited County Durham a few years previously and declared, 'Conditions like these make me ashamed to be an Englishman'.[14] They stood four deep with their capes as protection against the heavy downpour, and eagerly awaited the King's passage. Unfortunately, due to the inclement weather, the procession was cancelled and the marchers barely glimpsed the King's car as it sped to the Houses of Parliament.

One service the Jarrow Crusade's historical inflation renders is that it overshadows the awkward episode of the abdication. In the official chronologies of British history, the Jarrow Crusade's rough coincidence with the abdication obscures a king with sympathies for Hitler, who repeated on several occasions that had he remained on the throne Britain and Germany would not have gone to war.[15] The dignified non-political protest of the humble shipyard workers of Jarrow contrasts with the King who dabbled politically and whose private life would have scandalised the sensibilities of the interwar period, if not even public opinion today.

On Tuesday evening, Crusade leaders organised one of the most important events of their stay in London; a public meeting in the Memorial Hall, Farringdon Street. In her novel, *The Clash* (1929), Ellen Wilkinson had described this venue where on 1 May 1926 the historic meeting of the TUC had ratified the decision to support the miners with a general strike.

As Joan walked into the stone and granite entrance-hall, she could not help feeling it a grim joke that this chilly temple of Nonconformist respectability should be chosen as the place in which a great social upheaval might be launched.[16]

The same might be said of the appropriateness of the hall for the Crusade. The public meeting was almost guaranteed to get more publicity for Jarrow and add to the pressure on the Government. Londoners were invited to 'come and hear the story of the Jarrow marchers – the fight of a town for work – its shipyards are banned – its steelworks closed – Jarrow appeals to parliament – meeting on the eve of presentation of petition to parliament'.[17] It was not until the last minute that the list of speakers was finalised. Canon H.R.L. 'Dick' Sheppard was one of the principal speakers.[18] He was the founder of the Peace Pledge Union whom the Bishop of Durham uncharitably referred to as Dick Sheppard's 'crew of fanatics'.[19] Chaired by the Mayor of Jarrow, the line-up of speakers also included the Conservative ex-mayor Councillor Dodds, Ellen Wilkinson, the marshal of the march Councillor Riley and three marchers – Councillors Scullion, Hanlon and Symonds. At the bottom of leaflets advertising the meeting, Sir John Jarvis's name was listed in smaller print, to speak 'if his engagements permit'. The manager of the Labour Exchange in Hebburn, Mr J. Robinson, who channelled information to the Ministry of Labour and the Home Office, initially expected the Lord Mayor of London, the Chairman of London County Council and the Bishop of Jarrow to speak at the meeting. Clearly the Bishop would no longer be welcome even if he were willing again to risk the wrath of the Bishop of Durham.[20]

The meeting began at 8 pm. Canon Sheppard addressed the audience of 350 which disappointingly only half-filled the hall,

> I do admire the extraordinary dignity of the way in which you have carried out this march. I congratulate you on the way in which you have carried out this pilgrimage. The heart and mind of every thinking person in England is with you today. I only wish to God that we could

march the people of London down to Jarrow to see the conditions there. The last time I went to Jarrow I could hardly lift my head for days afterwards at the thought not only of what you were going through but of the extraordinary patience with which you are carrying on. I would have loved to have been with you on the march, not because I have anything to teach you but because I could have learned something from you. You have so aroused the conscience of this country that things are bound to happen now and if they don't come again, come every month until they do. I wish you good luck and tell you that crowds are with you and that we shall do everything in our power to assist you.[21]

But it was Sir John Jarvis who grabbed the headlines with his dramatic announcement of new jobs for Jarrow. The journalists' reaction was that 'a rich Santa Claus had suddenly appeared to solve all Jarrow's problems at a stroke.'[22] Surprising everyone on the platform, Sir John announced a plan for a steel tubes mill on the site of the boiler room at Palmer's. He explained that the reason he had not mentioned the project was that he had been abroad investigating the possibilities. He had secured investment from a major bank but he would be in sole control of the finances of the plant and would take no profit. The works would open next spring. Further disconcerting the march leaders, Sir John even supported the Government's refusal to see the men:

Jarrow is not the only distressed area and if the Government were to receive you and promise all that you asked then marchers would start from every quarter and demand similar treatment, which it would not be in the power of the Government to give.[23]

Despite Sir John saying in the Commons in July that 'on the matter of Jarrow we are like brother and sister', he had already clashed with Ellen Wilkinson immediately prior to the Crusade.[24] His letter which appeared three days before the Crusade's departure spoke optimistically of his achievements. Two new industries – ship-breaking and furniture making – had started and more than a thousand men had been employed on job schemes for a month each.[25] The letter clearly angered Ellen Wilkinson, who suspected Tory sabotage but replied in measured tones. Jarrow had 'suffered from his over sanguine optimism. It would be a pity if the glow of pleasure from his letter … suggested that fundamentally Jarrow was now alright'.[26] He also met with Runciman's officials from the Board of Trade immediately before the meeting, conniving with them to diffuse the political embarrassment to, and pressure on, his Government. When Board of Trade mandarin Leonard Browett CBE outlined his master's view that all Jarrow's shipyard workers would find employment in the other yards on the Tyne, Jarvis concurred that this 'confirmed the impression which he had formed'. If one believed this (rather implausible) proposition, why would there be any need for the Crusade? And why would one support it? Jarvis said that this information would be unsuitable for the meeting because it would 'exasperate' the men. Sir John pointed to the situation of the unskilled workers in Jarrow and the benefits of creating local industry, which had been his project for the last two years. His plan was to produce steel tubes for shells to be sold to the Admiralty. He also mentioned a plan for a paper plant that would employ thousands. Clearly Jarvis was pursuing his own agenda and using the Crusade as leverage for his own schemes for Jarrow, but in so doing he was presenting his Government with the opportunity to get off the hook.[27] In correspondence between government officials later that month, Jarvis's plans were cited as justification for waiting and doing nothing about Jarrow.[28] When the metal works did eventually open, not in spring 1937 as Jarvis had predicted, but in December 1937, it employed only 200 skilled and semi-skilled men from Jarrow.[29] Sir John skilfully secured three interest-free loans totalling £90,000 from the Government because of the location of the new works.[30]

Speaking immediately after Sir John, Ellen Wilkinson did not refer to the plan. Admitting her surprise, she later explained to the *Chronicle* that despite speaking to Sir John directly before the meeting he had not alerted her to his revelation. The meeting collected £8 7s 8d for the march funds. The shock of Sir John's news diffused the public clamour for the Government to find a solution to Jarrow's woes. It also eclipsed Ellen Wilkinson's powerful rhetoric and the council's plan for a Private Member's bill to allow the council to create new industries.[31] The bill proposed a grant from the Commissioner for the Special Areas to buy Palmer's as a national industrial training yard which would apprentice shipyard workers and give refresher courses to those who had not worked in some time. The minority report of the Royal Commission on Local Government on Tyneside agreed with Jarrow council's desire for the government to grant these new powers to local councils. But this would encroach on the dogma that government should not interfere with the market and the emerging orthodoxy that central government should be responsible for regional policy and regeneration. Eventually in 1939 the Jarrow bill was passed, but in a much watered-down form. The new law did little to alleviate Jarrow's unemployment problem: rearmament and war did that.[32] The rest of the yard could be cleared for new industries. The bill would also include a clause to remove the 40-year ban on shipbuilding. In addition, David Riley proposed a plan to provide the Ministry of Transport with road signs and other equipment from the Palmer's site. Whilst Sir John's announcement 'buoyed up the spirits of the men', the two schemes were mutually exclusive because the political will would not exist to support both, but also because both sought to use the Palmers' site.[33] Here was another reason why the political truce could only be temporary and superficial.

The results of council elections in England and Wales appeared in the newspapers on Tuesday 3 November. In net terms, Conservatives and Independents gained control of 44 and 42 councils respectively, at the expense of the Liberals who lost five councils and Labour which lost 81 councils. In the North East, Progressives held Newcastle while Labour held Sunderland and Blyth. In South Shields and Gateshead, the elections left Labour and their rivals neck and neck.[34]

Wednesday 4 November: You Knew You Were Finished
The Petition and the House of Commons

On Wednesday, bright morning sunshine faded to a grey London fog. At ten in the morning, Ellen Wilkinson ushered the men around the House of Commons. After time to reflect on Sir John's announcement, during the tour she and David Riley both made their opinions known. She cautioned:

> I would not like to throw water on any scheme that would bring work to Jarrow, but these men have had promises before and they have not come to anything. We have got the Government cornered and on no account must this latest offer enable it to avoid its responsibilities.

'We in Jarrow believe it', David Riley continued, 'when we see the men come home with black faces from the works.'[35] In *The Town That Was Murdered*, Ellen Wilkinson suggested that the press reaction to Jarvis's announcement dispelled the discomfort felt by government supporters in the Commons and that Jarvis 'is the type of rich man who, with the very best of intentions, desires to be the fairy-godfather to what he assumes to be a derelict town of down-and-outs'.[36]

The cabinet met at 11 am but, according to the minutes, ignored the Jarrow issue. Foreign affairs once again dominated the agenda with the five-power conference approaching and the difficult situation in Spain worsening. The Palestinian situation and defence also required cabinet discussion before it came to the more mundane matters of railway freight, trade, the Red Cross Convention and electrification. Meanwhile the Crusaders lunched with Reverend H. Clapham in St. Thomas's Church Hall, Westminster Bridge Road.

At two in the afternoon, the men embarked on the steamboat for a sight-seeing trip along the Thames paid for by Sir John Jarvis. Unbeknown to the men, Ellen Wilkinson had arranged this with the police to prevent a possible outcry in the House of Commons.[37] At a quarter to three, she presented Jarrow's petition to the House. In accordance with parliamentary ritual, it was deposited in a bag behind the Speaker's chair. Likewise, Sir Nicholas Grattan-Doyle, Unionist MP for Newcastle North (1920-40), the senior Tyneside MP, presented a second petition of 68,502 signatories collected across Tyneside in Jarrow's favour. As agreed at the all-Tyneside conference in support of Jarrow on 16 September, Alderman W. Locke, the Lord Mayor of Newcastle, had launched this second petition on 15 October.[38] This petition needed a last minute amendment because it was addressed to the Government rather than the Commons as procedure required. In the Distinguished Strangers' Gallery, the civic dignitaries of Tyneside – the Lord Mayor of Newcastle, the Mayors of Gateshead, South Shields, Wallsend and Jarrow – lent their weight to the proceedings.[39] Ellen Wilkinson read from the Jarrow petition:

> During the past fifteen years Jarrow has passed through a period of industrial depression without parallel in the town's history. Its shipyards closed. Its steelworks have been denied the right to reopen. Where formerly 8,000 people, many of them skilled workers, were employed, only 100 are now at work on a temporary scheme. The town cannot be left derelict and therefore your petitioners humbly pray that His Majesty's Government and this honourable House should realise the urgent need that work should be provided for the town, without further delay.[40]

As she handed over the black leather bound petition with gold letters, she broke down in tears, amid cheers and applause. Major Milner and an assistant steadied her, as she was overwhelmed by the emotion of the moment before returning to her seat. Sir Nicholas Grattan-Doyle then followed with a similar speech presenting the Tyneside petition.[41] Baldwin admitted that he had received 66 resolutions and letters in similar form from public bodies, together with one telegram, five postcards and eight letters from individuals since 1 July.[42]

According to parliamentary procedure, petitions had to be handwritten and addressed to the House. They could not criticise institutions such as the Houses of Parliament and had to conclude with the phrase 'And your petitioners, with duty bound, will ever pray'. The House would not debate the petition but it would instead be referred to the Committee on Public Petitions.[43] The Tyneside petition fell at a number of these procedural hurdles: it was addressed to the Government (and then amended, which was also not permitted), the petition text was typewritten, and its phraseology did not conform to that required. When the Commons Committee on Petitions reported, it recorded 61,766 for the Tyneside petition, that had claimed 68,502, and 11,046 on Jarrow's petition. Many signatures were disqualified, for a variety of reasons. Some were disqualified for being, in the committee's opinion, in the same handwriting, or without addresses. Because most of the original sheets of the Tyneside petition were addressed to the Government and not the House of Commons then it was officially credited with only 20 signatures.[44] Such were the famed 'checks and balances' of British parliamentary democracy, and thus was the Crusade's momentary audience with the-powers-that-be diffused by procedure and belittled by convention. The whole drama in the House of Commons re-enacted the short shrift given to the great Chartist petitions a century earlier.

In the House of Commons, Tom Magnay, the National Liberal MP for Gateshead, who had initially opposed the Crusade, asked if the ban on shipbuilding at Palmer's could be lifted.[45] Instead of a direct answer, the President of the Board of Trade read out the numbers of unemployed shipyard workers, which must have infuriated anyone sympathetic to the Crusade. Chuter Ede, the Labour MP for South Shields, described the Government's complacency as 'an affront to the national conscience'.[46] Sir Walter Runciman pointed to the improvement in the unemployment situation in recent months. Again responding to Tom Magnay, the First Lord of the Admiralty, Sir Samuel Hoare, pointed out that National Shipbuilding Securities Ltd, not the Government, owned the yard and that the situation in Jarrow would improve because Admiralty orders had been placed elsewhere on the Tyne.

After their boat trip, at around half past four, the Crusaders returned to the Commons for tea as guests of Sir Nicholas Grattan-Doyle in the members' dining room. The grand interior of the British Parliament with its great spaces and the play of light and dark, like the medieval cathedrals they had traipsed through in the previous weeks, were intended to be a humbling experience, to inspire awe, even religious devotion. Parliament had, indeed, cast its spell over many a young firebrand MP, but the powerful feat of architecture did not have this effect on the Crusaders, many of whom had seen the steel interiors of great ocean liners, oil tankers and battleships built with their own hands. The House of Commons was the site, instead, of the profound disillusionment of the marchers. Special Branch reported on their shock when they learned that the petition had been presented in their absence:

> .... they appeared very disheartened as they anticipated this ceremony would be the crowning feature of their march; and that they would have participated in proceedings.[47]

Several of the marchers connected their visit with the failure of the march. Crusader John Kelly remembered, 'We got nowt out of it. The petition was just hoyed out. But we expected that. There was nobody working.'[48] Billy MacShane echoed that sentiment, 'We got turned down. We got a cup of tea, they gave us a cup of tea. When we got turned down in the House of Commons, that was it ... You knew you were finished.'[49] The feeling amongst rank and file Crusaders that the Crusade did not succeed is all too often ignored. Out of work for ten years by the time he set out on the Crusade, Eddie Stead, one-time caulker at Palmer's, commented at the departure of the Jarrow '86 march that:

> I wish the lads better luck this time. Our march didn't do us a bit of good – we were still out of work at the end of it. The spirit's exactly the same and very little has changed. We were hungry and we just didn't know where the next meal was coming from. Did it achieve anything? Not a bit, we were still out of work.[50]

Con Whalen, the last survivor of the Crusade, caused a public controversy on local television news and in the local papers when he underlined this point:

> It was a waste of time, but I enjoyed every step. Politically it was a waste of time. It had no effect on unemployment. The only thing that saved Jarrow was the war when the shipyards were needed again. The thing about the march was that it was the best feed I've ever had. I was young and I liked walking. It was much better to be walking than working in the shipyards. It was like a holiday. Being the last survivor doesn't mean much to me. Somebody has to be last.[51]

Peter Flannery's acclaimed TV drama *Our Friends in the North* also dwelt on the failure of the Crusade. The beginning of the final episode, set in 1995, returned to the question of Crusader Felix's sense of personal failure and the failure of the Jarrow Crusade. The local Roman Catholic priest who was to conduct Florie's funeral told Nicky that his father, now suffering from Alzheimer's, had an acute sense of failure all his life because the Jarrow Crusade failed to secure jobs for the town. Going through his mother's possessions, Nicky found a copy of Tom Pickard's *Jarrow March*, with a letter from a Mrs Wilson to Florrie. It recounted her experience of the Crusade as a young girl in a Yorkshire village. In order to redeem their relationship and his father's sense of failure, Nicky drove Felix to meet Mrs Wilson. Nicky asked Mrs Wilson to recall what the marchers had sung as they passed through her village. He also asked her to remember what her father had said to her as the Crusaders left the village. The words that had stayed with her for all her life were that you had a choice in life, whether to be downtrodden or to stand up for yourself. Even now Peter Flannery allowed no room to sentimentalise the father-son relationship or to romanticise the Crusade. In a moment of great dramatic poignancy and pathos, Nicky turned to Felix and told him that his life was not a failure. Now incontinent, Felix's face purpled and he shat himself. In the car on their journey back to the North East, Nicky angrily shouted at Felix that he was a bastard. As a result, Nicky was unable to redeem his own sense of failure because of the unsettling truth about the Crusade.

***

In the late afternoon of 4 November 1936, David Riley described the events of the morning to the dumbfounded Crusaders. The petition was 'handed over' he said:

> as if no more than a minute had been spent in organising it. I heard the answers of the Prime Minister and Mr Walter Runciman. It means you have drawn a blank …They are certainly not going to do that with Jarrow. It does not matter what the consequences are, we are determined. Let us prove to these people that we are not going to suffer that kind of thing.[52]

As the march marshal delivered his speech, anger welled up in the throats of the marchers. In an instant when spontaneity and fury fused, one Crusader called out, 'Don't move, boys. We want to see the Prime Minister'. Just as the idea of the march had started from the gallery of the council chamber two months earlier, so the spontaneous voice of Jarrow's workless, proposed a stay-in strike so that the PM would hear them out.[53] Only two nights before, the Crusaders had seen Len Fox's play, *Stay Down Miner*, about the underground occupation of a pit.[54] In South Wales, the same tactic had been adopted in the struggle against company unionism and had caused such concern that the cabinet had discussed it and, that summer, hundreds of thousands of French workers occupied their factories. Indeed, workers across the globe seemed to be infected with this new form of protest. Later in November, the famous sit-down strike at Flint, Michigan won hard-fought union recognition for the United Automotive Workers at Ford's in the United States. Only after lengthy persuasion were the march leaders able to regain control over the situation and halt the protest so that Ellen Wilkinson and the march leaders could pursue matters on their behalf. Advised not to cause a scene, the marchers left in groups of half a dozen, presumably so that the police could ensure that they did not try to take further protest action. Ellen Wilkinson recalled that:

> They had imagined an imposing ceremony and a long discussion. But they were very sporting about it, as we explained that that was just how the most important petitions of the past had been presented to Parliament, and the interest and value of the presentation was seen in the later debates on the subject, not at the actual moment.[55]

After the drama of the threatened sit-in, there was a meeting to put Jarrow's case to MPs in one of the House of Commons Committee Rooms. Ellen Wilkinson had organised it as a cross-party event. Sir Frederick Mills (Leyton East), Megan Lloyd George (Anglesey), Tom Magnay (Gateshead), Jack Lawson (Chester-le-Street) sponsored the meeting showing the breadth of sympathy for Jarrow.[56] It was attended by over 100 MPs of all parties, including Clement Attlee, the leader of the Labour Party, who remained silent and did not or could not offer the Party's official support for the Crusade. In his wig and robe of office, Charles S. Perkins, the Town Clerk, was the first to address the gathering. He revealed that since 1922 unemployed in Jarrow had fluctuated between 41% and 74% and that it now stood at 51.3% (this figure was an underestimate because from 1935 Jarrow and Hebburn Labour Exchanges were merged). The cost of relief was enormous: since 1923, £1,794,000 had been paid in relief.[57] After the restrained formality of the Town Clerk, John William Thompson, Jarrow's mayor rose to his feet, dramatically throwing his gold chain of office onto the table. He said of it:

> The first Mayor of Jarrow, Sir Charles Palmer, was a Member of this House. When he was made mayor he gave this chain, which represents a ship's cable and at the bottom of it you see a ship's anchor. That was to represent the industry of a busy town.

The heavy object, with a thousand gold links representing the ships built in the town, crashed onto the table silencing the room. It was as if the weight of those ships had fallen onto the table. He hesitated with emotion, before returning to his speech:

> I find it very hard to speak to you today of what is taking place in my own town but I do feel that if you would come to see how we are held up you would be prepared to help us. The people of Jarrow have been promised first one thing and then another. Sir John Jarvis came along two years ago with some friends of his to our assistance with various schemes. We had the idea to build a park which would give employment – a month's work at a time for batches of 80 men. It has been said that the men of Jarrow don't want to work and won't work. We ask for volunteers for this job and we immediately had 1,400 applicants for this job which represented only one month's work for them.[58]

He continued, 'Now we cannot build ships for 40 years. A town of 35,000 starved for £ s d.'[59] When he sat down, sympathetic applause filled the committee room and the MPs, Government and Opposition, were 'distinctly uncomfortable … even the oldest shell-backs began to feel that Jarrow had a case, and that some nasty work had been afoot'.[60]

David Riley followed the mayor, expressing his frustration at the apparent failure of the march. 'I am getting fed up as a result of continuing to talk about the position of Jarrow without the slightest hope of anything being done.'[61] Then the former mayor, Councillor Robert Isaac Dodds, rose accusing the north-east industrialists who had blocked the scheme for a steel works and saying that it was 'strange' that the Brassert report had been unfavourable to their case when one of the advisors was a Consett industrialist who was clearly opposed to the scheme from the outset. Sir John Jarvis revealed that the failure to start the steel works at Jarrow in 1934 and 1935 had cost investors £65,000. He spoke of his plans for the tube works and the furniture works he had established. He also suggested that the Government subsidise employers who established new industries in the Special Areas.

The truce, which had been strengthened by local receptions on the route, strained when Jarrow Conservatives and Labour offered rival solutions for their town at the end of the march. This truce had involved a formal agreement between the parties in Jarrow not to contest the council elections taking place across the country on 2 November, but the sense of cross-party cohesion quickly evaporated. C.H. Vincent, President of the Jarrow Conservative Association, wrote a letter to *The Times* outlining the Conservatives' attitude to the Crusade. He explained that he agreed with the Government about the ill-advised nature of hunger marches but he claimed that the Crusade did not come under this category and that he had sought assurances from the organisers that it would be non-political and well-organised. He praised David Riley for dispensing his duties admirably in this regard. Jarrow was a special case, as it was dependent on Admiralty contracts and had therefore fallen victim to the Washington Disarmament Conference. He and the town's former Conservative MP, W.G. Pearson, believed that their only course of action was to lobby the Admiralty to provide work for Jarrow.[62] His colleagues believed that this was still the only solution for the town.[63] In contrast, the mayor announced the publication of *Jarrow – Its Plight and it Case* which suggested other remedies. But even Jarrow's Labour group did not speak as one. David Riley submitted a scheme to the House of Commons for the Ministry of Transport to employ 2,000 men in Jarrow.[64]

Back at the Mile End Institute, emotionally exhausted after the day's disappointment, the men had a fish and chip supper, followed by an evening concert performed by St. Thomas's Hospital medical students.

Thursday 5 November: Tears and Fireworks
The Return to Jarrow

It was a full month to the day since the marchers had left Jarrow. After a breakfast of boiled eggs, bread, butter and tea, there was nothing left to do but pack their kit onto the bus and return home.

Because of all the gifts received on the way, the cooking equipment (which Jarrow boy scouts had loaned them) and the clothing would not fit into the grey bus – which had been purchased from Northern Bus Company for £25 on the understanding that it would be re-purchased at the end of the march. Len Lomax from South Shields, the bus's driver, took four of the men along with him. The rest marched from the Smith Street Institute, which had provided their home for the last four nights, to King's Cross Station. Setting out in the rain must have felt like a badly written postscript to their heroic journey south. Their banners were unfurled and then taken down because of the rain, although the weather improved later in the morning. Instead of the cheers that had greeted them on Sunday, there were no crowds and only the curious stares of Londoners going about their business. The Crusaders' feelings were mixed. They anticipated a warm welcome from their loved ones but were cruelly disappointed at the Government's reply to their petition in the House of Commons. David Riley articulated his disenchantment and determination:

> I must confess I was bitterly disappointed. I believe the only way we will bring this matter before the cabinet with sufficient strength is not by easing up in our efforts to bring Jarrow's plight before the whole country in an organised way. ... I will not personally give up until something has been done to resuscitate industries in the town.[65]

Amongst the hundreds who gathered to give the Crusade a send off, an unexpected well-wisher waited at King's Cross Station. In what was widely interpreted as a snub to the Government, Malcolm Stewart, the Commissioner of the Special Areas, addressed the men before they boarded their train. He told them:

> I have not been invited to meet you but was determined that you should not go back without a word of encouragement. Your march has done good. I fail to understand how any sober-minded person could have associated your march with revolutionary ideas or

intentions. I admire you. You have demonstrated to the country that patience and courage with which you have borne the sufferings of unemployment for many a long year. I am not making promises or raising hopes – but don't lose courage, I have hope for Jarrow.[66]

The Crusaders left London on a special train at 1.08 pm. Two of the Crusaders did not return: John Farndale, the youngest Crusader, who had taken up a job offer as a baker's assistant in London and had gone to live with his sister; the other, Thomas Dobson, was still in hospital in Hendon.[67]

Back in the House of Commons Willie Gallacher, the Communist MP for East Fife, asked why the Prime Minister had refused an audience to the Jarrow and blind marchers. Jarrow was also mentioned again in the House on 9 November when Clement Attlee proposed a motion in support of the National Hunger March. On that occasion, the Minister of Labour, Ernest Brown, suggested that because of the numbers of juvenile and female unemployed, the problem of joblessness was exaggerated in Jarrow.[68] But, essentially, the Government had seen out the tempest and hoped that the Jarrow Crusade would be forgotten. And in a sense it was. It was not until the 1970s that interest revived in the Crusade and its legend grew.

Whereas the journey to the capital had taken four weeks of monotonous footslogging and blisters, on the return trip the countryside sped past the carriage windows and nearly the length of England was spanned in just five and a half hours. Scenes of 'riotous jubilation' greeted the Crusaders' arrival. Their train was due to pull in at 6.46 pm. Bob Maugham, who had worked in Wallsend pit and as a labourer at Palmer's, remembered the day sixty years later:

> It was fantastic. You couldn't get moved at Jarrow train station. We were supposed to have marched back to the Town Hall. We couldn't. It was more than the VE-day celebrations. I was proud of myself to be part of it. In my opinion, there will never be another one like it.[69]

The *Gazette* captured the atmosphere: the large, highly-charged crowd waiting at the railway station complemented the banging and flashing fireworks of Guy Fawkes's night against the darkness of the November evening. The crowd surged around the march leaders, letting off a frenzied cheer as the station doors were opened. Children rushed to pat the dog. David Riley addressed the crowd, 'This is not an end; it is a beginning'. A sobbing woman pressed a child into the arms of Alderman Symonds. Flashes of camera illuminated their faces. 'Where's Ellen?' townsfolk cried in the confusion. The diminutive MP called out, 'I'm here. I've been here all the time.' She echoed Riley's sentiments: 'I do not think this march is an end. It is not. It is only a beginning.' She paused to find her voice and continued:

> It is the beginning of the fight for our right to work. It is a great night for Jarrow. The march has put Jarrow on the map and has made Parliament realise, even if the Government did not, that something has to be done for Jarrow. We will not rest until we have made the Government take notice of us. We have lit a fire of sympathy in the House of Commons that will not be put out by any ministerial cold water. I don't think this march is an end, it is a beginning of a real fight for Jarrow.[70]

David Riley added that 'the credit goes to all the lads who have done their job so magnificently. They have aroused a sympathy throughout the country which will compel the Government to act.' Symonds, Hanlon and Scullion followed with speeches. Amid all the excitement one woman fainted. Naturally the question on many people's lips was what would happen now? Paddy Scullion was cheered as he defiantly said that they would continue the fight and march down to London again if necessary.[71] Councillor Mrs Scott told the *News Chronicle* that a women's march would be organised if there was no improvement for Jarrow.[72] 'Will you march again?' asked the *Gazette* reporter. 'I hope it won't be necessary,' Ellen Wilkinson said, 'but if it is, then I will march again. I will go on marching with them, if need be, until we win.'[73] She told *The*

Northern Echo, 'I did not expect that we should come back with a shipyard under one arm and a steelworks under the other, but I really think that the march has done good notwithstanding that the Government might have been a bit warmer to us.'[74]

Within a day, the march leaders' rhetoric of continuing their fight, of epic achievement, replaced the Crusaders' realisation of the failure of the march. Out of this rhetoric grew the myth of the Crusade's success. At the time it was more than rhetoric for those who had led the Crusade were determined to carry on, to launch another march if necessary. But those who had insisted initially on the non-political character of the march were not willing to go through it all again, fearing that another march might jeopardise the approach of lobbying government. The frustration of the 'four laddies' – Hanlon, Riley, Scullion and Symonds – was such that they quit Labour in order to carry on the battle.

Go to Jarrow today and you will notice that the memory of the Crusade forms part of the landscape itself. From the old railway station, now a metro stop, with Vince Rea's steel relief sculpture of the Crusade, you can walk a hundred yards into the town through the underpass with a colourful tile mural commemorating the route of the march designed by Jarrow school children. Some of their names on the plaque next to the image match those of the Crusaders, showing how the event lives on in family traditions, landscape and local folklore. Continue into the shopping centre, turn right, and you cannot miss Graham Ibbeson's bronze sculpture 'The Spirit of the Crusade' in the car park of a local supermarket. Turn left from the shopping centre and you find 'Ellen Hall' and 'Wilkinson Hall' flats across the way, the Town Hall where it all started with its commemoration plaques, and slightly further on the Jarrow Crusaders public house. Flick through your A to Z and you will discover Riley Street and Crusade Walk not five minutes from where you are. In Jarrow, landscape and memory have fused together just as the red hot rivets once fastened great sheets of steel in Palmer's Yard.

Conclusion

The Jarrow Crusade for a New Generation

'Gi-ro, gi-ro, to work we cannot go,
Sign on at ten, back home again, gi-ro, gi-ro.'
Chanted on the Jarrow 86 march.[1]

'Who sows misery, reaps anger.'
Slogan of the French unemployed during 1997-98 protests.[2]

Does the Jarrow Crusade still have anything to offer? Recycled hundreds of times through a multitude of media, it is tempting to think that it is exhausted and bears no relevance to the younger generation.

It is easy to dismiss the Jarrow Crusade as the British Establishment's pet protest. They patronized it on its way down to London, were pleased at its meekness and non-political stance, and have celebrated this ever since. The Labour Party leaders, old and 'New', the trade union bureaucracy, the British state through the educational system and the BBC, local councils and leisure industries, even big corporations like McDonalds and Morrisons, continue to nurture this image of the Crusade. Social historian Robert Colls observed that the 'Jarrow banner was a plain statement of appeasement' to the Conservatives.[3] It has become a mascot, like Paddy the dog eating out of a silver tureen, given special treatment to trivialise and obscure the truth about the Crusade and about the past more generally. The Jarrow Crusade is part of a usable past approved of by the institutions of the British state.

If the Jarrow Crusade is a legend, then there are some distinctively modern features to it. One indication of this is that the Crusade is being turned into a commodity in a globalised process of commercialisation. The internet has rapidly accelerated this. Nothing symbolised this phenomenon more graphically that when Cornelius Whalen, attending the unveiling of the 'Spirit of the Crusade' sculpture at Morrisons in Jarrow, was pictured with a badge bearing the Morrisons' logo. For some time now corporations have been obsessed about branding, and here was a marketing strategist's dream come true. We should not underestimate the continued usefulness of mythology for modern capitalism as a means of masking antagonisms of, in this instance, class. Thus, symbolically transcending the class divide, the multi-millionaire supermarket tycoon could clasp the hand of the ageing Crusader who was surviving on his state pension and living in a council house.

Alongside the Angel of the North and Gateshead's Baltic Centre, the Jarrow Crusade is used to market the north-east region. Read the official websites and the tourist information about the region, visit its museums and you will realise just how important the Jarrow Crusade has become in selling the region. At the time of writing, there were exhibitions in Bede's World museum and the South Shields Museum and Art Gallery about the Crusade. Such use of the Crusade is connected to the growth of leisure and heritage industries. There is nothing inherently wrong with investigating the past through these media. The problem arises if the form distorts the content and, in the desire to have a marketable past, uncomfortable truths are suppressed. At the same time, some have consciously sought to deploy the newer post-industrial symbolism of the Angel and the Baltic as an alternative to the Crusade and representations of the region's industrial past (and present). That is why it would be wrong to dismiss the Crusade.

The Jarrow Crusade, as we understand it today, requires demystification. Take the most widespread assertion that it was a crusade and not a hunger march. After moment's serious reflection, this assertion collapses. The crusades are an unfortunate historical analogy at the best of times. Christian and heroic mythology have not entirely obscured the brutal historical reality of these barbaric attacks on a more sophisticated, if stagnating, Islamic civilisation. But October 1936 was the worst time to adopt such rhetoric given the metaphor of the crusade as a central to Franco's propaganda. The Spanish nationalists sought to drive out and exterminate their enemies in 1936 just as crusaders had expelled Moors and Jews in the Catholic kings' 'reconquest' of Spain completed in 1492. Perhaps conscious of this, the *Evening Chronicle* tended to prefer the term 'pilgrimage', which conveyed David Riley's intended meaning more precisely. The march marshal's insistence on the term crusade, however, has not registered with stubborn Jarrow folk who by habit refer to the 'Jarrow march' or simply 'the march'.

Another aspect of the legend is what might be called the myth of universal support. The reception of the Crusade along the route was not, as is often suggested, uniformly good. In places such as Chester-le-Street, Wakefield, Ripon, Northallerton and Darlington there was less than an enthusiastic welcome from all or the food and sleeping arrangements left something to be desired. Likewise, the newspapers provided less than universal support. Whilst the press were generally sympathetic, this was on their terms and there was a minority of newspapers that condemned the march. The support for the Crusade could not match that achieved by the National Hunger March as measured by the numbers attending the reception demonstration in Hyde Park on 8 November. In terms of the march funds, despite the generosity of individuals, the Crusade would have struggled without the contributions of the Co-operative movement.

To underline the need to demystify the Crusade, certain inconsistencies exist between the Crusade legend and Crusaders' reminiscences. The common themes of that oral testimony emerge as being the food, the holiday feeling, the absence of politics, the good receptions along the route and the failure of the march. To a certain extent these testimonies reflect an internalisation of the language of the march leaders, but on some counts they do not. Whilst the myth was constructed and reconstructed from the shared agenda of the march leaders and newspapers, the marchers' views disclose much about the experience of everyday life in Jarrow. It would be wrong to see the concentration on food as simply a failure to remember more significant aspects of the march or a trick of memory emphasising the trivial. In the context of long-term unemployment, this tells us how deeply ingrained the hunger of the interwar period was for the people of Jarrow.[4] The most glaring discrepancy between these interviews and the official legend was the failure of the Crusade. Whereas other have hailed the Crusade as a success, the rank and file marchers rarely if ever made such a claim.

The question of identity provides a clue to why this should be so. The Jarrow Crusade has been remoulded for the purposes of local or even national identity, in a way that ignores the politics of its leaders and stresses its consensual and even classless character. It was not an essentially English march, despite its rhetoric and the appeal to the respectability of the Anglican Church. The larger part of the marchers were of Scottish and Irish descent. The framework of identity can provide mistaken assumptions at the regional level as well. While this book was being written, the Jarrow Crusade was even drawn into the 2004 Referendum on the proposed North-East Assembly, when some of those in favour argued that Jarrow was victim of a distant London-based government. This is a distorted view of what happened. In fact *local* plutocrats and MPs – Runciman, the Middlesbrough steel barons, Ramsay MacDonald, the Bishop of Durham – played the decisive roles. Indeed, the Crusaders commented how at home they felt in the strongly working-class East End of London, whereas their reception in parts of the North East was distinctly lukewarm.

Such emphasis on identity has obscured the questions of class and politics. The world of the 1930s, as today, was one of extremes of wealth and poverty. The Jarrow Crusade was inescapably a working-class protest and stands in a tradition of popular radicalism. Its leaders were left-wing firebrands, although the claim to be above politics disguised this. During the course of the Crusade, the march leaders firmly stuck to their non-political stance and their alliance with local Tories. However, the mayor had imposed this approach upon them, and they abandoned these failed tactics as soon as they returned from London. Indeed, the 'four laddies' moved further to the left in the aftermath of the Crusade. They were expelled from the Labour Party and proposed a second march more than once. In their efforts to build a left alternative to Labour, they had considerable support within Jarrow but not enough to overturn the local Labour Party. As regards Ellen Wilkinson, she reluctantly accepted the non-political position out of respect for David Riley and the decision of the council. She had privately argued against it and her speeches on the Crusade – though she was careful not to score party political points – were hardly apolitical given their radically anti-capitalist character. As she observed shortly after the Crusade:

> To say foreign politics does not matter to Jarrow is the silliest assertion when one realises that Jarrow is the meeting point of the rationalisation of the two great world industries, shipping and iron and steel.[5]

The non-political stance may have been an aspiration; it was not a reality. Political parties at the local level played a crucial role in providing support for the Crusade. Local Conservative support came at the price of an exaggerated respectability and anti-communism. The march was also political in a more profound sense, given that it was pitted against the power of the state: not only the police surveillance and the hostility of the Government but also the denial of benefits to marchers. 'No to politics' therefore was a myth, a politically expedient fiction, and Jarrow's experience in this regard cannot be held up as a model for current protest.

To anticipate an obvious criticism, all this is not to replace one myth with another – more left wing – myth. The postmodern approach, with its scepticism and relativism, denies the possibility of appealing to historical reality or truth. Rejecting postmodernism, the method employed in these pages has identified and retraced the legend of the Crusade to its sources in the march leaders' pronouncements, the embedded journalists and *The Town that Was Murdered*. These are the well-springs of the myth that have revitalised each stranger who has sought knowledge of the Crusade. The growth of legend over time can also be tracked through the representations of the Crusade. We discover that rather than being an ephemeral and purely discursive phenomenon, the legend has a real physical dimension: a chronological and geographical pattern of dispersal and implantation. After a long period of general silence and folk memory concentrated in Jarrow, from 1976 onwards the Crusade legend became institutionally consolidated and national in its scope. By the 1990s, it entered a new epoch in which its reach was becoming truly global. By analysing a fuller range of sources my aim has been to restore the richness and complexity of the Jarrow Crusade as a historical event. In this way, it has, I hope, been possible to break the circle of the myth where every new representation of the Crusade took these original sources of the myth as their starting point. To do so is to challenge various misconceptions associated with the legend. This takes us closer to the reality of the Crusade.

This approach also allows us to understand the uses to which the Crusade has been put. It exposes the shallowness of the claims that institutions such as the Labour Party, the TUC or the British state (through the Church of England, the BBC, or the education system) have over the Crusade. These institutions have formed long-standing and multiple associations with the Crusade. These powerful symbolic and emotional bonds suggest support for the march that was not in reality forthcoming in 1936. These myths of institutional support demonstrate the vested interests in perpetuating a distorted understanding of this event. Selective nostalgia for protest allows such institutions to act as arbiters of what constitutes legitimate protest in the past and present. It is an irony of history that the same institutions simultaneously celebrate the Crusade and discourage present day protests. New Labour and the BBC serve as good illustrations of this point. The New Labour Government has severely curtailed the right to protest and other civil liberties, whilst it has reveled when opportune in its connections with the Crusade.[6] The occasion for New Labour's Jarrow nostalgia was when the People's Fuel Lobby claimed in autumn 2000 to be following the footsteps (or 4X4 tyre tracks!) of the Crusade. Voices from Jarrow, including Con Whalen, ridiculed the idea and Tony Blair condemned the comparison in the Commons. Perhaps, this was an opportunistic exception to New Labour's generalised amnesia. It remains to be seen what their response will be to the seventieth anniversary coming up in 2006. The BBC for its part has repeatedly recalled the legend of the Crusade, whilst giving little voice to present day protests such as mass domestic opposition to the war in Iraq.[7] A proper understanding of the Crusade entails a critical reflection upon the institutions that seek to use the Crusade. It means contesting their right to distort our pasts.

The Jarrow Crusade highlights something wider about the shaping of public awareness of history in Britain. In an effort to forget unnerving truths and to fashion British or English national identity, soothing figures or episodes reinforce widespread misconceptions about the past. For that period, the Battle of Britain, Churchill and the Jarrow Crusade displace the Blackshirts, communist-led hunger marches, the abdication and appeasement.

Sometimes justification of these distortions is made explicit through the argument that social cohesion is premised on forging a common national identity. This requires a shared and usable past, a past as the BBC History mission statement puts it, to 'reflect, celebrate and anticipate'. The Jarrow Crusade can only form part of this national celebratory past in distorted form. As Eric Hobsbawm has observed, with the accelerating and unsettling processes of global change come greater efforts to create a secure refuge in an over-hyped sense of collective identity.[8] Thus a Labour Government and public historians now try to revise history so as to reclaim the supposed glories, benevolence or good intentions of the British Empire.[9] Like Home Office surgeons forcibly feeding a suffragette by , Simon Schama or Niall Ferguson drive a tube down our gullet and pump in the national mystique. History is taken out of the realm of rational debate and put into the arena of identity and belonging, of blood and soil. Not only are we being sold myths, we are being told simultaneously that these myths constitute who we are.

The celebratory aspect of heritage and the consensual interpretations of the Crusade underestimate the deep class divisions of Britain in the 1930s and the Crusaders' awareness of this. The physical landscape of the North East attests to these cleavages. Whilst images of the Crusade invite us to the North East, the streets in which the Crusaders lived have been flattened in slum clearance and the memory of these streets wiped from view. As for the other side of the class divide, we can visit the cathedrals, official residences, stately homes of the Crusaders' opponents in the North East. The contrast of the powerful and the powerless is apparent throughout the story of the Crusade. It is not a great exaggeration to characterise Labour and Conservative on Jarrow council as respectively the parties of the unemployed tenants and ratepaying landlords. The class divide stretched to knowledge and access to the truth. When one considers the closure of the shipyard or the fate of the steelworks, the folk of Jarrow were kept in the dark about the decisions that were affecting their lives.

The memory of the 1930s has informed contemporary politics in a special way. In particular, appeasement has become a crucial point of political reference for the discussion of international crises. The Jarrow Crusade acted as a snapshot of British attitudes on this question. There were those who were publicly critical of the policy such as Ellen Wilkinson and the Bishop of Durham. The appeasers we discover along the route of the Jarrow Crusade were wholly different from the caricature recent governments draw each time it seeks to justify war or discredit the anti-war movement. The appeasers were not a uniform group. Those (like Runciman, Baldwin and Chamberlain) opted for it as a result of a calculation of British imperial commitments and the desire to maintain great power status. Others (like Edward VIII, Grattan-Doyle and Lord Londonderry) were sympathetic to Nazism and Hitler's Germany. Appeasement had a diplomatic dimension, as with Sir Walter Runciman and his mission to Germany, and an economic dimension exemplified by the international steel cartel with amongst others, Nazi Germany. This cartel set the international context for the failure of the proposal for a steelworks in Jarrow. Appeasement understood in this way was exclusively a phenomenon within the British ruling class and the political elite. This is an uncomfortable truth. Appeasement cannot be meaningfully stretched to others that the Crusade encountered. It cannot sensibly include pacifists – like Dick Sheppard, who proposed that a group of human shields should stand between the lines during the Spanish Civil War. Pacifism had existed during the First World War and it simply did not weigh in the balance of decision-making for the British Government. Neither can appeasement include those anti-imperialists – and Ellen Wilkinson and several hunger marchers were in this camp – who were against a repeat of the First World War but who were willing to support the Spanish Republican war effort. Some were even prepared to fight and die for the anti-fascist cause in Spain, while their Government allowed Spanish and then Czech democracy to fall.

Although care must be taken in generalising from this event, the Jarrow Crusade does suggest a number of broader connections. Fresh evidence about the relationship between Edward VIII and the unemployed undermines the historical tendency to present the abdication as a trivial event, as a romantic drama rather than a political crisis. Constitutional difficulties could have quite rapidly become enmeshed with the social question. Indeed, this was the strategy of the leaders of the NUWM, and after his trip to South Wales Edward VIII knew very well that he could mobilise sympathy and anti-Baldwin feeling on the question of unemployment. The Crusade, which was conceived of as a non-political event appealing to all, not only exposed the sharp inequalities of wealth and power but also the fact that class interests shaped the character of the support that it received. Ruling-class, establishment and Conservative support was short-lived, always conditional and ultimately duplicitous. These supporters followed their own agendas, sometimes using the Crusade as a vehicle for their internal wrangles. It could not really be otherwise. This is bad news for those who see consensus and a nation at ease with itself, citing the acts of patrician generosity to support this. Another striking aspect of Jarrow's story is that these structures of wealth and power have reproduced themselves since and were present in the town decades later with the return of plant closures and mass unemployment.

Viewed in a wider perspective, the Jarrow Crusade was part of a decisive moment of truth in world history. For a spell, between February 1934 and May 1937, the momentum of events turned against reaction. Fascism, which had scored victories in Italy, Germany and Austria, was stalled in France, Britain and Spain. The mass organisations of the working class, devastated by the slump, made historic if temporary gains, with waves of unionisation in countries such as the United States and France. The epitome of this new militancy was the occupation tactic. In Britain, a recovery of working-class confidence after the demoralisation that followed the General Strike was tentative but sustained. It expressed itself in political campaigns like support for Republican Spain or the hunger marches, in trade union terms through rank-and-file organisations on the buses and in the aircraft industry as well as in the battle against company unionism in the coalfields. This situation coloured the Jarrow Crusade and its participants in many ways: in the threat of a stay-in at the House of Commons and in the attempt to create a new socialist party in Jarrow. More widely it reflected itself in those who volunteered for Spain, in the Tyneside apprentices' strikes of the following years, and in the Jarrow riot of 1939. Crucially the direction of European history was decided on the battlefronts of Spain. Starved of foreign policy success, the cracks in the fascist regimes would begin to show. That momentum shifted in 1937-8 and working-class people and the left were faced with the non-choice of appeasement or rearmament: that is suing for peace with fascist powers or a war for empire.

***

With large demonstrations against war and against the G8 in recent times, the history of dissent is of renewed interest. The question is what does Jarrow have to offer this new generation of protesters? In its own ways the Jarrow Crusade confronted the same system – though one that has evolved somewhat – and similar tactical choices that protesters face today. Although there is a temptation to claim everything is new about the anti-capitalist movement, a tradition of protest connects the Jarrow Crusaders, the blind marchers and the hunger marchers with the present and for that matter those who fought the fascists in Spain, South Shields or the East End of London. In some ways the Jarrow Crusade has a strikingly contemporary feel. As war approached and the Depression lingered, people were thinking globally and acting locally.

Then, as today, the world seems to be set on a course of mass hunger and war. Power is exercised anonymously through organisations known by their acronyms. The initials change – from EIC (European Iron Cartel), BISF, BIDC, NSS to IMF, WTO, EU, NATO – but the distance between the people and the real exercise power remains as wide as ever. The individuals who hide behind the insignia remain in relative anonymity, their actions closeted in a secretive world and only history, as with Jarrow, will be able to reveal fully their complicity and deceit. Then, as now, the powerful disguise brutal realities with neutral – or even pleasant-sounding – euphemisms.[10] Rationalisation, like globalisation in the 1990s, was the prevailing dogma through which economic decision-makers interpreted policy. Then the buzz-words for the unspeakable act that was done to Jarrow were rationalisation, self-pruning and sterilisation. Ellen Wilkinson, Jarrow's MP, could not see the rationality in 'murdering' the town.

Facelessness abetted by official and corporate secrecy render the establishment of responsibility for decision-making difficult. Only hindsight and the release of public records after 30 years or more allow fuller insights. As part of the process of writing this book, the accelerated release of two files of Home Office documents was secured. They were not due for open public scrutiny until 2036. Other documents were selected for accelerated release at the same time. Amongst these documents, a number of folders had been destroyed: their only record is red biro comment registering their obliteration. The lack of transparency shows the stunted nature of the democratic process over the most vital decisions affecting our lives, then as now. Amongst this batch of documents there were other embarrassing truths: those suspected of pro-German sympathy in the event of a German invasion, notably the Duke of Bedford and close friends of the Duke of Windsor, and Churchill's desire to force unemployed marching miners back to South Wales in 1927.

Secrecy prevented public accountability and sanctioned plausible denial. It was within the power of government to save Jarrow. Sir John Jarvis was certainly of this opinion. Writing to Neville Chamberlain, he suggested that a mere word from the Prime Minister to the British Iron and Steel Federation 'would do the trick'.[11] The President of the Board of Trade's infamous injunction to Jarrow to find its own salvation rested on the principle that the Government should not interfere in the workings of the market, or as Margaret Thatcher put it at the time that Jarrow's steelworks was closing the 1980s, 'You cannot buck the market'. The invisible hand of the market absolved decision-makers of responsibility for their actions. On Runciman's part, it was the height of hypocrisy to rely on this argument in an industry to which the Government afforded special import duties and powers of price fixing. The Government and the Bank of England had very considerable leverage because of this, and the opposition of particular steel interests to the Jarrow plan even antagonised other steel barons precisely because it put their special treatment on public view. It was not market forces that Runciman was unwilling to interfere with but the prerogatives of big business. In a sense as a great shipping magnate, they were his own prerogatives too. Whereas the organisers insisted the Crusade was non-political, in the corridors of Whitehall and the boardroom of industry, power politics was determining the fate of thousands back in Jarrow.

J.B. Priestley highlighted this shortcoming in British democracy's dealings with Jarrow. It is what the anti-globalisation movement today calls the 'democratic deficit':

> A stranger from a distant civilisation, observing the condition of the place and its people, would have arrived at once at the conclusion that Jarrow had deeply offended some celestial emperor of the island and was now being punished. He would never believe us if we told him that in theory this town was as good as any other and that its inhabitants were not criminals but citizens with votes. The only cheerful sight I saw there was a game of Follow-

my-leader that was being played by seven small children. But what leader can the rest of them follow?[12]

What leader, indeed? Didn't Ellen Wilkinson fill the role that Priestley identified as so pressing for Jarrow? The same passion that put her at the side of her constituents marching to London for work also put her at the side of German or Spanish workers under the iron heel of fascism. In different ways, for Ellen Wilkinson, they were all victims of the system. Whilst her pamphlet *Terror in Germany* concentrated on the torture cellars of the Nazis, her book *Why Fascism?* proved that a sophisticated understanding and a keen intellect lay behind her great passion. There is a certain nostalgia for Ellen Wilkinson, especially in the Labour Party, as a naïve, moralistic and idealistic campaigner who was manipulated by the men in her life. She was more than a gadfly flitting from one issue to another, because she had a rounded socialist understanding of the world. She connected together her different 'causes' and saw their solution in the overthrow of capitalism.

Ellen Wilkinson's book *Why War?* written in 1934 with her refugee friend Edward Conze is a classic anti-war tract with contemporary relevance, for it addresses many of the arguments that exist in the anti-war movement today. She observed the cynicism of a government taking its people into war for the economic interests of the rich through 'a suitable propaganda, the right excuse at the [right] psychological moment'. She noted contemptuously how in 1924 party officials justified the bombing of Iraq during the first Labour Government in terms little different from the Tories. Talking of the cost of the 1914-18 war, she observed the distorted priorities of the world:

> Such a sum would have re-housed Europe in garden cities, would have paid for electrification of the entire continent, abolished preventable disease, given a chance of health and straight limbs to a new generation of children. Thirty six thousand millions intelligently spent could have re-equipped Europe to the standard worthy of a scientific

century. It could have irrigated the Sahara and made the desert into a fertile land.[13]

She linked the permanent state of war in the world to the nature of capitalism and its imperialist character. She discussed the range of anti-war opinion: pacifists, those who looked to the League of Nations, and those who were anti-imperialists. She asked a question of the League of Nations that is as pertinent today to the Security Council of the United Nations – how can imperialist designs be held in check by an organisation whose membership was imperialist statesmen? She noted that the effectiveness of the League only covered minor disputes. In cases that directly affected the interests of the major powers, the League 'not only broke down but was humiliated'.[14]

Writing decades before debt campaigner Susan George, Ellen Wilkinson also perceptively addressed imperialism's relationship to debt, development and global poverty:

> We said that finance-capital consists of a combination of industrial and banking capital – industrialists taking part in banking and bankers taking part in industry. The banks, as organs of finance-capital, have a surplus of money which they lend to 'backward' governments. They not only demand very high interest, but since they are combined with industrialists through interlocking directorates, they demand concessions as a condition of their loans. In other words, they stipulate the forms that loans will take – railways, harbours, etc. The Government, suitably bribed, allows its country to be 'developed', railways to be built, and for these loans the natural resources of the country stand pledged. Even where a country is already groaning under the burden of debt, if its natural resources (or geographical position) are valuable, corrupt politicians are sometimes induced to accept bigger loans, only a small part of which is really used for the ostensible purpose for which they were

borrowed – especially when the capitalists are out for 'control'.[15]

Many of the complaints of the critics of the World Trade Organisation or the G8 are here: 'briberisation', debt as a weapon of control, the power of big business and the plundering of the world's resources.[16] In the same book, she connected capitalism's drive to war with its failure to provide work for all. She noted how unemployment is a hated part of the experience of working-class life. As she and Edward Conze put it:

> Unemployment on the scale of the nineteen-thirties is a double nuisance to capitalism. The unemployed not only yield no profit, but they must be provided with some sort of subsistence out of the existing profits. They form in themselves a discontented mass. More serious from the capitalist point of view, they are a vivid object lesson in the failure of capitalism as a system, and form the best argument for anti-capitalist propaganda.[17]

With the Crusade as the principal illustration, this hatred of unemployment has become deeply embedded in the culture of the North East. The dole was a key theme of Alex Glasgow's songs not only in its 1930s incarnation but also in its ugly, unheralded return from the late 1960s onwards. Born in Gateshead, the son of a miner, Alex Glasgow raised the alarm in his song 'The Magic Million' when the jobless total breached that number. In a sense we live with the long-term corrosive effects of mass unemployment on working-class communities. Behind Conservative and New Labour Governments' claims to have conquered mass unemployment have been measures of even greater social control to combat its effects: Anti-Social Behaviour Orders (ASBOs), more prisons and more police with greater powers. In contrast, the hunger marches were a crucial part of the history of civil liberties in this country. The National Council of Civil Liberties was established because of the repression of the unemployment movement in the 1930s, and the Citizens' Advice Bureau movement borrowed from the advice work done by the NUWM and others.

In the first instance, the memory of the Jarrow Crusade survived because of family connections. Second and third generations transmit the stories with pride. Through this oral tradition, the fables of the Crusade have become part of the local folklore – sometimes distinct from what might be termed the official legend. The audience of the children and grandchildren of Crusaders transcends Jarrow or even Tyneside, reaching a national and international audience. Even where they do not directly address the Crusade through their work, as Peter Flannery has, Crusader family members in the public eye make known their family connections: John 'Mr Music' Miles, folk singer Norma Waterson, journalist Terry Kelly and poet Tom Kelly. It is an indicator of just how much talent goes to waste at times of mass unemployment. But the return of unemployment has compounded this desire to remember. Three marchers on the Jarrow 86 protest – John Badger, William Orr and Wayne Scott – had family connections with the original Crusade. Wayne, who had been unemployed for six months, observed, 'I was just walking in the footsteps of my grandfather, but I wasn't just copying. I believe very strongly in the cause we are fighting'.[18]

By 1975 history had turned full circle. At a tube works, which had boasted 'we bring jobs to Jarrow', the threat of closure led to a workers' occupation. On 10 May, a Right to Work conference took place in the Labour Club in Jarrow in its support. The leaflet produced for the occasion stated that there would be 'no more Jarrow marches', preferring more direct tactics to fight job losses.[19] With the high tide of militancy of the early 1970s there were a number of workplace occupations to prevent closure, the most famous of which were the Upper Clyde Shipbuilders and Fisher-Bendix of Kirby on Merseyside. Yet these events have been forgotten. The memory of the Crusade is stronger than that of other more militant, more successful, methods of combating job losses because it has the powerful institutional backing of the trade unions and the Labour Party. The coincidence of the return of mass unemployment and the fortieth anniversary of the Crusade in 1976 marked the changeover when commemoration displaced the forgetting of the march.

In 1979, Magaret Thatcher came to power with a plan drawn up by Nicholas Ridley to destroy the power of the unions. One by one unions were to be defeated in industrial conflict. The first in the firing line were the steelworkers, who were defeated in 1980. By the early 1980s, the militancy of the previous decade had gone, and the heartache of closure returned to Jarrow 50 years after the Crusade. British Steel announced in November 1984 the closure of the same rolling mill whose opening Sir John Jarvis had trumpeted at the Crusade's public meeting in London in 1936. The plant, which employed 250 steel workers finally shut on 25 July 1986, making Jarrow once again the borough with the highest unemployment in the country.[20]

At the moment when the public was rediscovering the Jarrow Crusade, Alex Glasgow wrote a play *Whistling at the Milestones* (1977). It sought to illustrate the way in which it is in the interests of ordinary people to challenge the legend of the Crusade and learn from its history. It took the form of Mr Adams, the veteran Crusader, telling his grandson Hughie the story of the march. Eventually, the moral of his grandfather's account dawned on Hughie: the youngster's generation should not allow politicians to get away with the injustice of unemployment as their forefathers' generation had.[21] It was a rallying call. Alex Glasgow intended *Whistling at the Milestones* to identify an important truth about defeated social struggles.[22] Defeat potentially bears within it the germ of future conquests. This play asserted that it is wrong to say, as those who wish to present a consensual 1930s say, that the Jarrow Crusade was a success. It was emphatically defeated, and Crusaders repeatedly pointed this out. But social conflict is a process. Reassessing strategies and adopting more effective methods has always been an intrinsic part of social movements. So too has been the unlearning of those insights as history is written from the perspective of our rulers. The history of the Jarrow Crusade can assist this process of learning from defeat. The consequence, even the function, of the myth in the hands of New Labour or the heritage industry is to prevent this happening.

The defeat of the Jarrow Crusade bore the potential for postponed victory in a second sense. The bitter struggles of the 1930s informed the post-war reforms of reconstruction: unemployment provision, regional policy, the National Health Service and the governmental commitment to full employment. For those inspired to join protest against war or Third World debt or environmental destruction, it is tempting to reject the past, its ideas and its defeats. That institutions like the Labour Party or the BBC have invested so much in the making of the legend of the Jarrow Crusade tells us just how important the legacy of yesterday's protests is for today. For those who seek identity in events such as the Jarrow Crusade for family, working-class, or regional reasons should be aware that these events were much less straightforward than the myth of national consensus would have us believe. However, uncovering the rich history of 1936 and the politics of Ellen Wilkinson can give us some insights into the issues, debates and protests of today.

Appendix:
Who Murdered the Jarrow Steelworks Project?

The most ambitious aspect of Sir John Jarvis's plans for Jarrow was the attempt to attract industry in the shape of a modern steelworks. He succeeded in assembling a syndicate of investors for a three to four million pound Bessemer blast furnace and rolling mill on the Palmer's site. The project took shape in 1934 but there were a number of formidable obstacles. Early in March 1935, Sir John wrote a letter to the Prime Minister Ramsay MacDonald appealing to his 'very human heart' and on behalf of 'the people of Durham whom you love so well'. Sir John wanted the Prime Minister to intervene in order to diffuse the opposition of Sir Andrew Duncan and the BISF. The steelworks would make his ship-breaking scheme a success and create an environment in which new industries could flourish in Jarrow. Without the steelworks all would flounder. His plan would bring full employment to the impoverished town but without the steelworks 'the whole edifice of my dreams will topple in ruins!'[1]

A few days later three representatives of big capital – Sir Horace Wilson, Chief Industrial Adviser to the Government, Sir Bruce Gardiner, of the Bankers Industrial Development, and Sir Andrew Duncan, the Chair of the British Iron and Steel Federation – discussed the matter before advising the Prime Minister on a reply. They had seen the consultant's report which concluded that the Jarrow proposal would be profitable.[2] They were more interested in how this would impact on their overriding objective: the rationalisation of the steel industry. Their goal therefore was how to use the possibility of a new plant to get greater co-operation, even amalgamation, amongst the steel producers of the North East. They used the fact that Brassert, the consultant, had not considered which would be the optimum site across the whole of the North East, instead looking only at the viability of Jarrow. They also countered Sir John's claim that the BISF and Sir Andrew were not blocking and could not block money for the Jarrow steelworks. Throughout this sorry saga the BISF and the Government maintained that they were entirely innocent and that Sir John, Ellen Wilkinson and Jarrow supporters falsely and ridiculously accused the BISF. For example in the Commons debate, Peat, the Conservative MP for Darlington, presented a lurid caricature of Ellen Wilkinson and Sir John's position,

> The suggestion has been made that the British Iron and Steel Federation, like some sinister octopus, has its tentacles around the neck of any new enterprise and that it strangles that enterprise at birth. Nothing is more false and foolish than that statement.[3]

Those who were deciding Jarrow's future were able to hide behind the secrecy of Whitehall and the boardroom, and present a partial and distorted version of the facts. Their tactic of concealment and bluff relied on the fact that the interaction of the Government, Sir Andrew Duncan and in particular the North East Coast Committee of the BISF was largely secret and that whilst they did not directly block (that is, withhold) money directly, they did so indirectly because without their assent no bank or stock-broking firm would approve such an investment. The statements of Sir Walter, Sir Andrew and the BISF were a script to stick to. The secrecy and the unconvincing public position invited suspicion and speculation and the allegations were substantially correct. The secrecy was such that the President of the Board of Trade, Sir Walter Runciman, would not reveal what he knew to Jarrow's sitting MP, W.G. Pearson, in October 1935, a fellow supporter of the National Government. Small wonder Pearson lost his seat within a month and the Conservatives have never won the Jarrow constituency since.[4]

When challenged, the President of the Board of Trade warned Tyne Improvement Commissioners against allegations that could not be substantiated and told them that Sir Andrew and the BISF denied blocking the scheme. A confidential note of a meeting between Runciman and Sir Andrew Duncan reveals the latter's manoeuvring. He had suggested to Brassert that Shroeders, the investment bank, that was prepared to pour money into the project, 'might appreciate' his 'qualifications' about Jarrow.[5] Sir Andrew had then been in touch with other north-east steel producers and got their consent for a second Brassert report that would consider the optimum site for the North East as a whole. This would certainly buy time and undermine the first report. His goal was to secure the cooperation of north-east producers for a new plant for which there was clearly enough demand. Sir Andrew was working for a position where new entrants could not get finance without consulting the BISF. Therefore public statements that the BISF could not block and was not blocking the Jarrow scheme were dishonest. Whilst this was going on behind the scenes, Sir John Jarvis was announcing to the press in the summer of 1935 that new work would soon be brought to Jarrow, perhaps hoping to force the hand of the Government.[6]

How the BISF would react to the second Brassert report would therefore be decisive. Sir Andrew Duncan planned to meet the North East Coast Committee members after its publication. There were three steel producers in the North East: Dorman Long, Cargo Fleet (of which South Durham was a subsidiary), both on the Tees, and Consett Iron Company near the Tyne. For some time the banks, which because of company indebtedness had a stake in iron and steel, and the Government had wanted rationalisation in the industry. Under the auspices of Barclays, Dorman Long and Bolchow Vaughan merged in 1929. In 1932 the Import Duties Act broke with free trade and established tariffs for iron and steel amongst other industries. The BISF was established to assist this process of merger and cartelisation in conditions of a protected market. Ellen Wilkinson described this as 'the pretty little garden arranged for them by the President of the Board of Trade'.[7] Here was a graphic illustration of the closer threefold relationship that had emerged between finance, industry and the state. The world of British manufacturing supremacy, great industrial pioneers and family firms had passed and had been replaced by competition between industrial powers with global empires for markets, raw materials and investment opportunities. Many like Ellen Wilkinson saw in this the cause of the drive to world war.

In the meantime, Sir John Jarvis mobilised opinion behind his project: Lord Midleton visited the President of the Board of Trade, Sir John telegrammed both Baldwin and Runciman, the Commissioner of the Special Areas Malcolm Stewart continued to lobby for Jarrow, as did the syndicate's stockbrokers Laurence, Keen and Gardner. The second report came out around the time of the November general election, so was very politically sensitive. It was at this moment that Sir Andrew seemed to favour Jarrow over other possibilities so long as he could secure cooperation from other BISF members in the North East. He contacted George of Consett Iron Company, the leader of the North East Committee, to this effect. Both were hopeful of Jarrow's prospects. This was the first indication that Sir Andrew was campaigning for Jarrow.[8] In the run up to the election, the syndicate's stockbrokers again tried to exert pressure on the Government. Unemployment in the depressed areas had become an important electoral issue and on 12 November the Prime Minister had spoken in Newcastle on this topic. Arnold-Forster, acting for the syndicate, pointed out that the option that had been purchased on the Palmer's site expired within three weeks and that the syndicate had waited a year now. In an implicit threat, he reflected that they had done nothing to embarrass the Government. If the option expired, the site would in all likelihood be sold off in parts and the steelworks would be lost for good.[9] If publicised this would be highly controversial, and potentially damaging to the Government.

When the meeting of the North East Coast Committee of the BISF took place in early December 1935, objections to the principle of a new plant were dropped but MacQuisten of Cargo Fleet Company proposed a Cleveland site, Arthur Dorman proposed

Clarence, near Middlesbrough, and George of Consett argued for Jarrow. Sir Andrew said that if the Teesside members did not cooperate, he would support Consett's Jarrow option. The Teesside members however were able to undo the resolution of Sir Andrew, who agreed to a third Brassert report on the Teesside sites by 19 December. One of the other sites would only be chosen if it was substantially better than Jarrow.[10] A further meeting of Sir Andrew and three north-east steel producers took place on 10 January 1936. Sir Andrew was 'fairly certain' that the Jarrow plan would go ahead and the BID was contacted for the finance. The only snag was that Lord Greenwood on behalf of Dorman Long had to wait for a decision from his board, but this was presented as a mere formality in Sir Horace Wilson's report of the meeting.[11]

The speech of Viscount Furness at the annual general meeting of the South Durham Steel and Iron Company should have alerted all concerned to the possibility of a Teesside veto. Marmaduke Furness had inherited shipbuilding, iron and steel and coal concerns from his father Sir Steven William Furness (1872-1914), who was in some ways in the mould of Charles Palmer as a major employer and Liberal MP (1910-14 for Hartlepool). It would be tempting to think that both family empires foundered because the roulette of inherited wealth could not guarantee that the Victorian entrepreneurs would produce talented scions. But by the 1920s the entire family ownership model looked antiquated and the profits of the heyday of British heavy industry had passed. Furness's speech warned against 'unwarranted political dictation or interference'.[12] This was a clear threat to veto the Jarrow project.

With the support of the BISF now seemingly forthcoming, the syndicate used their option to buy the site from Thomas Ward Ltd. On 21 January 1936 the press declared the steelworks now certain and the £4 million investment was lined up. Most importantly, to the delight of the whole of Jarrow, 2,500 to 3,000 would be employed in the blast furnace and rolling mill when construction was complete in two years' time. Jarrow would be saved and, with the ancillary industries, there would be as many jobs as there had been at Palmer's in normal times. For several months Jarrow basked in this luminescent but false dawn. Five months of optimism in Jarrow were cruelly and dramatically cut short.

References

Introduction pages 1-20

1. Poetry of the Crusade – Tom Paulin, *The Invasion Handbook* (Faber and Faber: London, 2002) pp.103-104, Jarrow poem; Tom Pickard, *The Jarrow March* (Allison and Busby: London, 1982); Carol Rumens, 'Jarrow' in Andy Croft and Adrian Mitchell (eds), *Red Sky at Night: an Anthology of British Socialist Poetry* (Five Leaves: Nottingham, 2003), p.194; in Ellen Wilkinson's cuttings unpublished E.H. Rowe (of South Shields) 'Jarrow Crusaders' Epic Trek' (1936), John J. Harney, 'The Jarrow Marchers' in Dougan, *Jarrow March*, p.104; Ann Roberts an Australian wrote a poem based on a George Patterson painting of the Crusade, *Shields Gazette* 20 September 1986 and *South Tyneside Post*, 28 August 1986. For the drama of the Crusade - five plays, an opera and two musicals have dramatically reconstructed the Crusade. *Heads Held High*, written by Alan MacDonald of Brookside fame, was part of the Jarrow '86 commemoration. Drama lecturer and poet Tom Kelly wrote the play *Between Today and Yesterday* about the Crusade. Gateshead-born socialist folk singer, writer and poet Alex Glasgow wrote the first play about the Jarrow Crusade, *Whistling at the Milestones* (1977). Ellen's old school in Ardwick, Manchester celebrated the centenary of her birth with a play *Red Ellen* (1991). Alex Ferguson's *A Woman's Walk* (2000) examines the experience of the women left back home during the Crusade. Rose Reeve's musical *Crusader* (2001) records the tale of the march and the life of Ellen Wilkinson. In 2004, Arthur McKenzie and David Whitaker wrote *Cuddy's Miles*, a second musical about the Crusade with John 'Mr Music' Miles, whose grandfather Cuddy Errington was a cook on the Crusade, supplying the music.

2. *Shields Gazette*, 29 August 1986.

3. Alan Price, 'Jarrow Song', Warner Brothers, released 25 May 1974. Alan Hull of the north-east folk group Lindisfarne also recorded a Crusade song called 'Marshal Riley's Army'. South Shields punks Angelic Upstarts paid tribute to the courage of the Crusade's wives in 'Jarrow Woman' on their

Last Tango in Moscow album. There was also a tribute album in 1986 called *Heads Held High*. It comprised songs from Tom Robinson, Billy Bragg, Heaven 17, Brendan Cocker and concerts took place in Jarrow, Sheffield, Leeds and London with entertainers including Andy Kershaw, Ben Elton and the Mekons.

4. Vincent Rea (ed.), *Jarrow: Impressions of a Town: an Exhibition in Celebration of the 50th Anniversary of the Jarrow Crusade* (Bede Gallery: Jarrow, 1986).

5. *Shields Gazette*, 15 December 1967.

6. Tom Pickard, *The Jarrow March* (Allison and Busby: London, 1982), p.115.

7. Rhodes Boyson, 'The shadow of failure behind Labour's Jarrow nostalgia', *Daily Telegraph*, 3 June 1981.

8. Quoted in the *Shields Gazette*, 4 November 1986 reporting on the *Nightline* programme on Tyne Tees on 3 November 1986.

9. Shields Gazette, 5 October 2001.

10. Others did not. David Riley's son (James) recalled very little story-telling about the march at home, although the march leaders remained friends and he remembers their visits.

11. Alan Plater, 'The drama of the North-East' in Robert Colls and Bill Lancaster (eds), *Geordies: Roots of Regionalism* (Edinburgh University Press: Edinburgh, 1992), pp.82-83.

12. An interview with John Miles about his grandfather, *Cuddy's Miles* and the Jarrow Crusade: http://www.britishtheatreguide.info/othersources/interviews/JohnMiles.htm.

13. *Shields Gazette*, 6 November 1996.

14. Ibid., 13 November 1996.

15. Michael Polley, 'The Long-Weekend revisited', *Literature and History*, 3rd series, vol.8, no.1, 1999, pp.74.

16. A.W. Purdue, 'The myth of the Jarrow march', *New Society*, 8 July 1982, pp.50-51; John Saville, 'Some random comments on the hunger marches of the 1930s', *North-West Labour History*, August, 1988, pp.39-45.

17. Richard Croucher, ' "Divisions in the movement": the National Unemployed Workers' Movement', in Geoff Andrews, Nina Fishman and Kevin Morgan (eds), *Opening the Books: Essays on the Social and Cultural History of the British Communist Party* (Pluto: London, 1995), p.24.

18. Ronald Blythe, *The Age of Illusion: England in the Twenties and Thirties, 1919-1940* (Phoenix: London, 2001); Noreen Branson and Margot

Heinemann, *Britain in the 1930s* (Weidenfeld and Nicolson: London, 1971); Ben Pimlott, *Labour and the Left in the 1930s* (Cambridge University Press: Cambridge, 1977).

19. John Stevenson and Chris Cook, *Britain in the Depression: Society and Politics 1929-39* (Longman: London, 1994), p.216.

20. Harry Harmer, 'Failure of the Communists: the National Unemployed Workers' Movement', in Andrew Thorpe (ed.), *The Failure of Political Extremism in Britain* (Exeter University Press: Exeter, 1988), p.45.

21. Andrew Thorpe, *The Longman Companion to Britain in the Era of the Two World Wars, 1914-45* (Longman: London, 1993), p.175.

22. Matt Perry, *Bread and Work: the Experience of Unemployment 1918-39* (Pluto: London, 2000), pp.113-124.

23. Eric Hobsbawm and Terence Ranger (eds), *The Invention of Tradition* (Cambridge University Press: Cambridge, 1983); Raphael Samuel and Paul Thompson (eds), *The Myths We Live By* (Routledge: London, 1990).

24. David Dougan, *History of North East Shipbuilding* (Allen and Unwin: London, 1968), p.221-22.

25. At a net cost of £1.33 million. (The BIDC was a financial holding company which had the participation of the Bank of England.) A. Slaven, 'Self-liquidation: the NSS Ltd. and the British Shipbuilders in the 1930s', in Sarah Palmer and Glyndwr William (eds), *Chartered and Uncharted Waters* (Trustees of the National Maritime Museum: London, 1982), pp.125-147.

26. Norman L. Middlemas, *British Shipbuilding Yards*, vol. 1: North-East Coast (Shield: Newcastle, 1993), pp.90-103. It was responsible for the first screw collier, the first roll armour plate ship, the first double bottom for water ballast. The yard uniquely undertook the entire process of production from iron ore to the finished article.

27. David Cummings, 'Marshall Riley's Army', in Valley Writers, *Monks, Miners and Moonshine: Northern History as it Should Have Been* (Valley Writers: Waterhouses, 2000), p.133; Pickard, *Jarrow March*, p.35; Robert Boothby MP, *New Economy* (Secker and Warburg: London, 1943) quoted in Michael Foot MP and Donald Bruce MP, *Who are the Patriots?* (Gollancz: London, 1949), p.89.

28. Dougan, *History*, pp.146-148.

29. Jim Cuthbert and Ken Smith, *Palmers of Jarrow 1851-1933* (Tyne Bridge Publishing: Newcastle, 2004), p.40.

30. Von Ribbentrop quoted in Lynn Picknett, Clive Prince and Stephen Prior, *War of the Windsors: a Century of Unconstitutional Monarchy* (Mainstream Publishing: Edinburgh, 2002), p.103.

31. Conze, *Memoirs*, p.17.

32. John Sleight, *Women on the March* (John I. Sleight: Gosforth, 1986), p.25. The author also mistakes the 'united front', in the Special Branch reference to Ellen Wilkinson, for an organisation to get women the vote at the age of 21; by the time of the Crusade women had the vote at 21 and the 'united front' was a communist policy of unity to oppose fascism. On the ambiguity of her joining and departure from the British Communist Party see Rajani Palme Dutt's papers. NMLH CP IND DUTT 01 01 Dutt's Confidential MS Easter 1970, and CP IND DUTT 06 03 her correspondence with Dutt (c. August 1923-June 1924). On her deciding to join the Communist Party, Dutt described an international student socialist conference in Geneva that they both attended in December 1919 where despite her initial strong objections ('This is the most ghastly, callous, inhuman machine I have ever witnessed') he won her round to joining the future Communist Party. On leaving the Communist Party, local communists felt that she misled them about her membership of the party. This was followed by her attempts to build bridges with Dutt by asking him for advice on reading up on Marxism.

33. Sleight, *Women*, p.29; Ellen Wilkinson, 'The women's movement in Soviet Russia', *Communist Review*, November 1921, pp.26-29.

34. Edward Conze, *The Memoirs of a Modern Gnostic* (Samizdat: Sherborne, 1979), p.17.

35. Billy Hughes, 'In defence of Ellen Wilkinson', *History Workshop Journal*, issue 7, summer 1979, pp.157-160 and David Rubinstein, 'Ellen Wilkinson re-considered', *History Workshop Journal*, issue 7, summer 1979, pp.161-169.

36. Ellen Wilkinson, *Division Bell Mystery* (Harrap: London, 1932), pp.145 and 187.

37. Ibid., p.167.

38. *Daily Herald*, 29 October 1936.

39. Wilkinson, *Town That Was Murdered*, p.197.

40. Sir Walter Runciman (1870-1949) in *Who Was Who? 1951-60*, vol.5 (Adam and Charles Black: London, 1961), p.1009; Sir Walter Runciman (1847-1937) in *Who Was Who? 1931-40*, vol.3 (Adam and Charles Black: London, 1941), p.1179.

41. Cato, *The Guilty Men* (Gollancz: London, 1940) written by Michael Foot, Peter Howard and Frank Owen this pamphlet caught the mood in 1940.

42. Wilkinson, *Town That Was Murdered*, p.163.

43. Paul Vyšný, *The Runciman Mission to Czechoslovakia, 1938* (Palgrave: Houndmills, 2003), p.343. '*Wir brauchen keinen Weihnachtsmann, Wir haben unseren Runciman*'.

44. *Who Was Who? 1951-60*, vol.5, (Charles and Adam Black: London, 1961), p.326.

45. TWAS T113 5 Miss T.P. Scarborough to The Town Clerk (Charles Perkins) of Jarrow, 15 September 1936.

46. Michael Foot MP and Donald Bruce MP, *Who are the Patriots?* (Gollancz: London, 1949), p.92.

47. PRO BT 64 10 Confidential memo of meeting (5 April 1935) between the President of the Board of Trade and Tyne Improvement Commissioners, written 9 April 1935.

48. Letter to the Right Hon. The Earl of Harewood, 2 April 1937, in Bradley, *More Letters*, p.119 and Letter to anon., 6 April 1938, in ibid., p.149.

49. Right Reverend E.A. Burroughs, Bishop of Ripon, who died in 1934, unlike Henson, was a leading Anglo-Catholic (a high church creed that that was ritualistic and evangelical in outlook). Evelyn Foley Bradley (ed.), *Letters of Herbert Hensley Henson* (SPCK: London, 1950), p.227; Henson, *Retrospect*, pp.275, 298, 305.

50. Chadwick, *Henson*, p.249.

51. G.I.T. Machin, 'Marriages and the churches in the 1930s: Royal abdication and divorce reform 1936-7', *Journal of Ecclesiastical History*, vol.42, no.1, 1991, pp.61-81.

52. TWAS G EMP2 1, *Sunday Despatch,* 7 Oct. 1934.

53. *The Times*, 4 October 1950.

54. Newcastle Central Library, Frank Ennis (ed.), *Jarrow Reminiscences*, (1982), p. 19.

55. *Who was Who? 1951-60*, vol.5 (Adam and Charles Black: London, 1961), p.1045.

1. *Shields Gazette*, 29 September 1936.

2. *King James Bible*. This was a very different approach to that of the National Unemployed Workers' Movement (NUWM). Their leaders espoused Marxism rather than Christianity. They stressed the need for the unemployed to organise themselves and that the unemployed would achieve nothing unless they fought for their rights.

3. *Evening Chronicle*, 5 October 1936.

4. Julia Beattie's recollections in National Sound Archive (NSA) 1CDR0016530 Radio 4, *The Last Crusade: Recollections of the Jarrow March*, 1986.

5. *Cumbrian Evening News*, 6 October 1936 and *Eastern Daily Press*, 6 October 1936.

6. *Church of England News*, 9 October 1936.

7. The route was as follows: White Mare Pool, Wrekenton Road and Springwell Bank.

8. On the iniquities of the legal system for the poor, see the study of the North East published in the year of the Crusade: Charles Muir, *Justice in a Depressed Area* (Allen and Unwin: London, 1936).

9. Tyne and Wear Archive Service (TWAS) MG SSH 3 1, Juvenile Court Register (Jarrow), 5 January 1933 – 4 April 1944; MG SSH 1 4 Police Court Register (Jarrow), 14 May 1935 – 23 March 1937.

10. *Shields Gazette*, Jarrow March Supplement, 1986, p.ii. He remembered the anecdote slightly differently on another occasion: when father told him that they were fighting for jobs, Don asked 'Well where are their guns?' *Sunderland Echo*, 31 July 1982.

11. Ibid., p.x.

12. *Shields Gazette*, 29 September 1986. The death of Ben, the babe in arms in the photo, at the age of 63 was recorded in the *Shields Gazette*, 6 September 1999.

13. Barbara Machin, 'Jarrow on the march once more', *The Observer Magazine*, 28 September 1986, pp.28-29.

14. *Shields Gazette*, 13 September 1999, ran a story the same day on Con's views with the headline 'Our March was a waste of time.' Tyne Tees TV, *North East Tonight*, 13 September 1999.

15. www.geocities.com the_jarrow_crusade Ralph_Smith on 26 October 2004: Ralph Smith was the barber but according to David Dougan, *The Jarrow March* (Bede Gallery: Jarrow, 1976), pp. 66-67, Larry Duggan and Willie Maugham surely intending Alex Duggan and Bob Maugham, and *Shields Gazette*, Jarrow March Supplement, 1986, p.xii., Alex Duggan was the barber.

16. *Evening Chronicle*, 30 September 1986.

17. *Chester-le-Street Chronicle and District Advertiser*, 9 October 1936. Allotments and leek shows were an important part of the local culture and the means of making two ends meet during the Depression. The article also pointed out that leeks were delicacies, to be eaten in puddings and broths and excellent in plate pie.

18. Arthur Barton, *Two Lamps in our Street: a Time Remembered* (Hutchinson: London, 1967), p.172.

19. See for example, James Cameron (ed.), *Yesterday's Witness: a Selection of the BBC Series* (BBC: London, 1979); David Renton, *This Rough Game: Fascism and Anti-Fascism* (Sutton: Stroud, 2001), pp.139-151.

20. National Council of Labour, was the leading body of the Labour Movement bringing together the General Council of the TUC and the leadership of the Parliamentary Labour Party.

21. Léon Blum was the leader of the *Section Française de l'Internationale Ouvrière* (SFIO), the French Socialist Party, and the prime minister of a centre-left coalition government, the Popular Front.

22. Speaking in Kingsway Hall, London (24 November), Barnsley (5 December), Bristol (11 December), *Sheffield Daily Telegraph*, 6 December 1934; *Manchester Guardian*, 15 November 1934 and 24 November 1934; *West Daily Press*, 12 December 1934; for the Comintern's account of Ellen Wilkinson's visit and the repression: *Inprecorr*, no.60, December 1934, pp.1605-1606.

23. *Sunday Chronicle*, 16 December 1934.

24. National Museum of Labour History (NMLH) Labour Party NEC minutes, 19 December 1934.

25. Labour Party, *Report of the 34th Annual Conference, Southport 1-5 October, 1934* (Labour Party: London, 1934), pp.12-13.

26. NMLH LP ID CI 26 press cutting, title of paper unknown, 22 September 1934.

27. NMLH Arthur Henderson's letter cited in the Labour Party NEC minutes, 28 December 1934.

28. On 27 July, 1936. Paul Preston, 'Franco and Azaña: Victor and Vanquished (Spain's Civil War)', *History Today*, May 1999, pp.17-23.

29. Paul Preston, *Franco: a biography* (Fontana: London, 1995), p.29.

30. Ian MacDougall (ed.), *Voices from the Hunger Marches: Personal Recollections by Scottish Hunger Marchers of the 1920s and 1930s*, 2 vols (Polygon: Edinburgh, 1991), vol.2, p.327.

31. *Evening Chronicle*, 6 October 1936.

32. Thomas Sharp, *A Derelict Area: a Study of the South-west Durham Coalfield* (Hogarth Press: London, 1935).

33. John Newsom, *Out of the Pit: a Challenge to the Comfortable* (Basil Blackwell: Oxford, 1936), p.11.

34. Jean Le Bel coined the Queen Phillippa myth. We known that she was in Ypres in Flanders at the time of the battle. Another fable of the battle is the humiliating capture of the Scottish king discovered under a bridge. Michael Prestwich, 'The English at the Battle of Neville's Cross', in David Rollason and Michael Prestwich (eds), *The Battle of Neville's Cross* (Shaun Tyas: Stamford, 1998), pp.1-14.

35. On the choice of politically neutral colours, *Evening Chronicle*, 6 October 1936.

36. They also claimed that there were three banners, but there were only two at this point. *Yorkshire Herald*, 6 October 1936; *Irish Free Press*, 6 October 1936; *Cork Examiner*, 6 October 1936; *Evening Chronicle*, 6 October 1936; *Cumbria Evening News*, 6 October 1936.

37. Interviews with members of Jarrow and Hebburn Local History Society, 5 April 2004 and conversation with Vince Rea, 2 November 2004.

38. Email from John Badger (son) to author, 6 April 2004.

39. Con Shields Letter to son (also Con Shiels), From Ripon, n.d. Also quoted in *Shields Gazette*, Jarrow March Supplement, 1986, p.vi. This also prints extracts from David Ramshaw's diary. These two contemporary sources from participants are very sparse in detail.

40. It is celebrated in *Cuddy's Miles* (2004) and *A Woman's Walk* (2000). One of the medical students recalled the event in NSA *The Last Crusade*.

41. Harry McShane, *No Mean Fighter* (Pluto: London, 1978), pp.263-264.

42. *Shields Gazette*, 20 May 1997.

43. *Evening Chronicle*, 7 October 1936.

44. Public Record Office (PRO) MEPO 2 3097 Memo, Sergeant A.E. Cattle, 30 October 1936.

45. On the experience of the welfare provision for the unemployed, Alan Deacon, *In Search of the Scrounger: the Administration of Unemployment Insurance in Britain, 1920-1931* (Bell: London, 1976).

46. *Shields Gazette*, 7 October 1936. For other less sympathetic reflections on later marches see Paddy Scullion in *Shields Gazette*, 11 December 1980 and Sam Rowan in *Shields Gazette*, 1 May 1981.

47. TWAS T 133 5 R.I. Dodds to the Editor of the Yorkshire Post, 12 January 1935, protesting at Peat's special pleading for Teesside steel producers and disparaging the Jarrow scheme.

48. Con Shields Letter to Son (also Con Shiels), From Ripon, n.d.

49. NSA *Last Crusade*.

50. *Shields Gazette*, 8 October 1936.

51. PRO HO 144 20696 MI5 to F. Newsam (Home Office), 19 August 1936.

52. *Shields Gazette*, 27 April 1987.

53. Matt Perry, 'The Jarrow Crusade's return: the 'New Labour Party' of Jarrow and Ellen Wilkinson, M.P.', *Northern History*, vol.34, no. 2, September 2002, pp.265-278.

54. *Evening Chronicle*, 27 April 1987.

55. Frank Ennis, 'The Jarrow March: a symbolic expression of protest', MA Thesis, Durham University, 1982, p.107.

56. For his public work, he became a Freeman of the Borough of Jarrow in 1955 and was awarded an OBE in 1957. He died on 29 March 1985. David Riley became a General, Municipal and Boilermakers' Union official.

57. *Shields Gazette*, Jarrow March Supplement, 1986, p.xii. For some reason he is called Dermottroe in the interview although Con Shiels confirmed that it was in fact Mick McDermott.

58. Maureen Turnbull, 'Attitude of government and administration towards the hunger marches of the 1920s and 1930s', *Journal of Social Policy*, vol.2, no.2, 1973, pp.131-142.

59. A version is quoted in South Shields Local Studies Library: C.T. Bell, *The Way We Were in Hendon, Sunderland in the 1920s and 1930s*, unpublished manuscript.

60. There is some ambiguity about the nature of these relationships. ee Betty D. Vernon, *Ellen Wilkinson 1891-1947* (Croom Helm: London, 1982), pp.29, 33-35, 122-29.

61. Later Sir William Lawther, after having shifted to the right, and becoming President of the Federation in 1939, was part of the centre-right coalition of trade union leaders who isolated the left in the TUC and Labour Party Conference. Having abandoned his former sympathies for the communists, honoured in 1948, his was a Cold War knighthood. His brother Clifford died in Spain in February 1937. See John Saville's entry 'Lord Blake', in C. S. Nicholls (eds) *Dictionary of National Biography, 1971-80* (Oxford University Press: Oxford, 1986), pp.487-488; W.R. Garside, *The Durham Miners, 1919-60* (Allen and Unwin: London, 1971), pp.78-79.

62. Matt Perry, 'The Jarrow Crusade, the National Hunger March and the Labour Party in 1936: a Re-Appraisal', *Socialist History*, no.20, 2001, pp. 40-53.

63. The two speeches were reproduced as a Labour Party pamphlet, Senor de Asua and Senora de Palencia, *The Agony of Spain: Socialist Appeal to British Democracy, Spanish Envoys tell the Truth* (Labour Party: London, 1936); see also Isabel de Palencia, *I Must Have Liberty* (Longmans: New York, 1940); Isabel de Palencia, *Smouldering Freedom: the Story of the Spanish Republicans in Exile* (Longmans: New York, 1945).

64. Don Watson and John Corcoran, *An Inspiring Example: the North East of England and the Spanish Civil War 1936-39* (McGuffin Press: London, 1996).

65. *Shields Gazette*, 9 October 1936.

66. Claude Robinson, 'How they tried to stop us marching', *Tribune*, 3 June 1983.

67. *Northern Despatch*, n.d., in NMLH CP IND HANN 06 14 Wal Hannington's press cuttings for 1936.

68. Infant mortality per thousand births remained at 104 against a national average of 57.

69. TUC library, HC 253 IJ: A.A. Rennie (secretary, Jarrow Labour Party and Trades Council) to J.S. Middleton (secretary, Labour Party), letter [requesting permission for a collection at conference], 30 September 1936. Also NMLH LP JSM UM 1-4 which includes the reply from the Secretary to the Standing Orders Committee to Rennie refusing permission.

70. Ellen Wilkinson, *The Town That Was Murdered: The Life Story of Jarrow* (Victor Gollancz: London, 1939), p.204.

71. Robinson, 'How they tried'.

72. Ralph Hayburn, 'The NUWM, 1921-36: a re-appraisal', *International Review of Social History*, vol.28, 1983, p.285.

73. H.G. Nicholas, *The British General Election of 1950* (MacMillan: London, 1951), pp.135 and 213; The poster read, '*Remember - Unemployment - Don't give the Tories another chance - Vote Labour*', NMLH Poster collection 1995 39, slide 1950 0171.

74. Frank Ennis noted that there was a view amongst local Conservatives that the Crusade was a Labour stunt in Ennis, 'The Jarrow March', p.165.

75. *Our Friends in the North* won three Bafta awards in 1997: best drama serial, the Dennis Potter writers' award and best actress award for Gina McKee. It came 25th in the British Film Institute (BFI) poll on 5th September 2000 of the UK TV industry's favourite British television programmes of all time.

76. NMLH LP DAC 6 1 Timetable for the North East Tour.

77. *Evening Chronicle*, 9 October 1936.

78. Claude Robinson, *J'Accuse: the Autobiography of a Headteacher in Jarrow, 1934-1963* (People's Publications: London, 1986), pp.49-50.

79. *North Mail and Evening Chronicle*, 9 October 1936.

80. *Shields Gazette*, Jarrow March Supplement, 1986.

81. *House of Commons Debates*, Fifth series, vol.317, November 3 to November 20 1936-7, col.1024-1025 and 1895.

82. TWAS DT JD 8 7 Rent books, 11 August 1936 to 18 October 1937.

83. Conversations with Harry Clarke and Con Shiels, 17 March 2005.

84. P.A. Dormer (Medical Officer of Health for Jarrow), *Annual Report of the Health Department for 1936* (Borough of Jarrow: Jarrow, 1937), p.20.

85. South Shields Library: Borough of Jarrow Corporation, Rate Book, 1934.

86. *Star*, 9 October 1936.

87. Brian Bennison, 'Profits of Doom: the financial management of the Jarrow Crusade', *Journal of Regional and Local Studies*, vol. 6, no. 2, 1985, pp.49-53.

88. *Ripon Gazette and Observer*, 8 October 1936.

89. Durham Cathedral Library (DCL): *Diary of Hensley Henson, the Bishop of Durham*, vol.68, 15 October 1936, pp.26-27.

90. There have been many examples of BBC sponsorship of the Crusade legend: two books have been published from the radio programmes, Pickard, *Jarrow March* and Cameron, *Yesterday's Witness*, pp.84-88; There have been two other Radio 4 documentary programmes: Radio 4, *The Last Crusade*, 1986 and Radio 4, *The Fiery Particle*, 1991. Also, TWAS LHNE DT BBC LH JAR Radio Newcastle, *The Jarrow March*: written by Frank Ennis, broadcast 1982; BBC2 aired a documentary about Ellen Wilkinson entitled *Red Ellen*, broadcast 21 October 1986; BBC2 three-part documentary *The Road to Jarrow*, presented by Sir Bernard Ingham; Sir John Hall presented *Beyond Jarrow*, a 1988 BBC2 documentary; *Century Speaks*, the BBC oral history project - http://www.bbc.co.uk/history/programmes/century/cspeaks.shtml; see front cover of Christopher Lee, *This Sceptred Isle: the Twentieth Century* (BBC, London: 1999) pp.177, 187, 194; Alex Ferguson, *A Woman's Walk Is Never Done*, Radio 4, 1 September 2000 was the first programme in the 'Walks of Protest' series; Radio 4, *Mapping the Town* series, on Jarrow 25 February 2004 was presented by archaeologist Julian Richards and included a discussion of the Jarrow Crusade with the author. BBC, *Eyewitness: a History of the Twentieth Century in Sound* (BBC Audiobooks: Bath, 2004) written by Joanna Burke.

91. Andrew Matthews, *The Road to London: a Tale of the Jarrow March* (Franklin Watts: London, 1997).

92. There are many examples of school work about the Crusade posted on the internet.

93. Ellen Wilkinson, 'Dope distributors: the wireless', *Plebs*, vol. 21, no. 3, 1929, pp.56-58.

94. *Evening Chronicle*, 30 September 1986.

95. *Ripon Gazette and Observer*, 15 October 1936.

96. Ibid.

97. Ibid.

98. *Shields Gazette*, 21 February 1972.

99. *Yorkshire Post*, 12 October 1936.

100. *Shields Gazette*, 12 October 1936.

101. On 10 December 1931, there was a demonstration of 10,000 in Newcastle at the Northumberland PAC; on 14 March 1932, 100,000 unemployed demonstrated on the Town Moor, Newcastle; on 5 October 1932 unemployed demonstrators were baton charged by police in North Shields; on 31 January 1935 10,000 unemployed demonstrated in North Shields;

on 10 February 1935 the unemployed protested against Oliver Stanley, the Minister of Labour, in Newcastle; on 24 February 1935, there was a Newcastle demonstration against the Unemployment Assistance Board scales. Wal Hannington, *Unemployed Struggles* (Lawrence and Wishart: London, 1977), pp.229-237 and 310-317.

102. *Evening Chronicle*, 13 October 1936.

103. *Ripon Gazette and Observer*, 15 October 1936.

104 *Shields Gazette*, 11 November 1936.

105. From the Bishop (£5), the Rotary Club (three guineas), the Conservative Association, the Constitutional Club (two guineas each), the local Transport and General Workers' Union (T&GWU) branch and individuals, *Ripon Gazette and Observer*, 15 October 1936.

106. The Conservatives got 46.9% of the vote. See, Maureen Callicott, 'The making of a Labour stronghold: electoral politics in Co. Durham between the two World Wars', and Ian Hunter, 'Labour in local government on Tyneside 1883-1921' in Maureen Callicott and Ray Challinor (eds), *Working Class Politics in North East England* (Newcastle-upon-Tyne Polytechnic: Newcastle-upon-Tyne, 1983), pp.63-78

107. A. W. Purdue, 'Jarrow politics, 1885-1914: the challenge to Liberal hegemony', *Northern History*, vol. 18, 1982, pp.182-198.

Week Two pages 53-88

1. *North Mail*, 13 October 1936.

2. *Northern Echo*, 13 October 1936.

3. *North Mail*, 13 October 1936.

4. Letter from its director J. Baker White published in the *Northampton Evening Telegraph*, 24 October 1936 and the *Peterborough Advertiser*, 23 October 1936. For the role of the Economic League: Arthur McIvor, ' "A crusade for capitalism": the Economic League, 1919-39', *Journal of Contemporary History*, vol. 23, 1988; Arthur McIvor and H. Patterson, 'Combatting the left: victimisation and anti-labour policies on the Clyde 1900-39', in Robert Duncan and Arthur McIvor (eds), *Militant Workers: Labour and Class Conflict on the Clyde 1900-1952* (J. Donald: Edinburgh, 1992).

5. *Northern Echo*, 13 October 1936.

6. Don MacRaild, *Faith, Fraternity and Fighting: The Orange Order and Irish Migrants in Northern England, c.1850-1920*, (Liverpool University Press: 2005).

7.   Tom Kelly, 'The Catholic Component: Irish Catholics in the North East and Jarrow from the Mid-Nineteenth Century', unpublished manuscript, pp.18-19; Ennis, 'The Jarrow March'; TWAS PA 1322 M.J. Young, *Catholic Jarrow, St. Bede's, 1860-1940* (n.p.,1940).

8 . Thanks to the help of Professor Tony Hepburn, Professor Don MacRaild, and Dr Malcolm Smith for their expert advice in this field; *Appendix to the 29ᵗʰ Report of the Registrar General: Special Report on Surnames in Ireland, with Notes as the Numerical Strength, Derivation, Ethnology, and Distribution,* cmd. 7289, 1894; John Foster, Muir Houston and Chris Madigan, 'Distinguishing Catholics and Protestants among Irish immigrants to Clydeside: a new approach to immigration and ethnicity in Victorian Britain', *Irish Studies Review*, vol.10, no.2, 2002, pp.171-192.

9.   Kelly, 'The Catholic Component', p.23.

10. Robinson, 'How they tried'.

11. Toc H was a charitable organisation which began in Belgium during the Great War, where a British chaplain, 'Tubby' Clayton, established a venue for the relaxation of troops. Returning to civilian life, the veterans associated with it spread this association. See http:www.toch.org.

12. *Harrogate Herald*, 14 October 1936.

13. Sam Rowan, 'We'll march down with it', Age Concern, *Tyneside Memories* (Age Concern: Newcastle, 1996), p.43.

14. *Leeds Mercury*, 13 October 1936.

15. *Harrogate Herald*, 14 October 1936.

16. Ibid.

17. *Commons Debates*, vol. 319, cols. 571-572, 25 January 1937. The figures are for March 1936.

18. Ibid., vol. 328, cols. 1897-1950, 11 November 1937, the second reading of the Bill.

19. Joyce M. Bellamy and John Saville (eds), *Dictionary of Labour Biography*, Vol. 4 (Macmillan: London, 1977), pp.165-166.

20. Robinson, 'How they tried'.

21. Mary, daughter of King George V. *Who was Who? 1941-50*, vol.4 (Adam and Charles Black: London, 1952), pp.500-501; *Evening Chronicle*, 13 October 1936.

22. W.R. Garside, *British Unemployment: 1919-39* (Cambridge University Press: Cambridge, 1990), p.41.

23. Asa Briggs, *Victorian Cities* (Penguin: Harmondsworth, 1968), p.159.

24. The Greenshirts followed the ideas of Major C.H. Douglas. John Hargreave founded the Social Credit Party of Great Britain which campaigned for economic recovery through the expansion of social credit.

25. After the November election, the situation was 61 Conservative seats, 41 Labour seats, 3 Liberal seats. *The Times*, 3 November 1936; *Yorkshire Observer*, 13 October 1936.

26. *Sheffield Independent*, 14 October 1936.

27. *Shields Gazette*, Jarrow March Supplement, p. xi.

28. Con Shiels letter to son, from Barnsley, 13 October 1936.

29. Vince Rea, in discussion at talk by Matt Perry and Tim Brennan, 'Jarrow Crusade: Fact and Myth', at Bede's World, 3 April 2004.

30. B. Machin, 'Jarrow on the march once more', *The Observer Magazine*, 28 September 1986, pp.28-29.

31. Colin Williams, Bill Alexander, John Gorman, *Memorials of the Spanish Civil War: the Official Publication of the International Brigade Association* (Allan Sutton: Stroud, 1996), pp.71-72.; for extracts from Bob Elliott's diary, Frank Graham, *Battle of Jarama: the Story of the British Battalion of the International Brigade in Spain* (Frank Graham, Newcastle: 1987), p.23, For the list of those who lost their lives from the North East. See also, on a more dubious aspect of Elliott's role, James K. Hopkins, *Into the Heat of the Fire: the British in the Spanish Civil War* (Stanford University Press: Stanford, 1998), pp. 279 & 322.

32. Nigel Todd, *In Excited Times: the People against the Blackshirts* (Bewick Press: Whitley Bay, 1995), pp.101-102; Dave Goodman, *From Tees to the Ebro: My Road to Spain* (Middlesbrough Communist Party: n.p., n.d.) knew both Elliot and Jobling.

33. Peter Kingsford, *The Hunger Marchers in Britain 1920-40* (Lawrence and Wishart: London, 1982), p.225; Watson and Corcoran, *An Inspiring Example*, pp.28-29; Richard Croucher, *We Refuse to Starve in Silence: a History of the National Unemployed Workers' Movement 1920-46* (Lawrence and Wishart: London, 1987), p.225; Bill Alexander, *British Volunteers for Liberty: Spain 1936-9* (Lawrence and Wishart: London, 1982).

34. *Blaydon Courier*, 21 November 1936. Other marchers were William Watson (Winlaton), S. Sutherland (Chopwell), D.Gorman (Winlaton), Olive Airey (Bleach Green) and Emmie Lawther (wife of County Councillor Steve Lawther).

35. *Shields Gazette*, 31 March 1937.

36. *Tribune*, 16 July 1937.

37. Valentine Cunningham (ed.), *Spanish Civil War Verse* (Penguin: Harmondsworth, 1980), p.180.

38. *Shields Gazette*, 13 October 1936 and 13 November 1936.

39. *Sunderland Echo*, 14 October 1936.

40. *Why We March: Programme of the National Protest March*, 1936. Ellen Wilkinson was on its reception committee. Newcastle contingent of the National Hunger March's route: Sunderland (13 October); Seaham Harbour (14); West Hartlepool (15); Stockton and Middlesbrough (16); Stokesley (17); Helmsley (18); Malton (19); York (20); Selby (21); Doncaster (22 and 23); Gainsborough (24); Lincoln (25); Newark (26); Grantham (27); Stamford (28); Peterborough (29); Huntingdon (30); Cambridge (31and 1 November); Saffron Walden (2); Bishop's Stortford (3); Dunmow (4); Chelmsford (5); Romford (6); Poplar (7); London (8).

41. Manuel Grossi, *L'Insurrection des Asturies* (Études et Documentation Internationales: Paris, 1972).

42. *Barnsley Chronicle and South Yorkshire News*, 17 October 1936.

43. *Evening Chronicle*, 30 September1986.

44. Rose Reeve, *Crusader: the Story of Ellen Wilkinson and the Town of Jarrow* (unpublished 2001).

45. Ellen Wilkinson, *The Clash* (Virago: London, 1989), p.7.

46. Vernon, *Ellen Wilkinson*, pp.234-235; for an introduction to Ellen Wilkinson's life, see also D.E. Martin, 'Ellen Wilkinson', in Anne Commire (ed.), *Women in World History: a Biographical Encyclopedia*, vol. 16 (Yorkin: Detroit, 2002), pp. 550-553.

47. *Shields Gazette*, 18 January 1934. As Prime Minister he had been impotent in his desire to release the 76-year-old Tom Mann who was jailed in late 1932 for his activities with the NUWM. PRO HO 144 19835 and PRO HO 144 19836.

48. PRO T 172 1826 Jarrow unemployment prospects, 28 February 1934.

49. Ellen Wilkinson, *Peeps at Politicians* (Philip Allen: London, 1930), pp.14-15.

50. Frederic M. Miller, 'Unemployment policy of the National Government 1931-36', *Historical Journal*, vol.19, no.2, 1976, pp.463-464. Another firm had put in a bid for the contract of a destroyer repair ship for £100,000

less. PRO CAB 27 502 Committee on Trade and Employment, Memorandum 28 February 1933 and sixth meeting.

51. PRO CAB 23 85 Cabinet conclusions, 14 October 1936.

52. *Daily Dispatch*, 15 October 1936.

53. PRO HO 144 20696 MI5 to F. Newsam (Home Office), 14 October 1936. These files were released in autumn 2004.

54. PRO HO 144 20696 Metropolitan Police Chief Constable's report, 16 October 1936.

55. Ibid., Major Alexander Hardinge to A.S. Hutchinson (Home Office), 21 October 1936; A.S. Hutchinson (Home Office) to Major Alexander Hardinge, 20 October 1936.

56. TWAS T 113 5 Ronald R. Dobbie to Mayor of Jarrow, 20 July 1936; Mayor's Secretary to Ronald R. Dobbie, 23 July 1936 stating 'an appeal to His Majesty has had some consideration, but it is thought that a petition to Parliament should be presented in the first place'.

57. *Commons Debates*, vol.317, 1936-37, 5 November 1936, col.235.

58. PRO HO 144 20697 Metropolitan Police Chief Constable's report, 3 December 1936. A more definitive account of these events is not possible partly because amongst the recent release of files there are several that have been destroyed.

59. Susan Williams, *The People's King: the True Story of the Abdication* (Allen Lane: London, 2003), pp.1-17 and 57-64; Phillip Zeigler, *Edward VIII* (Sutton: Stroud, 1990), pp.301-2; Brian Inglis, *Abdication* (Hodder Stoughton: London, 1966), pp.229-235; for the journalist Bill Deedes, the King's statement 'reverberated around the country like a thunderclap', W.F. Deedes, *Dear Bill: W.F. Deedes Reports* (MacMillian: London, 1997), p.40; Robert Bernays registered doubt about the actual phrase 'something will/ought to be/must be done' in his diary on 9 December 1936, Nick Smart (ed.), *The Diaries and Letters of Robert Bernays, 1932-1939: an Insider's Account of the House of Commons* (Edwin Mellen: Lewiston, New York, 1996), p.278; Sir Larry Lambe, the courtier and part of the King's entourage on that tour, unconvincingly claimed that the quotation 'something must be done' resulted from the mischief of the *Daily Herald's* Hannen Swaffer in, Oliver Warner, *Admiral of the Fleet: the Life of Sir Charles Lambe* (Sidgwick and Jackson: London, 1969), p.68; *Times*, 24 Novemeber 1936, Geoffrey Dawson, the editor, argued against the interpretation that it was a rebuke to the Government; for the route and planning of the tour PRO MH 58 309 King Edward VIII's visit to South Wales, November 1936; for contemporary accounts *Western Mail and*

South Wales News, 19 and 20 November 1936 and *South Wales Argus*, 19 and 20 November 1936, these indicate that the King used the phrase 'something will be done' in Blaenavon and in Dowlais he said 'something should be done'.

60. *Labour Research*, December 1936, pp.279-281; The *Daily Worker*, 20 November 1936, saw the purpose of the visit to 'conciliate the people, but keep the attention from the main issue [the means test and the UAB]'. Indeed, Hardinge wrote to Baldwin that the King's visit would be a 'shock for the communists' and that it had gone 'extremely well', Keith Middlemas and John Barnes, *Baldwin: a Biography* (Weidenfeld and Nicolson: London, 1969), p.996.

61. Brian Inglis, *Abdication* (Hodder and Stoughton, London, 1966), p.234.

62. PRO 30 69 1753 Ramsay MacDonald's Diary, 21 November 1936.

63. There were now five Crusaders missing: McCourt, Queenan, Guy, Coyne, McGuckin.

64. *Shields Gazette*, Jarrow March Supplement, 1986.

65. Con Shiels, letter to Con Shiels (son), 17 October 1936, from Notts.

66. *Northern Echo*, 15 October 1936.

67. *Evening Chronicle*, 15 October 1936.

68. *Daily Herald*, 16 October 1936.

69. Durham Cathedral Library (DCL): *Diary of Hensley Henson, the Bishop of Durham*, vol.68, 6 October 1936, p.9.

70. Ibid., 8 October 1936, p.14

71. Durham Cathedral Library: *The Correspondence of Hensley Henson, the Bishop of Durham*, vol. 112: 23 January 1936-1 June 1945, letter to Marquis of Londonderry, 29 January 1937, p.58 it reads, 'I am very anxious to put an end to their extravagances of opinion and speech, which, in the recent past, have secured so much public attention in the diocese'.

72. *North Mail*, 15 October 1936.

73. *Shields Gazette*, 24 September 1986.

74. Ibid., 15 May 1939 and 25 May 1939.

75. Ibid., 18 May 1939.

76. The Home Office's reply was that an investigation would have to be deferred until after the hearings. *Commons Debates*, vol.345, 1938-39, 25 May 1939, col.2533.

77. *Barnsley Chronicle and South Yorkshire News*, 24 October 1936.

78. Ibid., 17 October 1936.

79. Bellamy and Saville, *Dictionary of Labour Biography*, vol.5, pp.124-128.

80. *Barnsley Chronicle and South Yorkshire News*, 17 October 1936.

81. Ibid., 17 October 1936.

82. NSA *Last Crusade*.

83. Ibid., 24 October 1936.

84. *Weekly Times*, 15 October 1936. Sir George Gillett (1870-1939), Labour MP, then in 1931, National Labour MP, Commissioner for the Special Areas 1936-9. He died on 10 August 1939.

85. Wilkinson, *Town That Was Murdered*, p.207.

86. *Evening Chronicle*, 18 October 1936.

87. *North Mail*, 17 October 1936.

88. Rowan, 'We'll march down with it', p.42.

89. George Orwell, *The Road to Wigan Pier* (Penguin: Harmondsworth, 1962), p.95.

90. J.B. Priestley, *English Journey* (Heinemann: London, 1984; first published, 1934), p.119.

91. A.D.K. Owen, Sheffield Social Survey Committee, *A Survey of the Standard of Living in Sheffield*, Survey Pamphlet no.9, June 1933, p. 24; A.D.K. Owen, Sheffield Social Survey Committee, *A Report on the Housing Problem in Sheffield*, Survey Pamphlet no.2, June 1931, p. 59; A.D.K. Owen, Sheffield Social Survey Committee, *A Report on Unemployment in Sheffield*, Survey Pamphlet no.4, July 1932, p. 56.

92. *Shields Gazette*, 17 October 1936.

93. Herbert Hensley Henson, *Retrospect of an Unimportant Life*, vol.3: 1939-46 (Oxford University Press: London, 1950), pp.80-81.

94. *Evening Chronicle*, 26 October 1936.

95. *Shields Gazette*, 17 October 1936.

96. *Diary of Henson*, vol.68, 30 October 1936, p.58.

97. *Derbyshire Times*, 17 October 1936.

98. *Shields Gazette*, 17 October 1936.

99. Alex Glasgow, *Respectable Men* (the 'skeleton script' for *Whistling at the Milestones*) (unpublished, 1977), pp.48-50.

100. PRO MEPO 2 3097 Chief Constable's report, 26 October 1936. According to this report 50 had set out from Edinburgh on 20 September but by the time they reached Jarrow on 2 October their forces were down to 21. Their leaders were disparaged as 'expelled from the British Legion for misappropriation of funds, or otherwise undesirable'.

101. PRO HO 144 20697 Inspector Vivian Wright's report, 17 November 1936.

102. Wal Hannington, *Never on our Knees* (Lawrence and Wishart: London, 1967), pp.314-316.

103. *Mansfield and North Notts Advertiser*, 23 October 1936.

104. *Sheffield Independent*, 21 October 1936.

105. Sheffield Archives (SA) LD 1541 Labour Party Hallam (Sheffield) Constituency, Divisional members' meeting, 12 October 1936; LD 1653 Sheffield Trades and Labour Council, Executive and Delegates Meetings, July 1936-December 1938;

106. NMLH GS JSM Labour Party NEC minutes, 25 November 1936.

107. SA ASLEF 7 *Sheffield Trades and Labour Council Annual Report*, 17th Annual report, 1936.

108. *Yorkshire Telegraph*, 17 October 1936.

109. Allan John Grant (1871-1955) in *Who Was Who? 1951-60*, vol.5 (Adam and Charles Black: London, 1961), p.444.

110. Wilkinson, *Town That Was Murdered*, p.187.

111. Sir Allan John Grant, *Steel and Ships: the History of John Brown's* (Joseph: London, 1950).

112. *Sunday Express*, 18 October 1936.

113. Monica Whatley, Ellen Wilkinson, Leonard W. Matters and V.K. Krishna Menon, *Condition of India: Being the Report of the Delegation sent to India by The India League in 1932* (Essential News, London: 1933); Suruchi Thapar-Björkert, 'Gender, nationalism and the colonial jail: a study of the women activists in Uttar Pradesh', *Women's History Review*, vol.7, no.4, 1998, p.590; NMLH LP ID IND 1 6iii for her continued commitment to the Indian cause, she seconded Laski's call on the Labour Party National Executive Committee for full dominion status within three years of the end of the war which was referred to a sub-committee at an NEC meeting in February 1940.

114. *Lathis* were three or five foot canes issued to police which could inflict vicious even fatal blows.

115. Edward Conze, *The Memoirs of a Modern Gnostic* (Samizdat: Sherborne, 1979), p.17.

116. *Shields Gazette*, 19 October 1936.

117. Ibid.

118. *Evening Chronicle*, 19 October 1936.

119. *The Times*, 17 October 1936. check

120. Hensley Henson in Henry Offley Wakeman (ed.), *Essays Introductory to the Study of English Constitutional History* (Longmans: London, 1891).

121. Wilkinson, *Town That Was Murdered*, p.201.

122. *Diary of Henson*, vol.68, 15 October 1936, pp.26-27.

123. Ibid., 17 October 1936, p.31.

124. Henson, *Retrospect* (vols 1 and 2 published as one: Oxford University Press: London, 1943), p.406.

125. Ian Kershaw, *Making Friends with Hitler: Lord Londonderry, the Nazis and the Road to War* (Allen Lane: London, 2004).

126. E.F. Bradley, *The Letters of Herbert Henson* (SPCK: London, 1950), p.97.

127. *Derbyshire Times*, 23 October 1936.

Week Three pages 89-120

1. *Derbyshire Times*, 23 October 1936.

2. *Burke's Peerage and Baronetage* (Burke's Peerage: Crans, Switzerland, 1999), pp.2733-2737. John Bowes (1811-1885) was the illegitimate eldest son of John Bowes, 10th Earl of Strathmore and Ringhorne (b.1769). John Bowes was therefore the great uncle of the late 'Queen Mum'. The Bowes family had possessed mining interests since 1726. John Bowes inherited 40,000 acres and a rent roll of £20,000 on the death of his father the tenth Earl of Strathmore and Kinghorne. He did not inherit the title because he was born out of wedlock, but became MP for South Durham (1832-47). Initially Charlie Palmer and John Bowes were partners from 1846 in the Marley Hill Coal Company, renamed John Bowes and Partners the following year. The relationship strengthened because Palmer's yard built colliers for John Bowes. John died in 1885 and his legacy was the fine collection of art and porcelain at the Bowes Museum, County Durham.

Charles H. Hardy, *John Bowes and the Bowes Museum* (Frank Graham: Newcastle-upon-Tyne, 1970). http://www.bowesmuseum.org.uk/

3. *Colliery Year Book and Coal Trades Directory* (Louis Cassier: London, 1933); William Page (ed.), *Victoria County History of Durham*, vol.2 (Constable: London, 1907). The company's output was 1.5 million tons from six pits.

4. South Shields Museum: TWCMS 2001 5009 2 South Tyneside Interviews, Harry Clarke. He became the secretary of the Labour League of Youth, the Young Communist League and was the Secretary of the Tyne Apprentices Committee and led an apprentices' strike at Swan Hunters in 1940. He also met Ruth First and became an honorary member of the African National Congress shortly after the Second World War.

5. Vince Rea (ed.), *Palmer's Yard and the Town of Jarrow* (Bede Gallery: Jarrow, 1975), pp.72-74.

6. Author's interview with Con Shiels, 23 September 2004.

7. *Mansfield and North Notts Advertiser*, 23 October 1936.

8. Ellen Wilkinson and Edward Conze, *Why Fascism?* (Selwyn and Blount: London, 1934), p.314.

9 . Ibid., p.315.

10. Author's interview with John Badger, 23 September 2004.

11. *Sunday Times Magazine*, 19 October 1975, p.29.

12. 'Nottingham and Mining Country', in D.H. Lawrence, *Selected Essays* (Penguin: Harmondsworth, 1950), p.119.

13. *North Mail*, 21 October 1936.

14. Cummings, 'Marshall Riley's Army', pp.132-136.

15. *Shields Gazette*, 21 October 1936.

16. *Shields Gazette*, 27 April 1984.

17. *Evening Chronicle*, 28 April 1984. Vince Rea's name was also spelled incorrectly in the plaque, *Shields Gazette*, 30 April 1984. Why such a monument should be accorded such symbolic significance at the time was due to the contrast between the quiescent dignified Crusade and the miners' strike. In the very same week of April 1984 local papers carried the story of twelve Durham miners on charges for picketing offences. The May Day Rally in the Community Centre, Cambrian Street, followed the unveiling. *Socialist Worker*, the newspaper of the Socialist Workers Party, was highly critical of Kinnock's role in the dispute.

18. *Shields Gazette*, 30 April 1984.

19. Alan Plater, *Close the Coalhouse Door (with Songs by Alex Glasgow)* (Bloodaxe: Newcastle, 2000), p.56.

20. R.W. Postgate, J.F. Horrabin and Ellen Wilkinson, *A Workers' History of the Great Strike* (Plebs League and the National Council of Labour Colleges: London, 1927), p.78.

21. Lionel Birch (ed.), *The History of the T.U.C. 1868-1968: a Pictorial Survey of a Social Revolution* (General Council of the TUC : London, 1968).

22. Christopher Hill, *Liberty against the Law: Some Seventeenth-century Controversies* (Penguin: Harmondsworth, 1996).

23. Stephen Knight (ed.), *Robin Hood: an Anthology of Scholarship and Criticism* (Brewer: Cambridge, 1991); J.R. Maddicott, 'The birth and setting of the ballads of Robin Hood', *English Historical Review*, vol. 93, 1978, pp.267-299; J.C.Holt, 'The origins and audience of the ballads of Robin Hood', Past and Present, no.18, 1960, pp.89-110; R.B. Dobson and J. Taylor, *Rymes of Robin Hood: an Introduction to the English Outlaw* (Sutton; Stroud, 1997), xv.

24. *Who Was Who? 1941-50*, vol.4 (Adam and Charles Black: London, 1952), p.53.

25. G.C.M. M'Gonigle and J. Kirby, *Poverty and Public Health* (Gollancz: London), 1936, pp.74-76.

26. *Manchester Guardian*, 21 October 1936.

27. Discussion of the legislative programme focussed on the Trade Marks Bill, the Trunk Roads Bill and the extension of unemployment insurance to agricultural workers. PRO CAB 23 85, 21 October 1936.

28. Interview with Margaret Lagan, at Jarrow and Hebburn Local History Society, 9 June 2004.

29. David M. Goodfellow, *Tyneside: the Social Facts* (Co-operative: Newcastle, 1940), p.73.

30. *Nottingham Guardian*, 22 October 1936.

31. *Leicester Daily Mercury*, 22 October 1936.

32. *Evening Chronicle*, 21 October 1936; On Professor H.M. Hallsworth CBE (1876-1953), at University of Durham, member of Unemployment Assistance Board and National Assistance Board (1934-49), *Who Was Who?* vol. 5, p.474.

33. *Daily Worker*, 25 October 1936; Harry McShane, *No Mean Fighter* (Pluto: London, 1978), p.217.

34. *Daily Sketch*, 26 February 1934.

35. She put her name to an appeal for funds of the NUWM supported miners' hunger march of 1927. She was one of only ten MPs to lend their support to the NUWM's 1935-6 campaign for extra winter relief, WCML NUWM NAC minutes, 8-9 February 1936. She also accompanied the 1934 hunger march at various stages, Winnifred Albaya, *Through the Green Door: Part II* (Sheffield District Education Committee: Sheffield, 1980), p.151.

36. *East Ham Echo*, 13 November 1936.

37. Wilkinson and Conze, *Why Fascism?*, p.313.

38. There were now six of the original crusaders missing: Cameron, Quennan, Guy, McGurkin, Coyne, Winship.

39. *Daily Mirror*, 22 October 1936.

40. *Leicester Daily Mercury*, 23 October 1936.

41. Wilkinson, *Clash*, p.103.

42. C. Seymour-Ure, 'The press and the party system between the wars', in G.Peele and C.Cook (eds), *The Politics of Reappraisal* (MacMillan: London, 1975).

43. Author's interview with Con Whalen, 26 August 1999.

44. M. Gribben, 'The Crusade continues', *Accent on the Wear*, no.2, October 1999, pp.14-15; *Sunday Express*, 21 November 1999; *Shields Gazette*, 10 September 1999; *Sunday Express*, 21 November 1999; *Shields Gazette*, 19 September 2003.

45. James Curran and Jean Seaton, *Power without Responsibility: the Press and Broadcasting in Britain* (Routledge: London, 1997), p.53.

46. Letter, Brian Buchanan to Mulligan, South Tyneside Metropolitan Borough Council, 14 November 1995.

47. *South Tyneside Times*, 27 October 1988.

48. *Shields Gazette*, 17 October 1988.

49. In the discussion at talk by Matt Perry and Tim Brennan, 'Jarrow Crusade: Fact and Myth', at Bede's World, 3 April 2004.

50. *Shields Gazette*, 28 October 1986. Reverend Frederick Lewis Donaldson (1860-1953) in *Who Was Who? 1951-60*, vol.5 (Adam and Charles Black: London, 1961), p.311. Canon Frederick Lewis Donaldson was vicar of St. Mark's from 1896 to 1918 before becoming Canon of Westminster (1924-51). He was a prominent Christian socialist, being one of the first members of the Christian Social Union chairing the Leicester branch (1896-

1906). He wrote a pamphlet *The Unemployed* in 1907 and *Socialism and the Christian Faith* the following year. He edited *Goodwill* between 1903 and 1906. He was a founder of the Christian Socialist League becoming its chairman (1913-16).

51. PRO MEPO 2 789 Leicester march to London, 1905; The Times, 15 May, 16 May, 27 May, 30 May, 3 June, 5 June, 10 June, 12 June, 19 June, and letters, 22 June, 24 June 1905. Richard Flanagan, *Parish-Fed Bastards: A History of the Unemployed in Britain 1884-1939* (Greenwood Press: New York, 1991), pp.60-63.

52. *Reynolds Illustrated News*, 8 November 1936 and *Daily Herald*, 24 October 1936.

53. *Shields Gazette*, 23 October 1936.

54. Ibid., 22 October 1936.

55. Pilgrim Trust, *Men without Work* (Cambridge University Press, 1938), p.47-56. The survey was conducted in November 1936.

56. Priestley, *English Journey*, p.101.

57. Wilkinson, *Town That Was Murdered*, p.207.

58. Sidney and Beatrice Webb, *Soviet Communism: a New Civilisation?* (Longmans: London, 1935). In subsequent editions the question mark was dropped.

59. Ellen Wilkinson, 'The Communist Manifesto', *New Dawn*, 4 May 1935, pp.272-273 and 279. This put her considerably to the left of the Communist Party.

60. NMLH CP IND MONT 4 10 various letters between Ivor Montagu and Ellen Wilkinson on this matter 1930-1; Centre d'Études et de Recherche sur les Movements Trotskyste et Révolutionnaires Internationaux, for Trotsky's correspondence with Marjorie Wells, Ivor Montagu and an anonymous English female recipient. It is highly likely that the latter is Ellen Wilkinson as Trotsky had so few English correspondents and she had intervened on the question of a visa for the Russian revolutionary, which is the subject of the letter in question and is dated 2 September 1930.

61. In a series of articles written after one of Ellen Wilkinson's trips to Spain: *Sunday Sun*, 25 April, 2, 9, 16, 23 May 1937. Orwell was critical of the British left (and Ellen explicitly) for their attitude to the repression of revolutionary Barcelona by the Popular Front Government, Sonia Orwell and Ian Angus (eds), *The Collected Essays, Journalism and Letters of George Orwell*, vol. 1: *An Age Like This 1920-40* (Penguin: Harmondsworth,

1970), p.332.

62. NMLH CP IND DUTT 31 03 A. Creech Jones MP to Ellen Wilkinson, 14 December 1938, a reply to her proposal for a British Popular Front with anyone who was anti-appeasement in December 1938 after Munich.

63. *Market Harborough Advertiser and Midland Mail*, 30 October 1936.

64. TWAS D X33 1 Leaflet for Market Harborough public meeting.

65. *Registrar-General's Statistical Review of England and Wales for the Year 1936*, New Annual Series, no. 16 (HMSO: London, 1937), pp.44-49.

66. P.A. Dormer (Medical Officer of Health for Jarrow), *Annual Report of the Health Department for 1936* (Borough of Jarrow: Jarrow, 1937), p.7. Even by the end of 1939 there were still 1,060 overcrowded houses in Jarrow, *Annual Report of the Health Department for 1939* (Borough of Jarrow: Jarrow, 1940), p.42.

67. Priestley, *English Journey*, p.101.

68. Ibid., p.236.

69. J.B.Priestley, *Wonder Hero* (Heinemann: London, 1933), pp.201 and 222-223.

70. Priestley, *English Journey*, p.237.

71. Ibid, pp.297-301. John Baxendale, '"I Had seen a Lot of Englands": J. B. Priestley, Englishness and the People', *History Workshop Journal*, no. 51, 2001, pp.87-111 surveys the debates over the anti-modern character of the book.

72. *Market Harborough Advertiser and Midland Mail*, 30 October 1936.

73. *Evening Chronicle*, 24 October 1936.

74. Robinson, *J'Accuse*, p.47.

75. *The Economist*, 4 July 1936, p.9

76. John Vaizey, *The History of British Steel* (Weidenfeld and Nicolson: London, 1974), pp.84-85.

77. Ibid., *Manchester Guardian*, 2 July 1936. Reporting on the previous Tuesday.

78. *Iron and Coal Trades Review*, 10 July 1936, p.60 for the statement with discussion, 17 July 1936, p.97; Ibid., *Daily Telegraph*, 7 July 1936.

79. Robinson, *J'Accuse*, p.64.

80. S.O. Davies (1886-1972), Vice-President of South Wales Miners' Federation (1924-33), Labour MP for Merthyr Tydfil (1934-70) and Independent Labour (1970-2). James Griffiths, President of South Wales Miners' Federation (1934-6), Labour MP for Llanelly (1936-70).

81. *South Wales Argus*, 26 October 1936.

82. In October 1999, the work was released on compact disc.

83. Dougan, *Jarrow March*, p.80.

84. *Shields Gazette*, 9 May 1997. The opera made its London debut on 9 October 1999 at the Central Methodist Hall, Westminster.

85. Dr Hensley Henson (1863-28 September 1947), the Bishop of Durham, *Who Was Who? 1941-50*, vol.4 (Adam and Charles Black: London, 1952) p.531; his autobiography, Henson, *Retrospect*.

86. *The Times*, 26 October 1936.

87. *The Economist*, 31 October 1936, p.202; *The Economist*, 4 July 1936, p.9 complained about clause six of the Finance Bill which allowed the BISF powers to import extra-quota foreign steel at low duties or even duty-free, and to allocate them among members as it saw it. The corporative state was the phrase used by the Italian fascists to describe their relationship between business and the state

88. Henson, *Retrospect*, p.398. Controversies such as at a guest lecture at the London School of Economics on 23 June 1932. His memoirs also reveal his annoyance at coal and wood thefts from his grounds and the recurrent controversies of his views on this subject.

89. Letter to anon., 3 January 1934, in Evelyn Foley Bradley (ed.), *More Letters of Herbert Hensley Henson: a Second Volume* (SPCK: London, 1954), p.91.

90. Letter to anon., 25 July 1930, ibid., p.62.

91. Letter to anon., 16 July 1925, ibid., p.39.

92. Letter to anon, 20 August 1935, ibid., p.148.

93. Letter to anon., 27 August 1936, ibid., p.62

94. *Commons Debates*, vol. 186, 30 July 1925, col. 466; Owen Chadwick, *Hensley Henson: a Study in Friction between Church and State* (Clarendon: Oxford, 1983), pp.166-174; *Durham Chronicle*, 1 August 1925; *Northern Echo*, 27 July 1925; The Ecclesiastical Commission received £400,000 a year in revenue from coal royalties, much of this from County Durham, though only a fraction of this would find its way to Henson. Henson also approved the prosecution of miners who were picking coal from his Bishop

Auckland residence and 23 were prosecuted during the year of the General Strike and miners' strike.

95.   Letter to anon., 14 August 1932, in Bradley, *More Letters*, pp.83-84.

96.   The Bishop had received a complaint from a parliamentary candidate about the vicar's partisanship during the election. Letter to an anon. vicar, 18 December 1935, ibid., p.105

97.   Herbert Hensley Henson, *Abyssinia: Reflections of an Onlooker* (Hugh Rees: London, 1936).

98.   *Church of England Newspaper*, 23 and 26 October 1936. Indeed the paper sympathised with Ellen Wilkinson's reply and criticised the Bishop of Durham for 'exaggerated language'.

Week Four pages 121-152

1.   *North Mail*, 27 October 1936.

2.   *First Report of the Commissioner for the Special Areas* (England and Wales), cmd. 4957, July 1935 (HMSO: London, 1935), pp.62-63; *Second Report of the Commissioner for the Special Areas* (England and Wales), cmd. 5090, February 1936 (HMSO: London, 1936), pp.97-99; *Third Report of the Commissioner for the Special Areas* (England and Wales), cmd. 5303, November 1936 (HMSO: London, 1936), pp.157-159; Matt Perry, 'The Limits of Philanthropy: Sir John Jarvis and the Attempt to Regenerate Jarrow, 1934-39' *North East History*, summer 2000 pp.35-59.

3.   Karl Marx, *Capital*, vol. 1 (Penguin: Harmondsworth, 1976), p.792. Marx called unemployment 'the reserve army of labour'.

4.   David Bell, *Ships, Strikes and Keelmen: Glimpses at North-Eastern Social History* (TUPS: Newcastle, 2001), p.106 citing a letter to the *Evening Chronicle* in 1991.

5.   Dougan, *Jarrow March,* pp.102-103.

6.   'Put Names to Faces' Exhibition organised by the Jarrow and Hebburn Local History Society, October 2001. The display is in the collection of the society. The six additional Crusaders were David Francis Riley, Paddy Scullion, James Lewis, Millet Pie, John McStravick (there is a Thomas McStravick listed), Bob Edwards. John George Tallack was named but he was a councillor who came to London for the final stage and the pictures of him are on the platform at Hyde Park. Con Shiels also named (a second) George Smith. This would imply that there were still eight or 15 Crusaders' identities that are unknown. Furthermore, Frank Ennis interviewed two marchers (Tim Newell and Nigel Marwood) who are not listed, Ennis, Jarrow march, pp.110 and 153.

7. PRO HO 144 20696 Chief Constable of Glamorgan to Under-Secretary of State for the Home Office, 23 October 1936.

8. Aaron Charlton Curry (1887-1957), accountant, MP for Bishop Auckland (1931-5), Whickham Urban District Council (1931-7), Lord Mayor of Newcastle (1949-50).

9. *Evening Chronicle*, 20 October 1936.

10. Gordon of Jarrow told the Bishop of Durham of the letter in *Diary of Henson*, vol.68, 24 October 1936, p.46; the Archdeacon's letter appeared in *The Times* on 17 October 1936.

11. PRO MEPO 2 3097 Inspector Wright's report, 5 November 1936.

12. *Shields Gazette*, Jarrow March Supplement, 1986.

13. PRO MEPO 2 3097 item 28A.

14. Author's interview with Con Whalen, 26 August 1999.

15. *Bedford Standard*, 30 October 1936.

16. *Time and Tide*, 31 October 1936.

17. PRO HO 45 16545 Inspector Wright's report, 1 November 1936.

18. *Blind Advocate*, vol. 33, no. 439, October 1936; see following issue for report on Glasgow demonstration and the march.

19. *Third Report of the Commissioner for the Special Areas* (England and Wales), cmd. 5303, November 1936 (HMSO: London, 1936), pp.57-59.

20. Lord Nuffield furthered his reputation as a philanthropist in 1936 by granting £1.3 million to medical research and giving £35,000 to the Royal National Institute of the Blind. He was later to be one of the investors – through the Nuffield Trust – in Sir John Jarvis's schemes to bring jobs to Jarrow.

21. Cameron, *Yesterday's Witness*, p.87.

22. *Diary of Henson*, vol.68, 27 October 1936, p.52; *The Times*, 27 October 1936.

23. *Birmingham Evening Despatch*, 29 October 1936.

24. Wilkinson, *Town That Was Murdered*, p.207.

25. *Birmingham Evening Despatch*, 29 October 1936. Elsewhere his age was quoted as 61 or 63.

26. Author's interview with Con Shiels, 23 September 2004.

27 *North Mail*, 29 October 1936.

28. *Evening Chronicle*, 28 October 1936.

29. Henderson told Hugh Dalton. Hugh Dalton, *The Fateful Years, 1931-45* (Muller: London, 1957), p.108 quoted in Pamela Brookes, *Women at Westminster: an Account of Women in the British Parliament 1918-1966* (Peter Davies: London, 1967), p.118.

30. Sleight, *Women*, p.35 noted more Nazi press attacks on Ellen as 'the Jew of all Jews' (despite the fact that she was a Methodist), a 'public enemy to National Socialism', and 'The Red-Haired Agitator'.

31. Sometimes referred to as the 'Nazi Black Book' or the 'Death List' and is reprinted along with the handbook for the German occupation of Britain in SS-General Walter Schellenberg, *Invasion 1940: the Nazi Invasion Plan for Britain* (St. Ermin's Press: London, 2000), p. 261 for Ellen Wilkinson's entry and p.174 for Edward Conze's.

32. Ellen Wilkinson, *The Terror in Germany* (London Caledonian: London, n.d., c.1934), p.4. She wrote a second pamphlet, NMLH LP ID 26 27 Ellen Wilkinson, *German Relief: Feed the Children: What Is Being Done to Relieve the Victims of the Fascist Regime* (London, n.d.[1933]).

33. Wilkinson, *Terror*, p.19.

34. Wilkinson, *Terror*, p.20.

35. NMLH LP FAS 34 300 Jarrow Division Labour Party reply to 1934 Labour Party Questionnaire.

36. For a history of the Arab community in South Shields, Richard I. Lawless, *From Ta'izz to Tyneside: an Arab Community in the North-east of England during the Early Twentieth Century* (University of Exeter Press, 1995).

37. *Shields Gazette*, 26 February 1998; Todd, *In Excited Times*, pp.68-74.

38. *The Times*, 30 October 1936.

39. *Commons Debates*, vol. 317, 4 November 1936, col.76.

40. PRO T172 1826 Sir John Jarvis to the Earl of Midleton, 25 July 1935.

41. PRO HO 45 16545 Inspector Wright's report, 6 November 1936.

42. Ibid., Inspector Wright's report, 1 November 1936 and Inspector's report, 6 November 1936.

43. Working Class Movement Library (WCML) National League of the Blind, Executive Council minutes, 20 June 1936.

44. *Shields Gazette*, 30 October 1936.

45. Ibid.

46. *Herts Advertiser and Saint Albans Times*, 30 October 1936.

47. For the years 1935-37, Goodfellow, *Tyneside*, p.20, 28.

48. Actually with the South East as an index figure of 100 Tyneside and Durham's malnutrition among school children was 263. South east including London county, Essex, Surrey, Kent, Middlesex and Hertfordshire. Goodfellow, *Tyneside*, p.53.

49. Ibid., p.71.

50. Ibid., p.51.

51. *Bedford Press*, 30 October 1936; *The Spectator*, 30 October 1936.

52. *Scots Mail*, 2 November 1936.

53. *Christian World*, 22 October 1936.

54. *Western Mail and South Wales News*, 9 October 1936.

55. *Royal Cornish Gazette*, 21 October 1936.

56. *Evening Chronicle*, 30 October 1936. One possible explanation that was not explored was that Special Branch was behind the confusion in some way. Although this was not common knowledge, they had infiltrated other hunger marches and were keeping the Crusade under surveillance.

57. *Left Review*, November 1936, pp.824-825. The National Hunger March, in a week of agitation, held a rally of 5,000-6,000 on their arrival in London, PRO HO 144 20697 minute sheet, 19 November 1936.

58. Information on Access to Archives, http://www.a2a.org.uk/; Albaya died in Spain and is celebrated by a plaque in Sheffield's Peace Gardens.

59. TWAS PA 1700 Newspaper cuttings re: Jarrow March, 1936: *Cambridge Daily News*, 2 November 1936.

60. *The Guardian*, 21 December 1998.

61. *The Times*, 17 June 2005. There was no Walter Harrison on the Crusade and it did not pass through York or Aldermaston. Davis's campaign team was trying to stress his humble background and the link with the Jarrow Crusade underlined this.

62. Margaret R. Pitt, *Our Unemployed: Can the Past Teach the Present* (Pitt: Harrow, 1982), p.83.

63. National Sound Archive, Millennium Memory Bank, William Sidney David Davey (b.1907), interviewed by Virtue Jones, recorded on 4 November 1998.

64. Ibid., Morris Moss (b.1907), recorded on 6 November 1998. The National Hunger Marchers held a public meeting of 1,200-1,000 hosted by Bethnal Trades Council with MPs and march leaders on 9 November 1936, PRO HO 144 20697, Sergeant East's report, 9 November 1936.

65. J.T. Reason and D. Lucas, 'Using cognitive diaries to investigate naturally occurring memory blocks', in J.E. Harris and P.E. Morris (eds), *Everyday Memory, Actions and Absent-Mindedness* (Academic Press: London, 1984), pp.53-70; Alan Baddeley, *Human Memory: Theory and Practice* (Psychology Press: Hove, 1997), p.215.

66. *Herts Advertiser and Saint Albans Times*, 6 November 1936.

67. *Morning Post*, 31 October 1936.

68. *News Chronicle*, 31 October 1936.

69. Thomas Cantrell Dugdale (1880-1952), 'Arrival of the Jarrow Marchers', is in the possession of the Geffrye Museum, London.

70. *Independent on Sunday*, 3 March 1996.

71. Vincent Rea (ed.), *Jarrow: Impressions of a Town: an Exhibition in Celebration of the 50th Anniversary of the Jarrow Crusade* (Bede Gallery: Jarrow, 1986), p.17.

72. *Daily Herald*, 31 October 1936. Otherwise, Harney was known as 'Dyke' according to Con Shiels.

73. Or Albert or John Dobson according to different press reports. He had travelled in the bus because of 'weak heart' since the Midlands. Dobson is not listed amongst the marchers in Dougan, *Jarrow March*, pp.102-103.

74. Newcastle Local Studies Centre, Frank Ennis, *Jarrow Reminiscences* (unpublished: Gateshead, 1982) – interview with Bob Maugham, 2 February 1982, p.24.

75. TWAS MF 1403 Jarrow Cemetery, 15 January 1925-15 February 1945. There is no obituary for Dobson in the *Shields Gazette*.

76. *Shields Gazette*, 5 January 1937.

77. TWAS DT JD 8 7 rent books 11 August 1936 -18 October 1937.

78. *News Chronicle*, 30 October 1936.

79. *Star*, 31 October 1936.

80. *News of the World*, 1 November 1936.

81. *The Times*, 30 October 1936.

82. *The Spectator*, 30 October 1936.

83. Edward Conze, *Spain Today: Revolution and Counter-Revolution* (Secker and Warburg: London, 1936).

84. Duchess of Atholl, MP, Eleanor Rathbone, MP, Ellen Wilkinson, MP, and Dame Rachel Crowdy RRC, *Report of a Short Visit to Valencia and Madrid in April 1937* (National Joint Committee for Spanish Relief: London, 1937).

85. C.R. Attlee MP, Ellen Wilkinson MP, Philip Noel Baker MP and John Dugdale, *We Saw in Spain* (Labour Party: London, n.d.[1937]).

86. *Sunday Sun*, 1 November 1936.

87. Ibid.

88. Con Shiels interview with George Smith, 7 February 2004.

89. *The People*, 1 November 1936.

90. *Shields Gazette*, Jarrow March Supplement, 1986, p.xi; *Evening Chronicle*, 30 September 1986 for interviews with Bill James.

91. *Shields Gazette*, 31 October 1936.

92. Author's interview with Con Shiels, 23 September 2004.

93. *Sunday Sun*, 1 November 1936.

94. *Sunday Pictorial*, 1 November 1936.

95. *Sunday Sun*, 1 November 1936.

96. *Northern Echo*, 5 October 1936. Stainthorpe hoped it would do some good now that all political differences had been sunk to help the town industrially.

97. *Shields Gazette*, 13 November 1936.

98. *Time and Tide*, 31 October 1936.

99. *Sunday Sun*, 1 November 1936.

100. *Shields Gazette*, Jarrow March Supplement, 1986, xi.

101. Ibid., p.xii.

102. *Sunday Chronicle*, 1 November 1936.

103. *Shields Gazette*, 31 October 1936.

104. Alex Ferguson, *The Pineapple King of Jarrow and Other Stories* (Iron Press: North Shields, 2004), p.15.

105. *Sunday Times*, 1 November 1936.

106. *Morning Advertiser*, 2 November 1936.

107. *Sunday Referee*, 1 November 1936.

108. '50,000 or so' is quoted in *Daily Herald*, 2 November 1936. The *Northern Echo*, 2 November 1936, claimed 5,000 were present. As is so often the case there is a large discrepancy between the police account which stated that there were 3,000. According to the police, there were 8,000-10,000 or elsewhere 12,000 on the reception demonstration for the National Hunger March (PRO HO144 20697), but *Daily Herald* put the figure at 250,000 and the *Daily Worker*, 9 November 1936, estimated 100,000. So according to these accounts, the crowd was four or five times larger than for the Jarrow Crusade.

109. *The Times*, 2 November 1936.

110. PRO MEPO 2 3097 Inspector Wright's report, 5 November 1936.

111. NMLH CP HANN 06 17 *Souvenir Programme of the Jarrow Men* (n.d., n.p.).

112. *North Mail*, 2 November 1936.

113. Wilkinson, *Town That was Murdered*, p.209.

114. *Daily Herald*, 2 November 1936.

115. *Daily Worker*, 3 November 1936.

116. *Birmingham Post*, 2 November 1936; *Western Mail*, 2 November 1936.

117. *Morning Post*, 2 November 1936.

118. *Northern Echo*, 2 November 1936.

119. *Jersey Evening Post*, 2 November 1936.

120. *Daily Herald*, 2 November 1936. William Richard Morris, Lord Nuffield (1877-1963), Chairman of Morris Motors Limited (1919-52). *Who Was Who? 1951-60*, vol.5 (Adam and Charles Black: London, 1961); Robert Jackson, *The Nuffield Story* (Muller: London, 1964). Like Lord Londonderry, the north-east coal baron, Lord Nuffield was on the Council of the Anglo-German Fellowship an organisation of Nazi sympathers from elite backgrounds which sought to make Nazi Germany respectable in Britain. Richard Griffiths, *Fellow Travellers of the Right: British Enthusiasts for Nazi Germany 1933-39* (Constable: London, 1980), p.185.

121. *Irish Daily Telegraph*, 2 November 1936.

122. *Daily Herald*, 2 November 1936.

123. *Belfast Telegraph*, 2 November 1936.

124. *North Mail*, 2 November 1936.

125. *Daily Herald*, 2 November 1936.

126. PRO HO 144 20697 Sergeant H. Williams's report 1 November 1936.

127. The Transport and General Workers (Leslie Pearmaine and Bernard Sullivan), South Wales Miners Federation (Arthur Horner, a communist), London Trades Council and NCL also had platform speakers The London Labour Party had a representative, G.R. Strauss (Herbert Morrison's right-hand man), on the March Reception Committee.

128. London Trades Council, *What the L.T.C. is Doing*, 77th Annual Report, 1936. The LTC annual report, written after questions were raised on the NCL about communist links with the National Hunger March, talked of its 'whole-hearted support' for the unemployed hunger marchers (and no mention was made of the Jarrow Crusade). It noted that the LTC bona fide credentials had been granted to the London Reception Committee of the Hunger March but made no mention of the connection with the NUWM which would have contravened the 'black circulars' – for which eleven trades councils had been stripped of recognition the previous year, Alan Clinton, *Trade Union Rank and File: Trades Councils in Britain* (Manchester University Press: Manchester, 1977), p.35.

129. PRO MEPO 2 3091 Report on the National Hunger March, 24 September 1936, and Chief Constable's report, 2 November 1936.

130. *Birmingham Post*, 2 November 1936.

131. *Daily Herald*, 2 October 1936.

132. PRO HO 45 16545 Inspector Wright's report, 1 November 1936.

133. WCML National League of the Blind, Executive Council minutes, 5 December 1936.

134. *Northern Echo*, 2 November 1936.

135. *Evening Chronicle*, 2 November 1936.

136. *North Mail*, 2 November 1936.

Week Five pages 153-176

1. *News Chronicle*, 3 November 1936. PRO MEPO 2 3097 minute sheet, 30 October 1936, reported that they were to see another Soviet film *Bed and Sofa* and the musical *Call of the Flesh*.

2. Sir Albert Levy was involved in various philanthropic activities: he was President and Treasurer of Eastman Dental Clinic, governing trustee of the Sir Albert Levy Benevolent Fund, Treasurer of the Royal Free Hospital. Andrew Kelly's suit went straight into the pawnshop, email from Tom Kelly to author, 19 March 2005.

3. PRO MEPO 2 3097 Inspector Wright's report, 5 November 1936.

4. Cameron, *Yesterday's Witness*, p.85.

5. Church of Rome, *Encyclical Letter (Nova impendet) of Pius XI to our Venerable Brethren ... on the Acute Economic Crisis, on the Distressing Unemployment of Large Numbers, on the Ever-increasing Output of Weapons of War* (Catholic Truth Society: London, 1931).

6. Paul Preston, *Franco: a Biography* (Fontana: London, 1995), pp.184-185.

7. See Hilari Raguer, *La Pólvora y el Incienso: la Iglesia y la Guerra Civil Española (1936-1939)* (Península: Barcelona, 2001), pp.83-98; Norman Cooper, 'The Church: from Crusade to Christianity' in Paul Preston, *Spain in Crisis: the Evolution and Decline of the Franco Regime* (Harvester: Hassocks, 1976); Mary Vincent, 'The martyrs and the saints: the construction of a Francoist crusade', *History Workshop Journal*, no. 47, 1999, pp.69-98; Isidro Goma y Tomas, *The Martyrdom of Spain* (J. Duffy for the Irish Christian Front, 1936).

8. Quoted in the Spanish right-wing daily newspaper, *ABC*, 2 April 1939.

9. Paul Preston, 'The discreet charm of Francisco Franco', in *Comrades! Portraits of the Spanish Civil War* (HarperCollins: London, 1999), p.53. Warren H. Carroll, *The Last Crusade* (Christendom Press: Chicago, 1996) takes a distinctly Carlist (the conservative rather than liberal of the two royal houses with a claim to the Spanish throne) perspective on the Civil War. Hitler liked to be portrayed as one of the Teutonic Order of Crusaders of the Thirteenth Century which launched raids against the heathens of Central and Eastern Europe. The SS also modelled themselves on this crusading religious order and the Germany army's iron cross was taken from the black crucifixes on their garments. However, adopting a language that fitted with the Communist Party's attempt at reconciliation with the Catholic Church, the left did on occasion use the term crusade in relation to the fight against fascism. For example, Dolores Ibarrúri who called the volunteers of the International Brigades 'Crusaders for Freedom', Jason Gurney, *Crusade for Spain* (Faber and Faber: London, 1974), p.189.

10. Reque Reuvia, 'Francisco Franco: vencedor de la Cruzada' (Franco victor of the Crusade), in Archivo Histórico Militar, Madrid.

11. For example, *Shields Gazette*, 3 November 1936.

12. Stella Davies, 'The Young Ellen Wilkinson', *Memoirs and Proceedings of the Manchester Literary and Philosophical Society*, vol. 107, no.3, 1964-65, p.4.

13. Northumberland Record Office 5021 B5 7 National Union of Mineworkers, Northumberland Mechanics branch, Northern Regional Council: The Labour Party: Back to Jarrow March, 1981; In 1986, there was the Jarrow '86 march from Jarrow to London; 1996 - Tim Brennan's Crusade Manoeuvres, a public art performance of the Crusade detailed in Tim Brennan, *Codex: Crusade* (Arts Editions North: Sunderland, 2004).

14. *News Chronicle*, 3 November 1936.

15. British Embassy in Korea website. The only entry in the chronology for the 1930s apart from the outbreak of war is the Jarrow Crusade. Accessed on 23 May 2000 at http://www.britain.or.kr/em/press/eplist1-2.htm.

16. Ellen Wilkinson, *The Clash* (Virago, London: 1989), p.26.

17. TWAS, D X33 11 Leaflet for the public meeting for 3 November in Memorial Hall, Farringdon Street.

18. For a biographies of Dick Sheppard: R. Ellis Roberts, *H.R.L. Sheppard: Life and Letters* (Murray: London, 1942); Carolyn Scott, *Dick Sheppard: a Biography* (Hodder and Stoughton: London, 1977).

19. *Diary of Henson*, vol.67, 5 September 1936, p.205.

20. PRO MEPO 2 3097 Robinson to Home Office and Ministry of Labour, 26 September 1936.

21. *Shields Gazette*, 4 November 1936.

22. Wilkinson, *Town That Was Murdered*, p.210.

23. *Shields Gazette*, 4 November 1936.

24. *Commons Debates*, vol.314, 15 July 1936. col. 2138.

25. *The Times*, 2 October 1936.

26. *The Times*, 3 October 1936. Philip Peebles, the chair of the Jarvis committee, replied in Sir John's defence, who was abroad at the time, 'How much he has already done many Jarrow people know; how much more he would have done but for unreasonable opposition is known over a wide area. ... Sir John's proposals have all been constructive, and those who know him best will weigh his work against Miss Wilkinson's criticism', *The Times*, 6 October 1936.

27. PRO BT104 12 report of meeting on 3 November 1936.

28. Ibid., letter from Tribe (Special Areas) to R. Somerville (Ministry of Labour), 14 Nov. 1936.

29. TWAS G EMP2 11: Ministry of Labour (Northern Division) Local Office, Jarrow and Hebburn 1935-41, n.d.

30. Under the Special Areas legislation, see Treasury files, PRO T161 1408 undated memo from N.S. Davison, Chief Accountant, Jarrow Metal Industries. Two interesting figures associated with this New Jarrow Steel Company/Jarrow Metal Industries were Sir Charles Bruce-Gardiner (as a director) and Lord Nuffield as a sponsor.

31. *Star*, 2 November 2 November 1936.

32. Military and defence spending as a percentage of total Government spending changed as follows: 1930 10.4%, 1935 12.6%, 1938 29.8%. A.T. Peacock and J. Wiseman, *The Growth of Public Expenditure* (Allen and Unwin: London, 1967), pp.186-187. In 1937, were five orders for George V class battleships, of which two were for the Tyne.

33. *Evening Chronicle*, 4 November 1936.

34. *Evening Chronicle*, 3 November 1936.

35. *Northern Despatch*, 4 November 1936.

36. Wilkinson, *Town That Was Murdered*, p.211.

37. PRO MEPO 2 3097 Chief Constable's minute sheet, 29 October 1936.

38. Sir Nicholas Grattan-Doyle (1862-1941) was a member of the pro-appeasement Anglo-German Fellowship and was director of Northern Newspapers Company Limited. *Who Was Who?*, 1941-50, vol.4 (Adam and Charles Black: London, 1952), p.461.

39. *Evening Chronicle*, 4 November 1936.

40. *Eastern Evening News*, 4 November 1936; Dougan, *Jarrow March*, p.101 for the petition in full.

41. Lord Mayor of Newcastle, W. Locke, opened the second petition for Jarrow being its first signatory in the offices on Grainger Street on 15 October.

42. *Yorkshire Telegraph*, 3 November 1936.

43. *Ipswich Evening Star*, 5 November 1936.

44. *Yorkshire Herald*, 30 November 1936.

45. Tom Magnay (1876-1949) MP 1931-45, an accountant by trade. Ennis, 'Jarrow march', p.127.

46. *Commons Debates*, vol. 317, 4 November 1936, cols. 75-77.

47. PRO MEPO 2 3097 Inspector Vivian Wright's report, 6 November 1936.

48. *Shields Gazette,* Jarrow March Supplement, 1986.

49. *The Guardian*, 20 June 1997

50. *Shields Gazette*, 6 October 1986.

51. *Evening Chronicle*, 11 September 1998.

52. *Morning Advertiser*, 5 November 1936.

53. Rowan, *Tyneside Memories*, p.39.

54. One indicator of the impact of this tactic can be witnessed by a novel of the same name, Ivor Montagu, *Stay Down Miner* (Lawrence: London, 1936).

55. Wilkinson, *Town That Was Murdered*, p.210.

56. Sir Frederick Mills Unionist MP for Leyton East (1931-45) whose parents were from Tynemouth; Jack Lawson MP (Chester-le-Street, 1918-50) had been Jarrow Labour MP Pete Curran's election agent in his losing election of 1910.

57. *North Mail*, 5 November 1936.

58. Ibid.

59. *Morning Advertiser*, 5 November 1936.

60. Wilkinson, *Town That Was Murdered*, p.210.

61. *North Mail*, 5 November 1936.

62. W.G. Pearson (d.1963), Conservative councillor since 1920, Deputy Mayor of Jarrow (1926-7), Mayor of Jarrow (1928-30), Jarrow MP (1931-5) gained a CBE in 1938, *Who was Who?*, vol.6, 1961-70 (Adam and Charles Black: London, 1971), p.880.

63. *The Times*, 4 November 1936, quoted in *Shields Gazette*, 4 November 1936. On this day, tragedy stuck Jarrow Conservatives, Elizabeth Bell, former Conservative Mayoress, died of pneumonia. She was the half-sister of W.G. Pearson.

64. *The Times*, 5 November 1936.

65. *Evening Chronicle*, 5 November 1936.

66. *News Chronicle*, 5 November 1936.

67. *North Eastern Daily Gazette*, 5 November 1936.

68. *Commons Debates*, vol.317, 1936, cols.235, 581-83,.

69. *Shields Gazette*, Jarrow March Supplement, 1986.

70. *Northern Echo*, 6 November 1936; *News Chronicle*, 6 November 1936; *Evening Chronicle*, 6 November 1936. The council did come in for criticism for failing to organise any official civic ceremony on the day.

71. *Newcastle Journal*, 6 November 1936.

72. *News Chronicle*, 6 November 1936.

73. *Shields Gazette*, 6 November 1936.

74. *Northern Echo*, 6 November 1936.

Conclusion pages 177-194

1. *Sunderland Echo*, 7 October 1986.

2. *Le Monde*, 17 January 1998.

3. Robert Colls, *The Collier's Rant: Song and Culture in the Industrial Village* (Croom Helm: London, 1977), pp.182-183.

4. For the deep psychological and physiological imprint of incessant hunger see, Max Cohen, *I Was One of the Unemployed* (Gollancz: London, 1945), p.42.

5. *Sunday Sun*, 30 May 1937.

6. The episode began when Andrew Spence of the People's Fuel Lobby at a meeting of hauliers and farmers in Cheshire, on 30 October announced, "I don't know if anyone has heard of the Jarrow crusade. Well, it's starting again, only bigger. We want as many vehicles on the road as possible.' *The Guardian*, 30 December 2000. For the exchange between Jarrow MP Stephen Hepburn and Tony Blair see *Commons Debates*, vol.355, 1 November 2000, col.707-708.

7. David Miller, 'The anti-war movement accuse the BBC of having a pro-war bias; the Government says it was too Baghdad-friendly. So who was right?', *The Guardian*, 22 April 2003; Justin Lewis and Rod Brookes, 'Reporting the war on British television' in David Miller (ed.), *Tell Me Lies: Propaganda and Media Distortion in the Attack on Iraq* (Pluto: London, 2004), pp.132-143.

8. Eric Hobsbawn, *The Age of Extremes: a Short History of the Twentieth Century 1914-1991* (Abacus: London, 1994), p.567.

9. John Kampfner, *Blair's Wars* (New York: Simon & Schuster, 2003), pp.3-4.

10. Michael Moore, *Downsize This!* (Boxtree: London, 1996), p.271 Among the terms for sackings, Moore selected from the *New York Times*, 'Downsized, rightsized, destaffed, degrown, dehired, involuntarily separated, personnel surplus reduction, transitioned, resource reallocation, a save, displaced, dislocated, disemployed, redundancy elimination, workforce imbalance correction, fired'.

11. PRO T172 1826 Letter Sir John Jarvis to Neville Chamberlain, 24 May 1936.

12. Priestley, *English Journey*, p.237; see also p.307 'Was Jarrow still in England or not?...'.

13. Ellen Wilkinson and Edward Conze, *Why War? a Handbook for those who will take part in the Second World War* (NCLC: London, nd: 1934?), p.28-29.

14. Ibid., p.46.

15. Ibid., pp.20-21.

16. Stiglitz coined the term briberisation to denoted the way in which governments are corruptly induced to participate in policies (especially privatisation) detrimental to their countries' economies, Joseph Stiglitz, *Globalisation and its Discontents* (Penguin: London, 2002).

17. Ibid., p.26.

18. *Shields Gazette*, 7 November 1986.

19. Jack Grassby, *The Unfinished Revolution: South Tyneside 1969-1976* (TUPS Books: Newcastle-upon-Tyne, 1999), pp.301-305. When the Palmer's Hebburn ship-repairs yard faced closure in 1970 South Shields Trades Council tried to get a regional one-day general strike, but the move was condemned by regional union officials.

20. *Shields Gazette*, 23 November 1984; *The Journal*, 26 July 1986; *Shields Gazette*, 24 May 1989.

21. South Shields Library, Local Studies, Alex Glasgow Folder contains a leaflet for *Whistling at the Milestones*; Gateshead Library, Local Studies, PL 17 24 and PL 13 43: contains leaflet and poster. Newcastle Library, Local Studies, has the 'skeleton script' at that time called *Respectable Men*.

22. Glasgow, *Respectable Men*, p.65.

    Hughie: Still, you were fobbed off. It was a waste of time.
    Lizzie: You're forgetting. The whole country got to know about Jarrow and the state it was in.
    Hughie: And a helluvalot of difference that made! What a waste of time.

Mr Adams: Aye. That's what folks say.

Hughie: And here's me 40 years later – still on the dole! Tell you what. If I was on a march like that now, I wouldn't be fobbed off like that. No fear.

Mr Adams: So it wasn't a waste of time after all.

Hughie: How come?

Mr Adams: You learnt something, didn't you?

END

Appendix pages 195-200

1. PRO BT 64 10 Sir John Jarvis to Prime Minister Ramsay MacDonald, 9 March 1935.

2. Ibid., Sir Horace Wilson's note for the Treasury, 14 March 1935.

3. *Commons Debates*, vol.314, 30 June 1936, col. 323.

4. PRO BT 64 10 W.G. Pearson to Sir Walter Runciman, 7 October 1935; Sir Walter Runciman to W.G. Pearson, 8 October 1935.

5. Ibid., Confidential note, 9 April 1935.

6. Ibid., *Daily Express*, 4 June 1935.

7. *Commons Debates*, vol.314, 30 June 1936, col. 338.

8. PRO BT 64 10 Proposed Steelworks at Jarrow memo, 31 October 1935.

9. Ibid., H.C. Arnold-Forster to President of the Board of Trade, 13 November 1935.

10. Ibid., Jarrow memo, 9 December 1935.

11. Ibid., Sir Horace Wilson, Jarrow Steelworks memo, 11 January 1936.

12. Ibid., *Financial News*, 19 December 1935.

Sources and Bibliography

Interviews

John Badger
Harry Clarke
James Riley
Con Shiels
Con Whalen

Private Collections

Tim Brennan: *Crusade Manoeuvres* including a letter on the Jarrow Cross from Brian Buchanan to Mulligan, South Tyneside Metropolitan Borough Council, 14 November 1995.

Alex Ferguson: script for *A Woman's Walk is Never Done.*

Jarrow and Hebburn Local History Society: *Put Names to Faces'* exhibition materials.

Tom Kelly, *The Catholic Component: Irish Catholics in the North East and Jarrow from the Mid-Nineteenth Century*, unpublished manuscript.

Tom Kelly: script for *Between Today and Yesterday.*

Rose Reeve, script for *Crusader: the Story of Ellen Wilkinson and the Town of Jarrow.*

Con Shiels: Letters to his Son, Con Shiels jnr.

George Smith: interviews with Lord Dixon, Con Shiels, Terry Kelly.

Gillian Fake: interviews with Eleanor Batey, Magaret Nisbett, Agnes Rogers, Bella Sanderson, Helen Scullion.

Gillian Fake, *Women and the Jarrow March*, unpublished undergraduate dissertation, University of Sunderland, 1993.

Archives and Archival Materials
General Government Papers

House of Commons Debates.

Appendix to the 29th Report of the Registrar General: Special Report on Surnames in Ireland, with Notes as the Numerical Strength, Derivation, Ethnology, and Distribution, cmd. 7289, 1894.

First Report of the Commissioner for the Special Areas (England and Wales), cmd. 4957, July 1935 (HMSO: London, 1935).

Second Report of the Commissioner for the Special Areas (England and Wales), cmd. 5090, February 1936 (HMSO: London, 1936).

Third Report of the Commissioner for the Special Areas (England and Wales), cmd. 5303, November 1936 (HMSO: London, 1936).

Royal Commission on Unemployment Insurance, First Report, cmd. 3872, 1931.

Royal Commission on Unemployment Insurance, cmd. 4185, (HMSO: London, 1932).

Report on the Effects of Existing Economic Circumstances on the Health in the Community in the County Borough of Sunderland and Certain Districts of Durham, cmd. 4886, (HMSO: London, 1935).

Ministry of Health, *Report on an Investigation into Maternal Mortality,* cmd. 5422, (HMSO: London, 1937).

Centre d'Études et de Recherche sur les Movements Trotskyste et Révolutionnaires Internationaux, (CERMTRI)
Leon Trotsky's correspondence.

Durham Cathedral Library (DCL)
Diary of Hensley Henson, Bishop of Durham.

The Correspondence of Hensley Henson, Bishop of Durham, vol. 112: 23 January 1936-1 June 1945.

Gateshead Library, Local Studies Collection
PL 17 24 and PL 13 43: contains leaflet and poster for *Whistling at the Milestones.*
Microfilm text of Alex Glasgow songs.

National Archives, formerly The Public Record Office, Kew (PRO)

Board of Trade files

BT 104 12 Proposal by Jarrow Corporation to acquire and clean Palmer's Yard, 1936-1937.

BT 10 112 Bankers Industrial Development Company: proposed promotion of works at Jarrow, 1937-1938.

BT 10 113 Proposed works at Jarrow for the production of bright steel bars etc., 1937-1938.

BT 55 15 Inter-Departmental Committee on Depressed Areas: Jarrow Slake Scheme – Information, 1935.

BT 64 10 Jarrow Steel Works Scheme. Press extracts, 1935.

BT 64 24 Jarrow Steel Works. Negotiations for purchase of site by Commissioner for Special Areas, 1937.

BT 64 32 Jarrow Steel Works. Acquisition and Leasing of site to New Jarrow Steel Co. Ltd, 1938.

BT 31 35733 342179 No. of Company: 342179; The New Jarrow Steel Company Limited, 1938.

Cabinet Office files

CAB 23 85. Cabinet Minutes, 1936.

CAB 27 502 Committee on Trade and Employment, Memorandum 28 February 1933 and sixth meeting.

Domestic Records of the Public Record Office.

PRO 30 69 469 Unemployment: unemployment in Jarrow: memo on recovery prospects 1929-1935.

Home Office files

HO 144 12143 Unemployed miners' march to London in 1927; march of the unemployed to London in 1929; hunger march to London in 1930. 1927-1930.

HO 45 16545 National League of the Blind: march to London, 1936.

HO 144 19843 National Hunger Marches to London: Communist influence, 1 November 1933 - 6 February 1934.

HO 144 19844 National Hunger Marches to London: Communist influence, 6-13 February 1934.

HO 144 19845 National Hunger Marches to London: Communist influence, 15-22 February 1934.

HO 144 19846 National Hunger Marches to London: Communist influence, 26 February 1934 – 29 January 1935.

HO 144 20696 Hunger March, 1936, 29 July – 23 October 1936.

HO 144 20697 Hunger March, 1936, 27 October 1936 - 19 January 1937.

Metropolitan Police files

MEPO 2 789 Leicester march to London, 1905.

MEPO 2 3064 National Unemployed Workers Movement Hunger March, deputation to House of Commons 1932-1934.

MEPO 2 3071 National Hunger March 1934: Police arrangements and reports of demonstrations 1933-1934.

MEPO 2 3091 Communist Party and National Unemployed Workers Movement: hunger march of 1936, 1936.

MEPO 2 3097 Jarrow march to London 1936.

Ministry of Health files

MH 58 309 King Edward VIII's visit to South Wales, November 1936.

Treasury files

T 161 777 Unemployment Relief: Special Areas: Jarrow; proposed paper pulp factory 4 November 1936 - 13August 1937.

T 161 1408 Jarrow Metal Industries Ltd and Armstrong Whitworth Ltd: Loan of £40,000 by Treasury under Section 6(1)(a) of Special Areas (Amendment) Act 1937 1939-1941.

T 163 120 2 Jarrow Corporation Bill 1939, 1938-1939.

T 172 1826 Jarrow unemployment prospects: proposed closure of Steel Works 1934-1935.

T 187 16 Jarrow Tube Works; proposals for the disposal of the interests of Sir John Jarvis 1937.

T 187 17 Jarrow Metal Industries Ltd, 1937.

T 187 18 Jarrow Metal Industries Ltd.; Draft Agreement between Sir John Jarvis and Tube Investments Ltd., and Stewart and Lloyds Ltd. 1937.

T 187 19 Proposal to form the New Jarrow Steel Co. 1937.

T 187 20 Proposal to form the New Jarrow Steel Co. 1938.

T 187 21 Proposal to form the New Jarrow Steel Co. 1938.

T 187 22 Proposal to form the New Jarrow Steel Co. 1939.

National Museum of Labour History (NMLH), Manchester

Communist Party of Great Britain (CP), Individuals (IND), Rajani Palme Dutt papers (DUTT).

CP IND HANN, Wal Hannington Papers.

CP IND MONT, Ivor Montagu Papers.

Labour Party (LP), LP General Secretary's Papers (GS), National Executive Committee minutes (NEC).

LP International Department (ID), Communist International, Ancillary Organisations papers (CI).

LP ID GER Reports on Germany.

LP ID IND Reports on India.

LP JSM J. S. Middleton papers.

LP DAC Distressed Areas Commission papers.

LP WI Ellen Wilkinson papers.

LP ID International Department.

LP FAS Reports on Fascism.

LP SCW Spanish Civil War collection.

Labour Party, *Report of the 34th Annual Conference, Southport, 1934* (Labour Party: London, 1934).

Labour Party, *Report of the 36th Annual Conference, Edinburgh, 1936* (Labour Party: London, 1936).

Poster collection 1995.39, slide 1950.0171: '*Remember - Unemployment - Don't give the Tories another chance - Vote Labour.*'

National Sound Archive, London

Millennium Memory Bank: William Sidney, David Davey, Lewis Greifer, Morris Moss.

BBC Radio 4, *The Fiery Particle*, 1991.

BBC Radio 4, *The Last Crusade*, 1986.

Newcastle Central Library, Local Studies Collection

Frank Ennis, *Jarrow Reminiscences* (unpublished: Gateshead, 1982).

Alex Glasgow, script for *Respectable Men* (the 'skeleton script' for *Whistling at the Milestones*) (unpublished, 1977).

Northumberland County Record Office

5021 B5 7 National Union of Mineworkers, Northumberland Mechanics branch, Northern Regional Council: The Labour Party: 'Back to Jarrow' 1981.

Sheffield Archives

LD 1541 Labour Party Hallam (Sheffield) Constituency, Divisional members' meetings.

LD 1653 Sheffield Trades and Labour Council, Executive and Delegates Meetings, ASLEF 7 Sheffield Trades and Labour Council Annual Reports.

South Shields Library, Local Studies Collection

Frank Ennis, 'The Jarrow March: a symbolic expression of protest', MA Thesis, Durham University, 1982.

Borough of Jarrow Corporation, Rate Book, 1934.

Press Cuttings Folders.

Alex Glasgow Folder contains leaflet for *Whistling at the Milestones*.

South Shields Museum

TWCMS 2001.5009.2: South Tyneside Interviews: Harry Clarke and Con Whalen.

Tyne and Wear Archive Service, Newcastle (TWAS)

DT JD 8 7 John Dobson Ltd Rent books, 11 August 1936 to 18 October 1937.

D X33 1 Leaflet for Market Harborough public meeting.

D X33 11 Leaflet for the public meeting for 3 November in Memorial Hall, Farringdom Street.

G EMP2 Papers relating to the 'Surrey Scheme', 1934-1993.

LHNE DT.BBC LH JAR: Radio Newcastle, *The Jarrow March*: written by Frank Ennis, 1982.

MB JA 3 Jarrow Municipal Borough Council, Local Board of Health Committee.

MB JA 4 Jarrow Municipal Borough Council Meeting minutes.

MB JA PH 1 1 12-13 P.A. Dormer (Medical Officer of Health for Jarrow), *Annual Report of the Health Department for 1936* (Borough of Jarrow: Jarrow, 1937); P.A. Dormer (Medical Officer of Health for Jarrow), *Annual Report of the Health Department for 1939* (Borough of Jarrow: Jarrow, 1940).

MB JA PH 4 Slum Clearance Records.

MF 1403 Jarrow Cemetery, 15 January 1925-15 February 1945.

MG SSH 3 1 Juvenile Court Register (Jarrow), 5 January 1933 – 4 April 1944.
MG SSH 1 4 Police Court Register (Jarrow), 14 May 1935 – 23 March 1937.
T 133 5 Jarrow Town Clerk's files.
Pamphlets collection: PA 1322: M.J. Young, *Catholic Jarrow, St. Bede's, 1860-1940* (n.p.,1940).
PA 1700 Newspaper cuttings re: Jarrow March, 1936: *Cambridge Daily News*, 2 November 1936.

Working-Class Movement Library, Manchester (WCLM)
National Unemployed Workers' Movement, National Administrative Committee minutes.
National League of the Blind, Executive Council minutes.
International Press Correspondence (Inprecorr)

Periodicals and Newspapers
Barnsley Chronicle and South Yorkshire News
Bedford Press
Bedford Standard
Belfast Telegraph
Birmingham Evening Despatch
Birmingham Post
Blaydon Courrier
Blind Advocate
Chester-le-Street Chronicle and District Advertiser
Christian World
Church of England Newspaper
Cork Examiner
Cumbria Evening News
Daily Dispatch
Daily Herald
Daily Mirror
Daily Sketch
Daily Worker
Derbyshire Times
Eastern Evening News
East Ham Echo
The Economist

Evening Chronicle

Harrogate Herald

Herts Advertiser and Saint Albans Times

Ipswich Evening Star

Irish Daily Telegraph

Irish Free Press

Iron and Coal Trades Review

Jersey Evening Post

Labour Research

Leeds Mercury

Left Review

Leicester Daily Mercury

Manchester Guardian

Mansfield and North Notts Advertiser

Market Harborough Advertiser and Midland Mail

Morning Advertiser

Morning Post

Newcastle Journal

New Dawn

News Chronicle

News of the World

Nottingham Guardian

Northampton Evening Telegraph

North Eastern Daily Gazette

Northern Echo

Northern Despatch

North Mail

North Mail and Chronicle

The Observer

People

Peterborough Advertiser

Plebs

Reynolds Illustrated News

Ripon Gazette and Observer

Royal Cornish Gazette

Sheffield Daily Telegraph

Sheffield Independent
Shields Gazette
South Tyneside Times
The Spectator
Scots Mail
Star
Sunday Chronicle
Sunday Express
Sunday Pictorial
Sunday Referee
Sunday Sun
Sunday Times
Sunday Times Magazine
Sunderland Echo
Tide and Time
Tribune
Weekly Times
Western Mail and South Wales News
West Daily Press
Yorkshire Herald
Yorkshire Observer
Yorkshire Post
Yorkshire Telegraph

Contemporary Literature

Duchess of Atholl, MP, Eleanor Rathbone, MP, Ellen Wilkinson, MP, and Dame Rachel Crowdy RRC, *Report of a Short Visit to Valencia and Madrid in April 1937* (National Joint Committee for Spanish Relief: London, 1937).

C.R. Attlee MP, Ellen Wilkinson MP, Philip Noel Baker MP and John Dugdale, *What We Saw in Spain* (Labour Party: London, n.d.).

Church of Rome, *Encyclical Letter (Nova impendet) of Pius XI to our Venerable Brethren ... On the Acute Economic Crisis, on the Distressing Unemployment of Large Numbers, on the Ever-increasing Output of Weapons of War* (Catholic Truth Society: London, 1931).

Max Cohen, *I Was One of the Unemployed* (Gollancz: London, 1945).

Edward Conze, *Spain Today: Revolution and Counter-Revolution* (Secker and Warburg: London, 1936).

Isidro Goma y Tomas, *The Martyrdom of Spain* (J. Duffy for the Irish Christian Front, 1936).

David M. Goodfellow, *Tyneside: the Social Facts* (Co-operative: Newcastle, 1940).

Manuel Grossi, *L'Insurrection des Asturies* (Études et Documentation Internationales: Paris, 1972).

Wal Hannington, *Unemployed Struggles* (Lawrence and Wishart: London, 1977).

Senor de Asua and Senora de Palencia, *The Agony of Spain: Socialist Appeal to British Democracy, Spanish Envoys tell the Truth* (Labour Party: London, 1936).

Herbert Hensley Henson, *Abyssinia: Reflections of an Onlooker* (Hugh Rees: London, 1936).

Herbert Hensley Henson, *Retrospect of an Unimportant Life* (2 vols published as one: Oxford University Press: London, 1943).

Herbert Hensley Henson, *Retrospect of an Unimportant Life*, vol.3: 1939-46 (Oxford University Press: London, 1950).

D.H. Lawrence, *Selected Essays* (Penguin: Harmondsworth, 1950).

National Hunger March, *Why We March: Programme of the National Protest March*, 1936.

John Newsom, *Out of the Pit: a Challenge to the Comfortable* (Basil Blackwell: Oxford, 1936).

Henry A. Mess, *Industrial Tyneside: a Social Survey* (E. Benn: London, 1928).

G.C.M. M'Gonigle and J. Kirby, *Poverty and Public Health* (Gollancz: London, 1936).

Ivor Montagu, *Stay Down Miner* (Lawrence: London, 1936).

Charles Muir, *Justice in a Depressed Area* (Allen and Unwin: London, 1936).

Sonia Orwell and Ian Angus (eds), *The Collected Essays, Journalism and Letters of George Orwell*, vol. 1: *An Age Like This 1920-40* (Penguin: Harmondsworth, 1970).

George Orwell, *The Road to Wigan Pier* (Penguin: Harmondsworth, 1962).

A.D.K. Owen, Sheffield Social Survey Committee, *A Report on the Housing Problem in Sheffield*, Survey Pamphlet no.2, June 1931.

A.D.K. Owen, Sheffield Social Survey Committee, *A Report on Unemployment in Sheffield*, Survey Pamphlet no.4, July 1932.

A.D.K. Owen, Sheffield Social Survey Committee, *A Survey of the Standard of Living in Sheffield*, Survey Pamphlet no.9, June 1933.

Pilgrim Trust, *Men without Work* (Cambridge University Press: Cambridge, 1938).

R.W. Postgate, J.F. Horrabin and Ellen Wilkinson, *A Workers' History of the Great Strike* (Plebs League and the National Council of Labour Colleges: London, 1927).

J.B. Priestley, *English Journey* (Heinemann: London, 1984; first published, 1934).

J.B. Priestley, *Wonder Hero* (Heinemann: London, 1933).

Thomas Sharp, *A Derelict Area: a Study of the South-west Durham Coalfield* (Hogarth Press: London, 1935).

Sidney James and Beatrice Webb, *Soviet Communism: a New Civilisation?* (Longmans: London, 1935).

Monica Whatley, Ellen Wilkinson, Leonard W. Matters and V.K. Krishna Menon, *Condition of India: Being the Report of the Delegation sent to India by The India League in 1932* (Essential News, London: 1933).

Ellen Wilkinson, *The Division Bell Mystery* (Harrap: London, 1932).

Ellen Wilkinson, *The Clash* (Virago: London, 1989).

Ellen Wilkinson, 'The Communist Manifesto', *New Dawn*, 4 May 1935, pp.272-273 and 279.

Ellen Wilkinson, *Peeps at Politicians* (Philip Allen: London, 1930).

Ellen Wilkinson, *The Terror in Germany* (British Committee for the Relief of the Victims of German Fascism: London, 1933).

Ellen Wilkinson, *The Town That Was Murdered: the Life Story of Jarrow* (Victor Gollancz: London, 1939).

Ellen Wilkinson and Edward Conze, *Why Fascism?* (Selwyn and Blount: London, 1934).

Ellen Wilkinson and Edward Conze, *Why War? a Handbook for those who will take part in the Second World War* (NCLC: London, nd: 1934?).

Ellen Wilkinson, 'The women's movement in Soviet Russia', *Communist Review*, November 1921, pp.26-29.

Secondary Literature

Bill Alexander, *British Volunteers for Liberty: Spain 1936-9* (Lawrence and Wishart: London, 1982).

Alan Baddeley, *Human Memory: Theory and Practice* (Psychology Press: Hove, 1997).

Arthur Barton, *Two Lamps in our Street: a Time Remembered* (Hutchinson: London, 1967).

John Baxendale, '"I Had seen a Lot of Englands": J. B. Priestley, Englishness and the People', *History Workshop Journal*, no. 51, 2001, pp. 87-111.

David Bell, *Ships, Strikes and Keelmen: Glimpses at North-Eastern Social History* (TUPS: Newcastle, 2001).

Joyce M. Bellamy and John Saville, with the assistance of David E. Martin (eds), *Dictionary of Labour Biography*, vols 1-10, (MacMillan: London, 1972-2000).

Brian Bennison, 'Profits of Doom: the financial management of the Jarrow Crusade', *Journal of Regional and Local Studies*, vol. 6, no. 2, 1985, pp.49-53.

Ronald Blythe, *The Age of Illusion: England in the Twenties and Thirties, 1919-1940* (Phoenix: London, 2001).

Rhodes Boyson, 'The shadow of failure behind Labour's Jarrow nostalgia', *Daily Telegraph*, 3 June 1981.

Noreen Branson and Margot Heinemann, *Britain in the 1930s* (Weidenfeld and Nicolson: London, 1971).

E.F. Brayley, *The Letters of Herbert Henson* (SPCK: London, 1950).

Asa Briggs, *Victorian Cities* (Penguin: Harmondsworth, 1968).

Pamela Brookes, *Women at Westminster: an Account of Women in the British Parliament 1918-1966* (Peter Davies: London, 1967).

Burke's Peerage and Baronetage (Burke's Peerage: Crans, Switzerland, 1999).

Maureen Callicott, 'The making of a Labour stronghold: electoral politics in Co. Durham between the two World Wars', and Ian Hunter, 'Labour in local government on Tyneside 1883-1921' in Maureen Callicott and Ray Challinor (eds), *Working Class Politics in North East England* (Newcastle-upon-Tyne Polytechnic: Newcastle-upon-Tyne, 1983), pp.63-78.

James Cameron (ed.), *Yesterday's Witness: a Selection of the BBC Series* (BBC: London, 1979).

Owen Chadwick, *Hensley Henson: a Study in Friction between Church and State* (Clarendon: Oxford, 1983).

Alan Clinton, *Trade Union Rank and File: Trades Councils in Britain* (Manchester University Press: Manchester, 1977).

Edward Conze, *The Memoirs of a Modern Gnostic* (Samizdat: Sherborne, 1979).

Robert Colls, *The Collier's Rant: Song and Culture in the Industrial Village* (Croom Helm: London, 1977).

Norman Cooper, 'The Church: from Crusade to Christianity' in Paul Preston, *Spain in Crisis: the Evolution and Decline of the Franco Regime* (Harvester: Hassocks, 1976), pp.48-81.

Richard Croucher, *We Refuse to Starve in Silence: a History of the National Unemployed Workers' Movement 1920-46* (Lawrence and Wishart: London, 1987).

Richard Croucher, ' "Divisions in the movement": the National Unemployed Workers' Movement', in Geoff Andrews, Nina Fishman and Kevin Morgan (eds), *Opening the Books: Essays on the Social and Cultural History of the British Communist Party* (Pluto: London, 1995), pp.23-43.

David Cummings, 'Marshall Riley's Army', in Valley Writers (eds), *Monks, Miners and Moonshine: Northern History as it Should Have Been* (Valley Writers: Waterhouses, 2000).

Valentine Cunningham (ed.), *Spanish Civil War Verse* (Penguin: Harmondsworth, 1980).

James Curran and Jean Seaton, *Power without Responsibility: the Press and Broadcasting in Britain* (Routledge: London, 1997).

Jim Cuthbert and Ken Smith, *Palmers of Jarrow 1851-1933* (Tyne Bridge Publishing: Newcastle, 2004).

Hugh Dalton, *The Fateful Years, 1931-45* (Muller: London, 1957).

Stella Davies, 'The Young Ellen Wilkinson', *Memoirs and Proceedings of the Manchester Literary and Philosophical Society*, vol. 107, no.3, 1964-5, pp.1-6.

Alan Deacon, *In Search of the Scrounger: the Administration of Unemployment Insurance in Britain, 1920-1931* (Bell: London, 1976).

W.F. Deedes, *Dear Bill: W.F. Deedes Reports* (MacMillian: London, 1997).

R.B. Dobson and J. Taylor, *Rymes of Robin Hood: an Introduction to the English Outlaw* (Sutton; Stroud, 1997).

David Dougan, *History of North East Shipbuilding* (Allen and Unwin: London, 1968).

David Dougan, *The Jarrow March* (Bede Gallery: Jarrow, 1976).

Alex Ferguson, *The Pineapple King of Jarrow and Other Stories* (Iron Press: North Shields, 2004).

Evelyn Foley Bradley (ed.), *More Letters of Herbert Hensley Henson: a Second Volume* (SPCK: London, 1954).

John Foster, Muir Houston and Chris Madigan, 'Distinguishing Catholics and Protestants among Irish immigrants to Clydeside: a new approach to immigration and ethnicity in Victorian Britain', *Irish Studies Review*, vol.10, no.2, 2002, pp.171-192.

Richard Flanagan, *Parish-Fed Bastards: A History of the Unemployed in Britain 1884-1939* (Greenwood Press: New York, 1991).

W.R. Garside, *British Unemployment: 1919-39* (Cambridge University Press: Cambridge, 1990).

W.R. Garside, *The Durham Miners, 1919-60* (Allen and Unwin: London, 1971).

Sir Allan John Grant, *Steel and Ships: the History of John Brown's* (Joseph: London, 1950).

Jack Grassby, *The Unfinished Revolution: South Tyneside 1969-1976* (TUPS Books: Newcastle-upon-Tyne, 1999).

M. Gribben, 'The Crusade continues', *Accent on the Wear*, no.2, October 1999, pp.14-15.

Richard Griffiths, *Fellow Travellers of the Right: British Enthusiasts for Nazi Germany 1933-39* (Constable: London, 1980).

Jason Gurney, *Crusade for Spain* (Faber and Faber: London, 1974).

Maurice Halbwachs, *On Collective Memory* (University of Chicago Press: Chicago, 1992).

Wal Hannington, *Never on our Knees* (Lawrence and Wishart: London, 1967).

Charles H. Hardy, *John Bowes and the Bowes Museum* (Frank Graham: Newcastle-upon-Tyne, 1970).

Harry Harmer, 'Failure of the Communists: the National Unemployed Workers Movement', in Andrew Thorpe (ed.), *The Failure of Political Extremism in Britain* (Exeter University Press: Exeter, 1988), pp.29-47.

Christopher Hill, *Liberty against the Law: Some Seventeenth-century Controversies* (Penguin: Harmondsworth, 1996).

Ralph Hayburn, 'The NUWM, 1921-36: a re-appraisal', *International Review of Social History*, vol.28, 1983, pp.279-295.

Eric Hobsbawm and Terence Ranger (eds), *The Invention of Tradition* (Cambridge University Press: Cambridge, 1983).

J.C. Holt, 'The origins and audience of the ballads of Robin Hood', *Past and Present*, no.18, 1960, pp.89-110.

James K. Hopkins, *Into the Heat of the Fire: the British in the Spanish Civil War* (Stanford University Press: Stanford, 1998).

Billy Hughes, 'In defence of Ellen Wilkinson', *History Workshop Journal*, issue 7, summer 1979, pp.157-160.

Brian Inglis, *Abdication* (Hodder Stoughton: London, 1966).

Robert Jackson, *The Nuffield Story* (Muller: London, 1964).

Ian Kershaw, *Making Friends with Hitler: Lord Londonderry, the Nazis and the Road to War* (Allen Lane: London, 2004).

Peter Kingsford, *The Hunger Marchers in Britain 1920-40* (Lawrence and Wishart: London, 1982).

Stephen Knight (ed.), *Robin Hood: an Anthology of Scholarship and Criticism* (Brewer: Cambridge, 1991).

Richard I. Lawless, *From Ta'izz to Tyneside: an Arab Community in the North-east of England during the Early Twentieth Century* (University of Exeter Press: Exeter, 1995).

G.I.T. Machin, 'Marriages and the churches in the 1930s: Royal abdication and divorce reform 1936-7', *Journal of Ecclesiastical History*, vol.42, no.1, 1991, pp.61-81.

J.R. Maddicott, 'The birth and setting of the ballads of Robin Hood', *English Historical Review*, vol. 93, 1978, pp. 267-299.

Andrew Matthews, *The Road to London: a Tale of the Jarrow March* (Franklin Watts: London, 1997).

Ian MacDougall (ed.), *Voices from the Hunger Marches: Personal Recollections by Scottish Hunger Marchers of the 1920s and 1930s*, 2 vols (Polygon: Edinburgh, 1991).

Ian MacDougall (ed.), *Voices from the Spanish Civil War*, (Polygon: Edinburgh, 1986).

Arthur McIvor, ' "A crusade for capitalism": the Economic League, 1919-39', *Journal of Contemporary History*, vol. 23, 1988, pp. 631-655.

Arthur McIvor and H. Patterson, 'Combatting the left: victimization and anti-labour policies on the Clyde 1900-39', in Robert Duncan and Arthur McIvor (eds), *Militant Workers: Labour and Class Conflict on the Clyde 1900-1952* (J. Donald: Edinburgh, 1992).

Harry McShane, *No Mean Fighter* (Pluto: London, 1978).

D.E. Martin, 'Ellen Wilkinson', in Anne Commire (ed.), *Women in World History: a Biographical Encyclopedia*, vol. 16 (Yorkin: Detroit, 2002), pp. 550-553.

Karl Marx, *Capital*, vol. 1 (Penguin: Harmondsworth, 1976).

Keith Middlemas and John Barnes, *Baldwin: a Biography* (Weidenfeld and Nicolson: London, 1969).

Norman L. Middlemas, *British Shipbuilding Yards*, vol. 1: North-East Coast (Shield: Newcastle, 1993).

Frederic M. Miller, 'Unemployment policy of the National Government 1931-36', *Historical Journal*, vol.19, no.2, 1976, pp. 453-476.

H.G. Nicholas, *The British General Election of 1950* (MacMillan: London, 1951).

C. S. Nicholls (eds) *Dictionary of National Biography, 1971-80* (Oxford University Press: Oxford, 1986).

A.T. Peacock and J. Wiseman, *The Growth of Public Expenditure* (Allen and Unwin: London, 1967).

Matt Perry, 'The Jarrow Crusade's return: the 'New Labour Party' of Jarrow and Ellen Wilkinson, M.P.', *Northern History*, vol.34, no. 2, September 2002, pp.265-278.

Matt Perry, 'The Jarrow Crusade, the National Hunger March and the Labour Party in 1936: a Re-Appraisal', *Socialist History*, no.20, 2001, pp.40-53.

Matt Perry, 'The Limits of Philanthropy: Sir John Jarvis and the Attempt to Regenerate Jarrow, 1934-39' *North East History*, summer 2000, pp.35-59.

Tom Pickard, *The Jarrow March* (Allison and Busby: London, 1982).

Lynn Picknett, Clive Prince and Stephen Prior, *War of the Windsors: a Century of Unconstitutional Monarchy* (Mainstream Publishing: Edinburgh, 2002).

Ben Pimlott, *Labour and the Left in the 1930s* (Cambridge University Press: Cambridge, 1977).

Margaret R. Pitt, *Our Unemployed: Can the Past Teach the Present* (Pitt: Harrow, 1982).

Alan Plater, 'The drama of the North-East' in Robert Colls and Bill Lancaster (eds), *Geordies: Roots of Regionalism* (Edinburgh University Press: Edinburgh, 1992).

Michael Polley, 'The Long-Weekend revisited', *Literature and History*, 3rd series, vol.8, no.1, 1999, pp.69-75.

Paul Preston, 'Franco and Azaña: Victor and Vanquished (Spain's Civil War)', *History Today*, no.49, May 1999, pp.17-23.

Paul Preston, *Franco: a Biography* (Fontana: London, 1995).

Paul Preston, *Comrades! Portraits of the Spanish Civil War* (HarperCollins: London, 1999).

A. W. Purdue, 'Jarrow politics, 1885-1914: the challenge to Liberal hegemony', *Northern History*, vol. 18, 1982, pp.182-198.

A.W. Purdue, 'The myth of the Jarrow march', *New Society*, 8 July 1982.

Hilari Raguer, *La Pólvora y el Incienso: la Iglesia y la Guerra Civil Española (1936-1939)* (Península: Barcelona, 2001).

Vince Rea (ed.), *Palmer's Yard and the Town of Jarrow* (Bede Gallery: Jarrow, 1975).

J.T. Reason and D. Lucas, 'Using cognitive diaries to investigate naturally occurring memory blocks', in J.E. Harris and P.E. Morris (eds), *Everyday Memory, Actions and Absent-Mindedness* (Academic Press: London, 1984).

David Renton, *This Rough Game: Fascism and Anti-Fascism* (Sutton: Stroud, 2001).

R. Ellis Roberts, *H.R.L. Sheppard: Life and Letters* (Murray: London, 1942).

Claude Robinson, 'How they tried to stop us marching', *Tribune*, 3 June 1983.

Claude Robinson, *J'Accuse: the Autobiography of a Headteacher in Jarrow, 1934-1963* (People's Publications: London, 1986).

Sam Rowan, 'We'll march down with it', Age Concern, *Tyneside Memories* (Age Concern: Newcastle, 1996).

David Rubinstein, 'Ellen Wilkinson re-considered', *History Workshop Journal*, issue 7, summer 1979, pp.161-169.

Raphael Samuel, *Theatres of Memory* (Verso: London, 1994).

Raphael Samuel and Paul Thompson (eds), *The Myths We Live By* (Routledge: London, 1990).

John Saville, 'Some random comments on the hunger marches of the 1930s', *North-West Labour History*, August, 1988, pp.39-45.

C. Seymour-Ure, 'The press and the party system between the wars', in G. Peele and C. Cook (eds), *The Politics of Reappraisal* (MacMillan: London, 1975).

A. Slaven, 'Self-liquidation: the NSS Ltd. and the British Shipbuilders in the 1930s', in Sarah Palmer and Glyndwr William (eds), *Chartered and Uncharted Waters* (Trustees of the National Maritime Museum: London, 1982), pp.125-147.

John Sleight, *Women on the March* (John I. Sleight: Gosforth, 1986).

Nick Smart (ed.), *The Diaries and Letters of Robert Bernays, 1932-1939: an Insider's Account of the House of Commons* (Edwin Mellen: Lewiston, New York, 1996).

John Stevenson and Chris Cook, *Britain in the Depression: Society and Politics 1929-39* (Longman: London, 1994).

Nigel Todd, *In Excited Times: the People against the Blackshirts* (Bewick Press: Whitley Bay, 1995).

Maureen Turnbull, 'Attitude of government and administration towards the hunger marches of the 1920s and 1930s', *Journal of Social Policy*, vol.2, no.2, 1973, pp.131-42.

Andrew Thorpe, *The Longman Companion to Britain in the Era of the Two World Wars, 1914-45* (Longman: London, 1993).

John Vaisey, *The History of British Steel* (Weidenfeld and Nicolson: London, 1974).

Betty D. Vernon, *Ellen Wilkinson 1891-1947* (Croom Helm: London, 1982).

Mary Vincent, 'The martyrs and the saints: the construction of a Francoist crusade', *History Workshop Journal*, no. 47, 1999, pp.69-98.

Paul Vyšný, *The Runciman Mission to Czechoslovakia, 1938* (Palgrave: Houndmills, 2003).

Oliver Warner, *Admiral of the Fleet: the Life of Sir Charles Lambe* (Sidgwick and Jackson: London, 1969).

Don Watson and John Corcoran, *An Inspiring Example: the North East of England and the Spanish Civil War 1936-39* (McGuffin Press: London, 1996).

Who Was Who? 1941-50, vol.4 (Adam and Charles Black: London, 1952).

Who Was Who? 1951-60, vol.5 (Adam and Charles Black: London, 1961).

Who Was Who? 1961-70, vol.6, (Adam and Charles Black: London, 1971).

Colin Williams, Bill Alexander, John Gorman, *Memorials of the Spanish Civil War: the Official Publication of the International Brigade Association* (Allan Sutton: Stroud, 1996).

Susan Williams, *The People's King: the True Story of the Abdication* (Allen Lane: London, 2003).

Phillip Zeigler, *Edward VIII* (Sutton: Stroud, 1990).

The Internet

An interview with John Miles about his grandfather, *Cuddy's Miles* and the Jarrow Crusade: http://www.britishtheatreguide.info/othersources/interviews/JohnMiles.htm

Jarrow Barber site: www.geocities.com the_jarrow_crusade Ralph_Smith

Century Speaks, the BBC oral history project - http://www.bbc.co.uk/history/programmes/century/cspeaks.shtml

http:www.lindisfarne.de marshall.txt

http://www.britain.or.kr/em/press/eplist1-2.htm

Television and Radio

BBC TV, *Red Ellen*, 1986.

BBC TV, *The Road to Jarrow*, 1996.

BBC TV, *Beyond Jarrow*, 1988.

BBC TV, *Our Friends in the North*, 1996.

Radio 4, *This Sceptred Isle: the Twentieth Century*, 1999.

Radio 4, *A Woman's Walk is Never Done*, 2000.

Radio 4, *Mapping the Town*, 2005.

Radio 4, *Before Jarrow*, 2005. (About 1920 blind marchers to London).

Radio 4, *Eyewitness: a History of the Twentieth Century in Sound*, 2004.

Radio 4, *The Last Crusade*, 1986.

Radio 4, *The Fiery Particle*, 1991.

Radio Newcastle, *The Jarrow March*, 1982.

Tyne Tees/Channel 4, *Crusade*, 1986.

Theatre

Tim Brennan, *Red Shoe Diaries*.

Tom Kelly, *Between Today and Yesterday*.

Alex Ferguson, *A Woman's Walk is Never Done*.

Alex Glasgow, *Whistling at the Milestones*.

Arthur McKensie and David Whitaker, *Cuddy's Miles*.

Rose Reeve, *Crusader: the Story of Ellen Wilkinson and the Town of Jarrow*.

Art, Poetry and Song

Mick Bisiker and Al Romanov, 'The Jarrow March' on the *Bisiker and Romanov* Album, Fellside Recordings, 1988.

Tim Brennan, *Codex: Crusade* (Arts Editions North: Sunderland, 2004).

Thomas C. Dugdale's oil painting, 'The Arrival of the Jarrow Marchers', 1936.

John J. Harney, 'The Jarrow Marchers' in David Dougan, *Jarrow March* (Bede Gallery: Jarrow, 1976), p.104;

Lindisfarne (written by Alan Hull), 'Marshal Riley's Army', on *Back and Forth* Album released December 1978.

Tom Paulin, *The Invasion Handbook* (Faber and Faber: London, 2002) pp.103-104, Jarrow poem;

Tom Pickard, *The Jarrow March* (Allison and Busby: London, 1982);

Alan Plater, *Close the Coalhouse Door (with Songs by Alex Glasgow)* (Bloodaxe: Newcastle, 2000).

Alan Price, 'Jarrow Song', Warner Brothers, released 25 May 1974.

Vincent Rea (ed.), *Jarrow: Impressions of a Town: an Exhibition in Celebration of the 50th Anniversary of the Jarrow Crusade* (Bede Gallery: Jarrow, 1986).

E.H. Rowe's poem 'Jarrow Crusaders' Epic Trek' (1936).

Carol Rumens, 'Jarrow' in Andy Croft and Adrian Mitchell (eds), *Red Sky at Night: an Anthology of British Socialist Poetry* (Five Leaves: Nottingham, 2003).

Ann Roberts's poem, *Shields Gazette*, 20 September 1986 and *South Tyneside Post*, 28 August 1986.

Will Todd's opera, *Burning Road*, 1996.

Index